Peasants into Citizens

Studien zur Sozial- und Wirtschaftsgeschichte Ostmitteleuropas

Herausgegeben von
Werner Benecke, Christoph Boyer, Ulf Brunnbauer,
Uwe Müller, Alexander Nützenadel und Philipp Ther

Band 31

2020
Harrassowitz Verlag · Wiesbaden

Peasants into Citizens

The Politicization of Rural Areas in East Central Europe (1861–1914)

Edited by Milan Řepa

2020

Harrassowitz Verlag · Wiesbaden

The series continues the »Frankfurter Studien zur Wirtschafts- und Sozialgeschichte Ostmitteleuropas«, whose volumes 1–16 have been published in the *Berliner Wissenschaftsverlag*.

All volumes of the series go through a peer-review process.

Cover Illustration: Young villagers, Moravian-Silesian borderlands, 1913.

Support for this volume has been provided by the Czech Science Foundation (Funding project No. 17-02986S).

Bibliografische Information der Deutschen Nationalbibliothek
Die Deutsche Nationalbibliothek verzeichnet diese Publikation in der Deutschen Nationalbibliografie; detaillierte bibliografische Daten sind im Internet über https://dnb.de abrufbar.

Bibliographic information published by the Deutsche Nationalbibliothek
The Deutsche Nationalbibliothek lists this publication in the Deutsche Nationalbibliografie; detailed bibliographic data are available in the internet at https://dnb.de

For further information about our publishing program consult our website https://www.harrassowitz-verlag.de

Printed on permanent/durable paper.
Printing and binding: Rosch-Buch Druckerei GmbH, Scheßlitz
Printed in Germany

ISSN 1867-6596
ISBN 978-3-447-11517-9

Contents

Foreword and Acknowledgements

This book was published as part of the Czech Science Foundation grant (no. 17-02986S) “The transformation and social activation of rural areas in Moravia and Austrian Silesia 1861–1914”. The aim of the project was to analyse how modernization processes connected with the principles of civil society and national ideology developed in peripheral rural areas of Moravia and Austrian Silesia, and to what extent these processes became established during this period. The research was based on a representative sample of villages and rural towns, chosen in order to cover Czech-speaking, German-speaking, Polish-speaking and linguistically mixed districts and to encompass various socio-economic environments (more fertile areas, mountain regions). The six-member team analysed the composition and activities of local “elites”, the activities of associations and clubs, elections, and modernizing impulses. A key aspect of the project was an investigation into the structures of communication and organization which enabled civic and national discourse to become established in rural areas, as well as how this discourse was perceived or modified in the context of these peripheral regions.

The book is the result of a workshop held in Prague in September 2018 with the participation of researchers from Europe, the United States and Japan. Its intention was to discuss the politicization of rural areas from a comparative international perspective. I am very grateful to all the active participants; beside the authors who contributed to the final manuscript, also to Daniel Brett (United Kindom), Marko Zajc (Slovenia), Milan Hlavačka and Pavel Cibulka (Czech Republic).

I would like to express my gratitude to Uwe Müller and Roman Holec for the comments and modifications they suggested, and to Graeme Dibble for improving the language. I am very thankful for the support from Harrassowitz Publishing House; namely I am grateful to Barbara Krauß, Michael Fröhlich, and Uwe Müller for their helpfulness, and also to Torsten Lorenz for the mediation.

Brno, May 2020 — Milan Řepa

Introduction

The Politicization of Rural Areas: The Case of East Central Europe

MILAN ŘEPA

The subject of this publication is—as its title suggests—the politicization of the rural, i.e. predominantly agrarian, milieu in the second half of the 19th and early 20th century. The politicization of the countryside was an integral part of a fundamental transformation in society commonly referred to as modernization. The essence of this extensive and long-term political and social change lay in the integration of both individuals and social groups into supra-regional and supra-class structures as the result of building a centralized, bureaucratically administered state, mainly to the detriment of traditional social, local, estate or confessional ties. We usually understand the term "politicization" to mean the increasing participation of the population in public affairs and their identification with certain political ideas, parties or prominent figures.

It was the historians examining modern French history who contributed significantly to our knowledge of the politicization of the countryside.[1] The turbulent transformations in political life in France as well as France's varied regional diversity provide ample material for studying this process. The paradigmatic shifts in the historiography of the 20th century also led to changes in approaches to this issue. After the initial prevalence of political, social and economic history (which dominated in the 1950s and 1960s), the 1970s marked a period when cultural-historical and anthropological approaches started to come to the fore. These enabled us to give detailed explanations of regional modernization, as well as the relationship between the state and its inhabitants, the metropolis and the region, and the town and the countryside.

The classic of the genre—*A Political Portrait of the French "West" During the Third Republic*—stands at the very beginning of a long series of works dealing with this topic. Despite being published as long ago as 1913, it has not dated and we can draw inspiration

---

1 It is such a specific and central field of research that several of its evaluations are already available. The most important include a learned study by an author who has devoted himself to this topic for a long time: Gilles PÉCOUT, *La Politisation des paysans au XIXe siècle. Réflexions sur l'histoire politique des campagnes françaises*, Histoire et Sociétés Rurales 1994, 2, pp. 91–125. The politicization of the folk milieu, i.e. not only the rural one, is dealt with in the study Louis HINCKER, *La politisation des milieux populaires en France au XIXe siècle: constructions d'historiens. Esquisse d'un bilan (1948–1997)*, Revue d'histoire du XIXe siècle, vol. 14, 1997, no. 1, pp. 89–105.

from it to this day.[2] The political profile of the individual regions and their geographic, economic, social and cultural contexts have become an attractive and almost inexhaustible model for analogous studies. They offered a suitable subject for doctoral theses, where candidates showed a mastery of their profession through their knowledge of a specific region. The 1950s and 1960s saw an upsurge in theses dedicated to both the socio-economic and political profile of selected regions, such as works by André Armengaud, Georges Dupeux, Christianne Marcilhacy and Philippe Vigier. The book which probably contributed the most to the issue of the politicization of the countryside was Vigier's *The Second Republic in the Alpine Region,* which regarded the years 1848–1852 as being fundamental for the politicization of the French countryside. Another historian who examined the Second Republic in detail was Maurice Agulhon. Agulhon is one of the most important representatives of the third generation of the Annales school, in which the approaches of cultural anthropology became more popular in French historiography. The key to learning about the politicization of the French countryside is to be found in his book *The Republic in the Village.*[3] While works from the first half of the 1960s stressed social and economic factors, Agulhon was already looking more at collective psychological phenomena. These helped him to explain the relatively sudden and radical movement of the population of the Var department towards democratic principles as well as socialism during the Second Republic.

Agulhon's work places him among those who contributed significantly to the resurgence of political history in the 1970s. It was a return to political history enriched by new methodological approaches which French historiography had picked up over the course of the 20th century. The resurgence of political history was linked to "histoire culturelle", which dominated French historiography in the last quarter of the 20th century in the era of the fourth Annales generation. One of its leading figures was Alain Corbin, whose innovative books practically became bestsellers and were translated into several languages. Those related to the politicization of the countryside include his works about Limousin and *The Village of Cannibals.*[4]

Anglo-Saxon researchers, such as Ted Margadant, Peter McPhee, Michael Burns, Peter M. Jones and Caroline Ford, have also made a considerable contribution to the topic of the politicization of the French countryside. France had always provided them with attractive topics, and the politicization of the countryside was one of the most alluring. This was augmented by the US historian Eugen Weber, who published a book in 1977 depicting how the peasants became "Frenchmen".[5] Of all of the works dedicated to the politicization of the French countryside and the formation of a nation, it was Weber's

2 André Siegfried, *Tableau politique de la France de l'Ouest sous la Troisième république*, Paris 1913.

3 Maurice Agulhon, *La République au village. Les populations du Var de la Révolution à la IIe république*, Paris 1970.

4 Alain Corbin, *Archaïsme et modernité en Limousin au XIXe siècle 1845–1880*, Paris 1975; Alain Corbin, *Le village des "cannibals"*, Paris 1986.

5 Eugen Weber, *Peasants into Frenchmen. The Modernization of Rural France 1870–1914*, London 1977.

monograph which received the most attention, mainly due to his forthright opinions which provoked a number of critical reactions, especially among French historians. According to Weber, the reason that politicization and centralization in France were advancing more slowly than the public generally presumed was because Weber believed "politicization" only referred to municipal issues which were perceived as being "big" in terms of state or national politics. Weber claimed that as late as the 1870s the French still did not fully identify with the state, and that for them a united France was more or less an abstract term. He saw the causes for this in the backwardness of most rural areas. In his opinion, at least until the mid-19th century, life in villages, farms and in remote areas continued according to the same model as before the French Revolution.

Each new regional study by historians dealing with the politicization of the French countryside added more precise findings to this field of research and helped to overturn some prejudices about the rural milieu which were and are widespread both generally and in the historiographical discourse. Naturally, the conclusions and findings contained in the above-mentioned syntheses, monographs and studies cannot be fully applied to other settings, but they can be inspiring. In addition, there might be a number of topics in common, such as the state's attempts at modernization and the resistance to them, the forms of the diffusion of national consciousness and the response from the rural environment of the individual regions, the role of the individual agents of modernization, whether they were institutions (the Church, associations, the army, schools, state and local authorities), participants (priests, intellectuals, teachers, journalists, local authorities) or phenomena and processes (the press, communications, industrialization, elections, secularization, labour migration, etc.).

The situation in East Central Europe (here represented by *Wielkopolska*, Galicia, the Bohemian lands, Hungary, and Romania) was naturally much more heterogeneous than in France and, therefore, in many respects, more specific. Political developments in the second half of the 19th and early 20th century were complicated here by the complex constitutional and ethnic situation that was characteristic especially of the Habsburg Empire, which most of the contributions in this book are related to. As was the case in France, 1848 also marked an important watershed here, which was, however, of even more fundamental importance for the Habsburg Empire. The eras that it divided were not the same as those in France. While in France the *Ancien Régime* ended in July 1789, in the Habsburg Monarchy people had to wait until spring 1848 for this historical moment. Only then were the inhabitants of the Habsburg Monarchy able to gain their first taste of modern politics. New perspectives opened up for all strata of society, including the peasantry. After all, prior to 1848 the peasants had not formed an indifferent mass, passively enduring their fate—this is documented not only by peasant revolts, but also by the number of disputes that subjects had with their landlords, as well as by the complaints they submitted to regional authorities or addressed to the monarch. These disputes with the landlords, which were part of life in the agrarian countryside until the revolution of 1848, mostly concerned the number of corvées and the use of pastures. At the beginning of the revolution in 1848 the subjects' first activities also took the form of requests or complaints. However, old forms of protest were soon replaced by the possibilities offered by civil society—uncensored press, freedom of assembly and elections. Not everyone trusted these innovations; the peasants were, however, discovering that the revolution was heading towards what they had been striving towards for so long—the removal of feudal duties, corvées and servitude in general.[6] After this was achieved, the continuation of the revolution was no longer important to them. "They had never been true revolutionaries," as Jerome Blum rightly pointed out.[7] On the other hand, Paul Himka used the term "very revolutionary reactionaries" for peasants, namely the peasants from Eastern Galicia, pointing out the paradox that although the Galician peasants hated their landlords, loyalty to the ruler and the influence of the Greek Catholic hierarchy finally brought them into the reactionary camp.[8]

The so-called neo-absolutist regime has a bad reputation but it contributed much to developing economic potential, improving state administration and education in the Austrian Monarchy, in particular in its Western areas. The 1850s was also important for the development of peasant socialization and public involvement—in at least two significant respects. Firstly, the creation of local self-government—no matter how limited—made peasants responsible for municipal affairs. For the rural population, local self-government was a great schooling in politics, though it also imposed large burdens on them as a result of the responsibilities passed on to them. Secondly, district agricultural associations started to be established as branches of the semi-governmental land agricultural societies. The state supported their establishment as a response to the complicated changes the rural population was undergoing after the abolition of serfdom within the process of incorporating agricultural production into the wider capital market. This network of agricultural associations was to improve conservative peasant production. Their development and significance for the modernization and politicization of the countryside in the following decades is examined in the contributions by Yuko Kiryu and Andrea Pokludová.

From the 1860s, the politicization of the peasantry in Cisleithania came from two sources—the mutual impact of "high-level" parliamentary politics and association life

---

6 For information about the transformation of the peasant world in the Habsburg Empire in the 19th century, see especially the summarising works by Ernst Bruckmüller: Ernst BRUCKMÜLLER, *Landwirtschaftliche Arbeitswelten und ländliche Sozialstrukturen*, in: Helmut Rumpler—Peter Urbanitsch (eds.), Die Habsburger Monarchie 1848–1918. Band 9, Soziale Strukturen, Teil 1/1. Von der feudal-agrarischen zur bürgerlich-industriellen Gesellschaft, Wien 2010, pp. 251–322; Ernst BRUCKMÜLLER, *Der Bauernstand. Organizationsbildung und Stadeskonsolidierung*, in: Helmut Rumpler—Peter Urbanitsch (eds.), Die Habsburger Monarchie 1848–1918. Band 9, Soziale Strukturen, Teil 1/2, Von der Stände- zur Klassengesellschaft, Wien 2010, pp. 783–811; Ernst BRUCKMÜLLER, *Bäuerliche Mobilisierung und nationale Frage in der Habsburgermonarchie. Zur Genese und Struktur von politischen Organizationen der Bauern*, in: Helga Schultz—Angela Harre (eds.), Bauerngesellschaften auf dem Weg in die Moderne. Agrarismus in Ostmitteleuropa 1880 bis 1960, Wiesbaden 2010, pp. 71–85.

7 Jerome BLUM, *The End of the Old Order in Rural Europe*, Princeton 1978, p. 371.

8 John-Paul HIMKA, *Galician Villagers and the Ukrainian National Movement in the Nineteenth Century*, London 1988, p. 28.

at the local level. It was natural that both currents interlinked. The introduction of electoral curiae, census suffrage and single-seat electoral districts with majority electoral rule significantly favoured certain electoral strata and meant that some social and professional groups were disproportionately represented amongst the deputies in comparison with the social structure of society. To a certain extent, the division of voters and deputies into electoral curiae mirrored the previous division of society into estates and mainly promoted the interests of certain groups in society. This system created a very complicated "electoral geometry;" for example, in the Bohemian lands. As the Czech population paid less tax than the German population overall, it often occurred that even in those electoral districts where the Czechs predominated, the German voters held sway as a result of census suffrage. For example, although German inhabitants formed only a third of the population in Moravia, the German Liberals maintained a majority in the Moravian Provincial Diet from 1861 practically until 1906.[9]

Societies and associations were evidently as important for the development of civil society as parliamentary politics. In the 1860s and 1870s, the network of agricultural associations was the backbone of the countryside. Their significance grew even more after the economic crisis in the 1870s. The owners of small or medium-size farms, who were primarily dependent on the sales of these products, responded to the crisis by increased involvement in associations. Through establishing numerous economic associations, consumer cooperatives, peasant joint-stock sugar refineries, malting plants, breweries and credit unions, peasant schools and academic journals, the peasants were not only looking for protection and non-economic guarantees of their economic prosperity, but also for forms of self-help and a means of making their own agricultural activities more effective. Only as a result of the agrarian crisis did the peasants realize that they could not rely on the existing political forces when pursuing their own ideas, but that they themselves had to be politically more active and organized than they had been until then. The gradual democratization of suffrage increased the weight of peasant votes. The diversification of the political scene in the late 19th century led to the creation of agrarian factions in different political parties or directly to the formation of agrarian parties.

The contributions in this publication reflect a number of crucial issues and questions outlined in this introduction. The aim of this book was to give a comparative perspective of the politicization of villagers in Prussian Poland (*Wielkopolska*), Bohemia, Moravia, Galicia, Hungary, and Romania. Seven historians from Europe, the United States and Japan investigate the processes by which civic structures were created in rural areas. They study the factors leading to the increased participation of the rural population in political life and in public affairs in general.

9 Jan Havránek, *Die ökonomische und politische Lage der Bauernschaft inden böhmishen Ländern in den letzten Jahrzehnten des 19. Jahrhunderts*, Jahrbuch für Wirtschaftsgeschichte 1966, part 2, pp. 97–136; Jiří Malíř, *The Moravian Diet and Political Elites in Moravia 1848-1918*. In Judit Pál—Vlad Popovici (eds.), Elites and Politics in Central and Eastern Europe (1848–1918), Frankfurt am Main 2014, pp. 101–128.

It seems that the "laboratory" for research into the politicization of the peasantry in Central Europe is Galicia, where a varied amalgam of social, ethnic and religious conditions was created. Based on material from Galicia, several now classic works were written on the politicization of the rural countryside. Paul Himka focused on Eastern Galicia and the Ukrainian national movement in his book *Galician Villagers and the Ukrainian National Movement in the Nineteenth Century* published in 1988. The Ukrainian national movement in the last third of the 19th century followed the pattern of the revolutionary years of 1848/1849, when the traditional peasant-landlord conflict became part of the Ukrainian-Polish conflict. Here the basic precondition for the politicization of the peasants was the great Austrian reforms of the 1860s, in particular the restoration of Parliament, the introduction of compulsory education and the guarantee of basic civil liberties such as freedom of the press and freedom of association. The democratization of political life that resulted from the Austrian reforms turned the attention of the national leadership to the peasantry, its only source of votes. By the turn of the century, the East Galician peasantry had been integrated into the Ukrainian nationally defined society, providing it with a strong backbone. On the other hand, national consciousness remained very weak among the Ukrainians living in Russia and Hungary.

In her book *The Nation in the Village,* Keely Stauter-Halsted dealt with the genesis of Polish national identity in Western Galicia during the period 1848–1918.[10] A national consciousness evolved there among many villagers only after the re-emergence of the Polish state in 1918. She stressed that national consciousness was by no means the only identity available to newly emancipated peasants in the former Polish territories, nor was a psychological attachment to "Poland" preordained. Identification with the Austrian state, the Catholic Church, the native region, and with "peasantness" remained strong until the turn of the 20th century.

The most extensive work about the politicization of the peasantry in Galicia was published by the German historian Kai Struve.[11] He showed that what prevented the diffusion of a Polish national consciousness was the fact that from the time of the Polish Commonwealth, peasants had continued to identify Poles with the landlords, and in a wider sense, the upper classes. Due to social tension and cultural differences in feudal society, the peasants regarded the Polish landlords as the "others", and thus nationality played no role in the self-identification of the broad mass of peasants until at least the turn of the 20th century. Similarly to Himka and Stauter-Halsted, Struve also examined the antagonism directed towards the Jews, which increased in particular after the economic crisis in the 1870s and with the foundation of the money economy. Struve also looks at Galicia in the introductory contribution to this collection. Here he expressed his belief that the nationalization of society was not solely the result of the diffusion of a national consciousness among the population, but it consisted primarily in the structuration of

---

10 Keely STAUTER-HALSTED, *The Genesis of Peasant National Identity in Austrian Poland, 1848–1914*, Ithaca 2001.

11 Kai STRUVE, *Bauern und Nation in Galizien. Über Zugehorigkeit und soziale Emanzipation im 19. Jahrhundert*, Göttingen 2005.

civil society according to national differences. Nationalism succeeded in the rural milieu because its advocates linked it to other more concrete offers and benefits (e.g. improvements in agriculture, entertainment) that made the national movement attractive for peasants.

A specific role in the politicization of the countryside was played by agricultural organizations. In their contributions, Yuko Kiryu and Torsten Lorenz emphasize their potential for civil society. Lorenz presented an ambivalent picture of the cooperative movement in the Prussian province of Posen—on the one hand, it had a role in the modernization of society, while on the other, it participated in national disintegration and the implementation of paternalistic leadership structures.

There are two contributions related to Moravia. Pavel Kladiwa explores material concerning one of the most backward and poorest regions of the Bohemian Lands—Wallachia. He considers the external impulses which were the main factors behind modernization (which reached Wallachia at the beginning of the 20th century)—the state education system and also initiatives of local activists. National ideology and civic activism were transferred to the rural Wallachian world from the urban milieu, mainly as a result of the activities of the members of the intelligentsia who migrated there and subsequently became firmly rooted, but also partially the result of local initiatives. Andrea Pokludová focuses on the role and function of clergymen and teachers as forces of progress in the agricultural and social life of the north-eastern Moravian countryside. Her findings disprove the stereotypical idea of clergymen as elements in society which were opposed to modernization; many of them, like teachers, contributed to the spread of the agrarian enlightenment among the peasants.

The political and social conditions in the Transleithanian part of the Habsburg monarchy were significantly different to those in Cisleithania—as well as to those in the Region of Posen, which was part of Prussia. In Hungary, the emancipation of the serfs only applied to half the peasant population. In addition, the emancipated serfs suffered as a result of the high state collection and they had no electoral rights due to the rigidly set census. Naturally, this did not apply to the German peasantry, which benefited from the more advanced agricultural economy. In his contribution, John Swanson investigated the German population and their collective identity in Hungary. Similarly to Struve, Swanson does not view the shift from a premodern identity to a modern one, or from an ethnic identity to a civic or national one, as a simple linear process. Swanson's research explores the forms of Germanness amongst the German minority in Hungary, focusing specifically on the notions of Germanness brought to the rural communities in Hungary from the German Reich.

Romania also offers valuable material for comparisons within the political geography of East Central Europe, as with the case of the Region of Posen, it was an immediate neighbour of the Habsburg Empire. Of all the territories looked at, the conditions here for the transformation of rural dwellers into citizens were undoubtedly the least favourable. This was also shown in the contribution examining electoral legislation in Romania from 1866–1918. Thanks to Sorin Radu, the topic of suffrage was also covered. The Constitution of 1866 introduced modern representative governing principles to Romania, but due to the limited suffrage, peasants were excluded from the franchise. This is persuasively shown by the statistical data. In Romania in 1911 only 6% of adult men had a direct vote for the Chamber and 1.5% had a direct vote for the Senate. These numbers are simply incomparable to those in Cisleithania, when in the same year there was the second election to the Imperial Council based on universal male suffrage. The state of the political culture and standing of the peasant population in Romania is also documented by Radu in the debate which was held on the issue of expanding the franchise. Radu also emphasized the fact that for over four decades, the Romanian educated class did little to prepare the rural world for public life.

This book extends the study of peasant politicization to territories that have remained rather neglected until now. This applies mainly to the Bohemian lands but also, to a certain extent, to Hungary and Romania. These new findings complement those from the longer tradition of research in this particular field, as in the case of Prussian Poland and Galicia. These contributions enable us to compare the different conditions leading to developments in the political life of various parts of East Central Europe. However, at the same time they identify some elements which this area had in common. There were three key agents of politicization in the East Central European countryside: national movements, agricultural associations, and the extension of the franchise.

Bibliography

Maurice AGULHON, *La République au village. Les populations du Var de la Révolution à la IIe république*, Paris 1970.

Jerome BLUM, *The End of the Old Order in Rural Europe*, Princeton 1978.

Ernst BRUCKMÜLLER, *Bäuerliche Mobilisierung und nationale Frage in der Habsburgermonarchie. Zur Genese und Struktur von politischen Organizationen der Bauern*, in: Helga Schultz—Angela Harre (eds.), Bauerngesellschaften auf dem Weg in die Moderne. Agrarismus in Ostmitteleuropa 1880 bis 1960, Wiesbaden 2010, pp. 71–85.

Ernst BRUCKMÜLLER, *Der Bauernstand. Organizationsbildung und Stadeskonsolidierung*, in: Helmut Rumpler—Peter Urbanitsch (eds.), Die Habsburger Monarchie 1848–1918. Band 9, Soziale Strukturen, Teil 1/2, Von der Stände- zur Klassengesellschaft, Wien 2010, pp. 783–811.

Ernst BRUCKMÜLLER, *Landwirtschaftliche Arbeitswelten und ländliche Sozialstrukturen*, in: Helmut Rumpler—Peter Urbanitsch (eds.), Die Habsburger Monarchie 1848–1918. Band 9, Soziale Strukturen, Teil 1/1. Von der feudal-agrarischen zur bürgerlich-industriellen Gesellschaft, Wien 2010, pp. 251–322.

Alain CORBIN, *Archaïsme et modernité en Limousin au XIXe siècle 1845–1880*, Paris 1975.

Alain CORBIN, *Le village des "cannibals"*, Paris 1986.

Jan HAVRÁNEK, *Die ökonomische und politische Lage der Bauernschaft inden böhmishen Ländern in den letzten Jahrzehnten des 19. Jahrhunderts*, Jahrbuch für Wirtschaftsgeschichte 1966, part 2, pp. 97–136.

John-Paul HIMKA, *Galician Villagers and the Ukrainian National Movement in the Nineteenth Century*, London 1988.

Louis HINCKER, *La politisation des milieux populaires en France au XIX*[e] *siècle: constructions d'historiens. Esquisse d'un bilan (1948–1997)*, Revue d'histoire du XIXe siècle, vol. 14, 1997, no. 1, pp. 89–105.

Jiří MALÍŘ, *The Moravian Diet and Political Elites in Moravia 1848-1918*. In Judit Pál—Vlad Popovici (eds.), Elites and Politics in Central and Eastern Europe (1848–1918), Frankfurt am Main 2014, pp. 101–128.

Gilles PÉCOUT, *La Politisation des paysans au XIX*[e] *siècle. Réflexions sur l'histoire politique des campagnes françaises*, Histoire et Sociétés Rurales 1994, 2, pp. 91–125.

André SIEGFRIED, *Tableau politique de la France de l'Ouest sous la Troisième république*, Paris 1913.

Keely STAUTER-HALSTED, *The Genesis of Peasant National Identity in Austrian Poland, 1848–1914*, Ithaca 2001.

Kai STRUVE, *Bauern und Nation in Galizien. Über Zugehorigkeit und soziale Emanzipation im 19. Jahrhundert*, Göttingen 2005.

Eugen WEBER, *Peasants into Frenchmen. The Modernization of Rural France 1870–1914*, London 1977.

Civil Society, Peasants, and Nationalism in Austrian Galicia from the 1860s until 1914

Kai Struve

Abstract

Recent studies of the Habsburg Monarchy, especially of its Austrian half since the 1860s, have emphasized the development of a vital civil society, public sphere, and increasingly broad political participation on the one hand, and on the other hand, they have highlighted the phenomenon of "national indifference". At the same time, civil society and the public sphere became increasingly segmented according to national differences. Using the example of the Galician crownland, the article argues that the new possibilities of political participation offered to broad layers of society by the reforms of the 1860s could be used by them effectively only via organizing and articulating their interests in civil society and the public sphere. The nationalist segmentation of society then appears as the result of the nationalist intelligentsia's crucial role in organizing and articulating these formerly excluded social interests in the public sphere and the political institutions of the Habsburg state.

This article aims to introduce the case of Galicia into two scholarly discussions about the Habsburg monarchy and nationalism. The first discussion relates to the internal development of that state during the nineteenth century. Here the older image of Austria as a "prison of peoples" has been replaced by a view emphasizing the existence of an active civil society and growing political participation, especially in the period from the 1860s until the eve of the First World War. The second discussion relates to the subject of "national indifference" that has attracted much attention in studies of nationalism in recent years.

Both discussions have mainly been inspired by research into Bohemia and German-Czech relations, though they clearly also refer to other cases. Until now Galicia has only been considered here in a marginal way. This article contends that research into the Polish and Ruthenian cases for that crownland can contribute significantly to unresolved questions and problems concerning these two interrelated discussions.

In an important article some years ago, Gary Cohen clearly and emphatically outlined the new view of the Habsburg monarchy as a state characterized by a vital civil society with broad democratic involvement in political decision-making.[1] Pieter Judson put forward a similar, more detailed view in his recent history of the Habsburg Empire.[2] Moreover, Gary Cohen stresses that the national movements were not a reaction against a state suppressing the nationalities, but part of the development of a strong civil society and public sphere.[3] However, neither Cohen nor Judson provide a clear and convincing answer to the question why the increased political participation and mobilization of society in this period took place primarily within national contexts.[4] This question appears even more puzzling when at the same time it is posited that most people were rather indifferent to the appeals of the nationalists.

The concept of "national indifference" developed by Tara Zahra in a more systematic way in an influential article in 2010 was also mainly based on research into Bohemia and Moravia, which she, Pieter Judson and others, had conducted over the previous years.[5] When researching the activities of nationalist organizations and activists, they discovered that the response from society was limited. Bilingualism, mixed marriages and close family ties, local customs and other factors hindered the nationalists' attempts to create clearly delineated national communities. Other studies emphasized the fact that although the German-Czech conflict in Bohemia was the most bitter national conflict in Austria, identification with the monarchy and the emperor, the crownland or local communities, remained strong across all layers of society compared to national identification.[6]

1 Gary B. COHEN, *Nationalist Politics and Dynamics of State and Civil Society in the Habsburg Monarchy, 1867–1914*, Central European History 40, 2007, pp. 241–278.

2 Pieter M. JUDSON, *The Habsburg Empire. A New History*, Cambridge (MA) 2016.

3 G. COHEN, *Nationalist Politics*, pp. 264–268.

4 To a certain degree only the Austrian Social Democrats were an exception here, but nationalist conflicts also increased within their ranks. Finally, in 1911 the Czech Social Democrats ended their cooperation with the German-dominated Austrian party, Jakub S. BENEŠ, *Workers and Nationalism. Czech and German Social Democracy in Habsburg Austria, 1890–1918*, Oxford 2017. In Galicia, Polish and Ruthenian Social Democrats split at the turn of the century, Kerstin S. JOBST, *Zwischen Nationalismus und Internationalismus. Die polnische und ukrainische Sozialdemokratie in Galizien von 1890 bis 1914. Ein Beitrag zur Nationalitätenfrage im Habsburgerreich*, Hamburg 1996.

5 Tara ZAHRA, *Imagined Noncommunities. National Indifference as a Category of Analysis*, Slavic Review 69, 2010, pp. 93–119. See also Pieter M. JUDSON, *Guardians of Nations. Activists of the Language Frontiers of Imperial Austria*, Cambridge (MA) 2006. This study also discusses Southern Styria and South Tyrol; Tara ZAHRA, *Kidnapped Souls. National indifference and the battle for children in the Bohemian lands, 1900–1948*, Ithaca 2008. A region that did not belong to the Habsburg Monarchy, but has appeared rather prominently in research on "national indifference" is Prussian Upper Silesia, see James BJORK, *Neither German nor Pole. Catholicism and National Indifference in a Central European Borderland*, Ann Arbor 2008; for a comparison of Galicia and Upper Silesia with respect to national indifference see Kai STRUVE, *Górny Śląsk na przełomie XIX i XX w.—nacjonalizacja społeczeństwa w perspektywie porównawczej*, in: Sebastian Rosenbaum (ed.): Górnoślązacy. Problemy społeczności pogranicza w XX wieku, Katowice 2014, pp. 16–36. For a recent contribution to the discussion on "national indifference" see also Maarten VAN GINDERACHTER—Jon Fox (eds.), *National Indifference and the History of Nationalism in Modern Europe*, London 2019.

6 Jeremy KING, *Budweisers into Czechs and Germans. A local history of Bohemian politics, 1848–1948*, Princeton 2002. Also the change of or unclear national identification can be considered to belong

Gary Cohen's above-mentioned article discusses the reasons for and consequences of increasing nationalist radicalization at the turn of the century, but it does not address the more basic question of why the increasing political participation and mobilization of society took place to a great extent within national frameworks.

In *Habsburg Empire*, Pieter Judson maintains the top-down perspective that had characterized his earlier study *Guardians of the Nation*. Mobilization for nationalist causes appears here mostly as the result of the intensive work of nationalist activists who ascribed political meaning to linguistic differences and instrumentalized them to integrate different social groups and classes.[7]

The following article proposes a somewhat different answer to the question of why nationalism became so influential despite the fact that national indifference was widespread. It refers to Rogers Brubaker's argument that nations should be considered more as "events" rather than "groups".[8] Brubaker does not discuss the "medium level" of organizations in the sphere of civil society in his critique of "groupness" in a more systematic way, but refers mostly to "entrepreneurs" and "actors" in the nationalist conflicts. Nevertheless, his argument suggests that nations appear over longer periods and can be analysed primarily as national movements. Organizations provide the "fluctuating relations" between individuals, as Brubaker also describes nations, with a certain stability over time and, no less importantly, they support and enable people's combined activity over larger territorial distances who have no direct personal contact with each other. Usually, national movements did not consist of one organization, but of a number of different organizations in the spheres of culture, politics, economics and agriculture. Additionally, these organizations usually did not have aims that were purely and solely "national", but provided their members with concrete benefits or allowed them to present more concrete problems and issues in public or in political institutions. Nevertheless, they acted in a national framework in the sense that they described their activities as national, that they were primarily concerned with the situation of the nation they considered themselves to be a part of and that they saw their work (also) as a contribution to the strengthening of their nations.

Therefore, the question to what extent a society was nationalized or indifferent to nationalism becomes the question to what extent civil society, politics and the public sphere were structured according to national differences. Another, more basic question,

---

to the field of "national indifference". On these phenomena, see: Gary B. Cohen, *The Politics of Ethnic Survival: Germans in Prague, 1861–1914*, Princeton 1981; Emil Brix, *Die Umgangssprachen in Altösterreich zwischen Agitation und Assimilation. Die Sprachenstatistik in den zisleithanischen Volkszählungen 1880 bis 1910*, Wien 1982.

7 P. Judson, *The Habsburg Empire*, pp. 269–275, 299–309. For a critique of the lack of the inclusion of broader organizational background and perspectives of local people in the analysis of "national indifference", see Laurence Cole, *Differentiation or Indifference? Changing Perspectives on National Identification in the Austrian Half of the Habsburg Monarchy*, in: Maarten van Ginderachter—Marnix Beyen (eds.), Nationhood from Below: Europe in the Long Nineteenth Century, Basingstoke 2012, pp. 96–119.

8 Rogers Brubaker, *Ethnicity without Groups*, Cambridge (MA) 2004, pp. 7–27.

however, is why indeed civil society and the public in many parts of Central Europe at the turn of the century were increasingly divided according to national differences and not according to other categories of belonging or interests that transcended national or linguistic boundaries.

This article will discuss these questions for the rural regions and village populations of Galicia. They provide an excellent case study because, on the one hand, national indifference remained quite strong (at least among the Roman Catholic population), and on the other hand, politics, civil society and the public sphere in rural regions were strongly separated along national divisions by the eve of the First World War.

In contrast to Bohemia and other western parts of the Habsburg state, hardly any industry developed in this the largest and most populous Austrian crownland. The economy remained dominated by agriculture and its peasants were mainly subsistence-oriented smallholder farmers. Urbanization was low and illiteracy high, though rates of school attendance rose from the 1880s and reached about 86% for school-age children in 1910/1911.[9]

In Galicia, Polish and Ruthenian nationalisms competed with each other. Traditionally, Ruthenians were those who belonged to the Uniate Greek Catholic church. During the nineteenth century they mostly consisted of peasants and priests, *chłop i pop*, as the somewhat derisive Polish saying went. The nobility of Ruthenian descent had been Polonized and in most cases had changed their religion to Roman Catholic since the Late Middle Ages. A secular Ruthenian intelligentsia only developed towards the end of the nineteenth century.[10]

In earlier decades, Ruthenians who had acquired a secular higher education usually changed their language to Polish and often identified themselves as Poles of the Ruthenian faith. These "gente Rutheni, natione Poloni", as they were often called after a term attributed to the sixteenth-century writer Stanisław Orzechowski, represented one of the main ways to grasp Ruthenian identity in a national sense during the nineteenth century. The two other options that competed with each other within the Ruthenian movement were the Russophile and the Ukrainophile concepts. These considered Ruthenians to either be part of the Russian or the Ukrainian nation.[11] While the Ukrainophile parties and organizations became predominant towards the turn of the century, it was only after the First World War that the Russophiles largely disappeared.[12]

9 On the crownland's economic structure and development, Klemens Kaps, *Ungleiche Entwicklung in Zentraleuropa. Galizien zwischen überregionaler Arbeitsteilung und imperialer Politik, 1772–1914*, Wien 2015; on school attendance, Podręcznik Statystyki Galicyi 9, 1913, part 1, p. 67.

10 Svjatoslav Pacholkiv, *Emanzipation durch Bildung. Entwicklung und gesellschaftliche Rolle der ukrainischen Intelligenz im habsburgischen Galizien (1890–1914)*, Wien 2002.

11 For an excellent discussion on the different concepts of identity among the Galician Ruthenians, John-Paul Himka, *The Construction of Nationality in Galician Rus': Icarian Flights in Almost All Directions*, in: Ronald Grigor Suny—Michael D. Kennedy (eds.), Intellectuals and the Articulation of the Nation, Ann Arbor 1999, pp. 109–164.

12 On the Russophile movement, Anna Veronika Wendland, *Die Russophilen in Galizien. Ukrainische Konservative zwischen Österreich und Rußland 1848–1915*, Wien 2001.

According to the Austrian census of 1900, 45.7% of the population was Roman Catholic, 42.4% Greek Catholic and 11.1% Jewish. The share of Polish speakers was somewhat higher than that of the Roman Catholics because there were more Greek Catholics who declared Polish as their language than Roman Catholics who declared Ruthenian. In addition, most Jews declared themselves Polish speakers because the Austrian census did not recognize Yiddish as a standard language. Greek Catholic speakers of Ruthenian mostly lived in the rural areas of the eastern part of the country, while the Roman Catholics lived mostly in the western part, but they also had the largest share in the urban population in eastern Galicia, especially in the larger cities. They were also a significant minority in some rural regions.[13]

The Early-Modern Legacy in Mid-nineteenth Century Galicia

A deep social and cultural divide between the gentry and the village populations characterized conditions in rural Galicia during the nineteenth century, as it did for most other parts of the early-modern Polish-Lithuanian Commonwealth. For the peasants, the partition in 1772 and the creation of the "Kingdom of Galicia and Lodomeria" under Habsburg rule had resulted in improvements to their legal status vis-a-vis the landlords, and a limitation to the corvée and other feudal duties.[14] Nevertheless, tensions between landlords and peasants remained high or even increased during the first decades of the nineteenth century. During the bloody *rabacja* of 1846, peasants burned down about 400 estates and killed up to 1,000 landlords or their officials in the central, mainly Roman Catholic and Polish-speaking regions of Galicia. This peasant *jacquerie* began when the Austrian *Landrat* of the Tarnów district called upon the peasants to defend the emperor against a Polish national uprising. The peasants quickly defeated the insurgents, who had support mostly among the landlords, but they did not stop at that point and continued to destroy the manors. Apparently, they expected to get rid of the corvée if the manors disappeared. This event demonstrated most strikingly the peasants' attitude towards the Polish national movement's aim of resurrecting the Polish state and towards Polish national identity. Most peasants were not only indifferent, but openly hostile to the Polish nation because they identified their landlords as Poles, remembered conditions in the pre-partition period as having been worse, and feared that the renewal of Polish independence would result in an increase of the landlords' power and more work on the land of the estates.[15]

---

13 Rudolf A. Mark, *Galizien unter österreichischer Herrschaft. Verwaltung—Kirche—Bevölkerung*, Marburg 1994, pp. 70–85, cited numbers on p. 80.

14 Roman Rosdolsky, *Untertan und Staat in Galizien. Die Reformen unter Maria Theresia und Joseph II.*, Mainz 1992 (first published in Polish 1962).

15 The basic study on the events of 1846 is still Stefan Kieniewicz, *Ruch chłopski w Galicji w 1846 roku*, Wrocław 1951; see also Thomas W. Simons, *The Peasant Revolt of 1846 in Galicia: Recent Polish Historiography*, Slavic Review 30, 1971, pp. 795–817. For newer research and the wider context of the events in rural Galicia see Krzysztof K. Daszyk—Tomasz Kargol—Tomasz Szubert (eds.),

The revolution of 1848 was another landmark event and two elements were very important for developments in the future. One was the abolition of the corvée and other feudal duties. The other was that for the first time, Ruthenians demanded recognition as one of the equal nationalities of the Habsburg state. Based mainly around the Greek Catholic church and with a strong role for the priests, "Ruthenian Councils" were established in most parts of eastern Galicia as regional organizations of the "Main Ruthenian Council" [*Holovna Rus'ka Rada*] in L'viv during spring 1848. The gentry and urban-based Polish national movement organized itself into "National Councils" [*Rady Narodowe*]. While the "Ruthenian Councils" also had support among the peasants, peasants saw the Polish "National Councils" as representing their landlords and mostly mistrusted them.[16]

The elections to the Austrian Reichstag of 1848 confirmed the peasants' overwhelming rejection of the Polish movement: 89 of 100 Galician deputies were elected in rural districts, 41 seats were won by Polish candidates, mostly landlords, but also some Roman Catholic priests and other members of the Polish intelligentsia, compared to 35 districts where peasants were elected. However, the mandates for three peasants were invalidated because of alleged violations of the electoral law. In fact, as Roman Rosdolsky has argued, it was not the peasant candidates, but most of the Polish deputies who had won seats in rural districts as the result of fraud, manipulation and violating the electoral law. Part of their mandates resulted from the fact that villages boycotted the elections because they did not understand them, sometimes even fearing a landlords' trap to collect declarations about the return of the corvée.[17] Nevertheless, these elections clearly revealed the ability of peasants to use modern political institutions to represent their interests. Despite the fact that the villagers had no previous experience of political elections, in nearly 40% of rural districts, peasant candidates were elected. Also most of the ten non-peasant Ruthenian deputies were elected only because of strong peasant support.

The Austrian Reforms of the 1860s and their Impact

After the failure of the 1848 revolution, only the Austrian reforms of the 1860s offered new opportunities for broader political participation. They created the basis for the

Rok 1846 w Krakowie i Galicji. Odniesienia, interpretacje, pamięc, Kraków 2016. Andriy Zayarnyuk discusses the repercussions of 1846 on the mostly Ruthenian Sambir region, Andriy Zayarnyuk, *Framing the Ukrainian Peasantry in Habsburg Galicia, 1846–1914*, Edmonton 2013, pp. 1–35.

16 Stefan Kieniewicz, *Pomiędzy Stadionem a Goslarem. Sprawa włościańska w Galicji w 1848 r.*, Wrocław 1980; on peasants and the Ruthenian movement in 1848, J.-P. Himka, *Galician Villagers*, pp. 26–36, and A. Zayarnyuk, *Framing the Ukrainian Peasantry*, pp. 36–75. Zayarnyuk tends to emphasize the distance between peasants and the mainly clerical activists of the Ruthenian movement. That is certainly true, but in the Polish case mistrust between both sides was clearly much greater, see for a comparison Kai Struve, *Bauern und Nation in Galizien. Über Zugehörigkeit und soziale Emanzipation im 19. Jahrhundert*, Göttingen 2005, pp. 85–94.

17 Roman Rosdolsky, *Die Bauernabgeordneten im konstituierenden österreichischen Reichstag 1848–1849*, Wien 1976, pp. 61–80.

development of an active civil society and public during the last decades of the Habsburg Monarchy.

One of the most important steps for the involvement of peasants in politics was the reform of the crownland diets in 1861. In Galicia, the ballot rules remained in force with only small changes until 1914 and gave the peasants a large degree of influence; 74 of 150 (later 161) seats were elected by the fourth curia of villages and small towns. The first curia of large landowners could only elect 44 deputies. The remaining seats were allotted to the larger cities and the chambers of industry and commerce. However, additional restrictions applied to the fourth curia. The elections were indirect and open. Voters chose electoral delegates who then elected the deputy. Both provisions created many opportunities for bribery and other manipulation. A tax census also applied which meant that only about half of the male population over the age of 24 could vote.[18] Nevertheless, the mainly peasant fourth curia had great political clout. From 1873 deputies were also elected to Vienna's *Reichsrat* according to similar rules. Here 27 of the 63 Galician seats were allocated to the fourth curia.[19]

The reform of communal (self-) administration that began in 1856 and received its final legal form in 1866 was another important step for the involvement of the rural population in political decision-making. It separated villages and the manor and gave elected mayors and village councils quite a wide range of competencies. Though village self-administration often functioned poorly in its initial phase due to many of the illiterate mayors' lack of qualifications, it allowed villagers to be part of a political process to improve conditions in their communities. It also taught mayors and other activists the mechanisms of state administration and how to use them in their own interest.[20]

The first elections to the Galician diet in 1861 and 1867 showed similar peasant attitudes to those in evidence during the Reichstag elections in 1848. Ruthenian candidates won nearly all of the eastern Galician seats from the fourth curia. In 1861, there were 26 Greek Catholic priests, three Ruthenians from the secular intelligentsia and 18 peasants among the elected Ruthenian deputies. The peasants' mistrust of the landlords and "Poles" remained deep, as was demonstrated by the outcome of the election in western

18 On the electoral rules for the Galician diet, Stanisław GRODZISKI, *Sejm Krajowy galicyjski 1861–1914*, vol. 1, Warszawa 1993, pp. 45–82. On the percentage of those eligible to vote, K. STRUVE, *Bauern und Nation*, pp. 114.

19 On the electoral rules for the Reichsrat elections, Harald BINDER, *Galizien in Wien. Parteien, Wahlen, Fraktionen im Übergang zur Massenpolitik*, Wien 2005, pp. 185–190; Józef BUSZKO, *Polacy w parlamencie austriackim 1848–1918*, Warszawa 1996, pp. 259–273.

20 On village self-administration and its problems, see Keely STAUTER-HALSTED, *The Nation in the Village. The Genesis of Peasant National Identity in Austrian Poland, 1848–1914*, Ithaca 2001, pp. 78–91, John-Paul HIMKA, *Galician Villagers and the Ukrainian National Movement in the Nineteenth Century*, London 1988, pp. 175–189; Jan MOLENDA, *Chłopi—naród –niepodległość. Kształtowanie się postaw narodowych i obywatelskich chłopów w Galicji i Królestwie Polskim w przededniu odrodzenia Polski*, Warszawa 1999, pp. 112–133. The role of peasants in district self-administration has not received much attention in research yet, for the legal aspect, see Konstanty GRZYBOWSKI, *Galicja 1848–1914. Historia ustroju politycznego na tle historii ustroju Austrii*, Kraków 1959, pp. 227–289.

Galicia. Despite the fact that no organized political movement competed against the Polish candidates, seventeen peasants were elected from the fourth curia, but only seven landlords and members of the Polish intelligentsia, and three Roman Catholic priests. One remarkable change in comparison to the 1848 elections was that the peasants now appeared to have a much better understanding of the meaning and significance of the elections. In contrast to 1848, the number of villages boycotting the elections, fearing a landlords' trap, was low. Although comprehensive statistical data only exists for elections since 1876, there are many indications that participation in these elections was higher than during the subsequent decades until the end of the century.[21] The fundamental politicization of the peasants was not so much the result of education and organization towards the end of the century, as it was obviously already in existence in the 1860s.

The main political aim of the peasants and their deputies during the 1860s and 1870s was to keep the "servitutes"—the rights of village communities to use pastures and forests—for the villages. When the corvée and other peasant feudal duties were abolished in 1848, the question of the "servitutes" had been left unresolved. Conflicts had already arisen in 1848 when landlords barred peasants from entering forests or driving their cattle to the pastures which they claimed as their property. From 1855 a state commission reviewed the numerous disputed cases, usually deciding in favour of the manors and assigning some compensation in the form of money or part of the pastures or forests to the villages or peasants. However, for the peasants most of these decisions were unsatisfactory and the proceedings and decisions led to great resentment. A large majority of the cases were decided during the 1860s and 1870s, but some judicial proceedings continued until the beginning of the 1890s.[22]

Not very much is known about the first peasant deputies in the Galician diet. The Ruthenian peasants were part of the Ruthenian club, though many did not participate actively or regularly in its meetings. In addition, the Ruthenian intelligentsia deputies and activists were unhappy about the large number of peasants in the diet. However, it was only in 1873 that a short-lived joint club of Ruthenian and Polish peasants emerged after the Ruthenian peasant deputies had left the Ruthenian club because they believed that the other Ruthenian deputies did not support their struggle for the servitudes strongly enough.[23] Here a shared social identity and common interests overcame religious and national divisions.

21 Józef Putek, *Pierwszy wstępy włościaństwa polskiego 1848–1861*, Kraków n. d. [1933], pp. 26–30; Ostap Sereda, *"My tu ne pryishly na smikh": uchast' skhidnohalyc'kykh selian u seimovykh vyborakh ta zasidanniakh u L'vovi (60-I roky XIX st.)*, in: Kazimierz Karolczak (ed.), L'viv—misto—suspil'stvo—kultura/Lwów. Miasto—społeczeństwo—kultura, vol. 4, Kraków 2002, pp. 165–186, here, p. 168, see also pp. 173–181. On electoral turnout in rural districts, Kai Struve, *Politische Mobilisierung und nationale Identifikation. Die Wahlbeteiligung der Landbevölkerung in Galizien 1861–1911*, Zeitschrift für Ostmitteleuropaforschung 54, 2005, pp. 377–398.

22 J.-P. Himka, *Galician Villagers*, pp. 36–56; A. Zayarnyuk, *Framing the Ukrainian Peasantry*, pp. 76–97; Krzysztof Ślusarek, *Uwłaszczenie chłopów w Galicji zachodniej*, Kraków 2002.

23 On the peasant club, Ihor Chornovol, *Ukraïns'ka fraktsiia halyts'koho kraiovoho sejmu 1861–1901 r.*, L'viv 2002, p. 77; K. Struve, *Bauern und Nation*, pp. 243f.; more broadly on Ruthenian peasant

Among the western Galician peasant deputies in the first Galician diet of 1861, Jan Siwiec, the deputy from Żywiec district on the western border with Silesia, was an outstanding figure. As the son of a wealthy peasant he studied for some time at L'viv University, but had to abandon his studies as a result of the 1848 revolution. Later he was drafted into the Austrian army for ten years after coming into conflict with officials from the imperial estates in the region. Siwiec was not only popular among the peasants, but he also shared their loyalty to the emperor and the Austrian state. In 1861 he published a forty-page pamphlet entitled *Dem Kaiserstaate Österreich gewidmet von einem seiner Bewohner*, with proposals to reform the Austrian state, among them democratization, improvement of elementary education, abolition of corporal punishment and regulations for church fees. However, he did not mention any Polish or other national aims. The German-language pamphlet had been written by an Austrian patriot. In 1863 Siwiec was deprived of his mandate because at the time of the election he had not fulfilled the legal requirements for becoming a deputy, although he did so after taking his seat.[24] Obviously, the well-educated and literate Siwiec was even more inconvenient for the Polish deputies than the other peasant deputies.

The high share of peasant and Ruthenian deputies in 1861 was never to be reached again. The possibility of a non-national peasant movement loyal to the Austrian state that appeared in the 1860s and 1870s never materialized, because neither then, nor later, did the intelligentsia activists support peasant emancipatory efforts within an non-national Austrian framework. During the following elections the Polish political activists succeeded in continuously reducing the number of peasant and Ruthenian deputies until the end of the 1880s. Between 1876 and 1889 no peasant candidate was elected in western Galicia. The number of Ruthenian deputies declined to eleven after the elections in 1883.[25]

The most important reason for the decline in the number of peasant and Ruthenian deputies was that before the election to the Galician diet in 1867, Polish politicians had established the Polish *Centralne Komitety Wyborcze* [CKW, Central Electoral Committees]—one in Kraków for the western part of the crownland and one in L'viv for the eastern part. Their task was to select candidates for the electoral districts and to organize support for them with the help of delegates or district committees. Despite their differences, both Polish conservatives and democrats participated in these committees because they shared the aim of preventing the election of Ruthenian and peasant

---

and non-peasant deputies, A. Zayarnyuk, *Framing the Ukrainian Peasantry*, pp. 97–113; O. Sereda, *"My tu ne pryishly"*, pp. 181–184.

24 *Dem Kaiserstaate Österreich gewidmet von einem seiner Bewohner*, Teschen 1861. The pamphlet was published anonymously, see Stefan Suchonek, *Poseł Jan Siwiec (Karta z dziejów ruchu ludowego w Galicji)*, in: Henryk Barycz—Jan Hulewicz (eds.), Studia z dziejów kultury polskiej, Warszawa 1949, pp. 539–562. See also K. Stauter-Halsted, *The Nation in the Village*, pp. 68–72.

25 There was even more substantial decline during the Reichsrat elections. In 1873 fifteen Ruthenian deputies were elected. In 1879 their number fell to three, A. V. Wendland, *Die Russophilen*, pp. 368–370.

candidates.[26] Due to the fact that nearly half of the seats in the Galician diet were from the fourth curia, it was crucial for the Polish political groupings to win a significant number of seats in that curia in order to maintain their traditional role of political leadership. This was even more essential against the backdrop of their accommodation with the Austrian state in the informal "Galician autonomy" which emerged before and after the constitutional reforms of 1867. This autonomy basically meant that a majority of the Polish elites declared their support for and loyalty to the emperor and the Austrian state. In return, they were allowed to oversee Galician affairs and gain some influence in Vienna. However, an essential element of this new informal arrangement of Polish self-rule was that the Polish conservative loyal elites held strong positions in the Galician diet and the Reichsrat. For this they needed seats from the fourth curia.[27] One of the consequences was that from the 1870s, elections were increasingly characterized by the bribery of electors and officials' biased or fraudulent activities.[28]

However, there were other reasons for the decline in the number of Ruthenian and peasant deputies. One was dissatisfaction among peasants about the effectiveness of their deputies who had been unable to safeguard the servitudes or bring about other significant improvements.[29]

Furthermore, the reduction in the number of Ruthenian deputies at the end of the 1870s was also the result of a crisis in the Russophile movement, which foreshadowed some of the reasons for its decline and the rise of the Ukrainophiles. In fact, at that time and later for most local activists the question of Russophilism vs. Ukrainophilism was unimportant compared to the shared belonging to the Ruthenians. However, on a crownland level, the Russophile influence had been increasing from the 1850s until the 1870s.[30] Towards the end of the 1870s, the print-run of the most important Ruthenian newspapers in the rural regions in that period, *Nauka* and *Russkaja Rada*, declined. One of the reasons was that the language of the newspapers had moved away from the Galician vernacular and closer to Russian, the language which the Russophiles aimed to introduce into Galicia as part of their nation-building project.[31] The fundamental problem which

26 On the CKW, H. Binder, *Galizien in Wien*, pp. 190–201; on the eastern Galician branch, Magdalena Semczyszyn, *Galicyjskie wybory. Działalność Centralnego Komitetu Wyborczego w Galicji Wschodniej w latach 1867–1906*, Warszawa 2014.

27 Christoph Freiherr Marschall von Bieberstein, *Freiheit in der Unfreiheit. Die nationale Autonomie der Polen in Galizien nach dem österreichisch-ungarischen Ausgleich von 1867*, Wiesbaden 1993.

28 On the example of the Sambir region, A. Zayarnyuk, *Framing the Ukrainian Peasantry*, pp. 169–176.

29 K. Struve, *Bauern und Nation*, pp. 247f.

30 This also had the religious dimension of strong tendencies towards Orthodoxy among the Greek Catholic clergy in this period, John-Paul Himka, *Religion and Nationality in Western Ukraine. The Greek Catholic Church and the Ruthenian National Movement in Galicia, 1867–1900*, Montreal 1999.

31 A. V. Wendland, *Die Russophilen*, pp. 399f.; K. Struve, *Bauern und Nation*, pp. 138f. On linguistic controversies and practices among Galician Ruthenians see also Michael Moser, *New Contributions to the History of the Ukrainian Language*, Toronto 2016, pp. 169-408

the Russophiles continued to struggle with was that most of their newspaper readers simply did not understand that language.

More generally, the Russophiles tried to compensate for the Ruthenians' lack of many of the elements of a modern nation (and to compete in that respect with the Poles) by defining the Ruthenians as part of the Russian nation. However, by referring to the prestige of Russian high culture and literary language, the political power of the Czar, and the Orthodox Church, they risked becoming alienated from the broad mass of the Ruthenian population. In addition to the language problem, there were other reasons why the Ukrainophile concept provided a better base for overcoming the social distance between the peasants and intelligentsia, and for developing joint organizational and communication structures. For the *narodovtsi*, as the Ukrainophiles were mostly called in nineteenth century Galicia, the basis of Ukrainian national identity was the *narod*, the people, and their language and culture. Such a concept greatly encouraged intelligentsia activists to become involved with the peasants on an equal base. With regard to politics, after the reforms of the 1860s the Ruthenian movement could only make capital from the issues of political participation, constitutional rights, and social justice. For this, the Ukrainophile concept provided a much better base than by referring to Czarist autocracy. On the one hand, the Ukrainophile concept was more open to the inclusion of peasant interests, and on the other, it was more attractive to the younger generation of intelligentsia activists who were more strongly influenced by various left-wing, socialist ideas than the Russophiles of the 1860s and 1870s.

More generally, political developments in the 1860s and 1870s showed the peasants to be highly politically mobilized, but with weak organizational and communication structures. They were too weak to resist the Polish side's more effective strategies in getting their candidates elected. Stable organizational and communication structures among the peasants and between the peasants and intelligentsia activists as the basis for political activity and electoral success developed only over the subsequent two decades.

The constitutional reforms of the Austrian state during the 1860s laid the groundwork for closer integration between peasants and intelligentsia activists in organizations combining national aims with the struggle for the improvement of conditions in the villages, real civic equality for the peasants and to promote their economic interests. The peasantry lacked the skills and means for developing and maintaining parties and other organizations on their own beyond small regions. This was only possible with the participation of intelligentsia activists who edited and distributed newspapers and participated in maintaining organizational structures. Usually, the intelligentsia activists in rural regions also had a national agenda and included national objectives among their activities.

Therefore, the effective representation of peasant interests within modern political institutions which required a pooling of interests in civil-society organizations and the public sphere only took place in national contexts. Peasant activists also had to accept the national goals. But many of them also realized that emphasizing the peasants' national identity provided them with an additional resource for legitimizing and publicly presenting their concerns. At the same time, the only intelligentsia activities who were successful in rallying peasant support were those who genuinely integrated peasants and peasant interests. Nevertheless, the result was a national separation in politics and the public sphere which was not based on the strong national feelings of the majority of the rural population, but on the fact that there were no other structures in civil society and the public sphere which supported peasants in the pursuit of their civic rights.

Civil Society

The Austrian reforms of the 1860s created the legal base for intelligentsia activities which aimed to improve the deplorable living conditions in the villages. The new political importance of the peasantry seems to have contributed to the increased interest.

The Ruthenian association for popular education, *Prosvita*, was founded in 1868 and initially produced popular books and pamphlets. Although the Ukrainophile *Prosvita* association was later to become the most important organization in Ruthenian civil society in Galicia, during the 1870s the *Kachkovs'kyi Society*—a Russophile educational association founded in 1874—was more successful and influential. A number of reading rooms were also established in villages in this period, but they were not stable yet and nearly all of them had disappeared again by the end of the 1870s.[32]

The first Polish associations for popular education were founded in the same period, but they were short-lived and had no major impact. This again indicates the larger social distance between the peasants and the Polish upper classes. The peasants' mistrust was deeper because of the role of the landlords in these activities, while the commitment of intelligentsia activists seems to have been weaker.[33]

At the start of the 1880s, new Polish associations for popular education were founded that were more permanent. They established a large number of small libraries and reading rooms in villages. In later years the libraries and reading rooms often served as educational centres, providing lectures and other activities. In contrast to the Ruthenian associations, which had a large peasant membership, these new Polish associations had been founded by the Polish upper classes for the peasants. They did not encourage peasants to become members, and as a result the peasants had no formal voice in organizational matters.[34] The only exception was an association which united the "agrarian circles" in its initial phase.

32 On the Kachkovs'kyi Society, A. V. Wendland, *Die Russophilen*, pp. 262–321; Paul Robert Magocsi, *The Kachkovs'kyi Society and the National Revival in Nineteenth Century East Galicia*, Harvard Ukrainian Studies 15, 1991, pp. 48–87; the most comprehensive treatment of *Prosvita* is still Stepan Pers'kyi, *Populiarna istoriia tovarystva "Prosvita" u L'vovi*, L'viv 1932; for a comparison of their early activities, K. Struve, *Bauern und Nation*, pp. 142–148; A. Zayarnyuk, *Framing the Ukrainian Peasantry*, pp. 126–145.

33 Ryszard Terlecki, *Oświata dorosłych i popularyzacja nauki w Galicji w okresie autonomii*, Wrocław 1990, pp. 25–38.

34 The basic study of these organizations is R. Terlecki, *Oświata dorosłych*. See also Józef Szocki, *Literatura popularna dla ludu na przykładzie Wydawnictwa Ludowego 1882–1920*, Kraków 1994; K. Struve, *Bauern und Nation*, pp. 158–170.

At the end of the 1870s, the Roman Catholic priest Stanisław Stojałowski initiated the foundation of "agrarian circles" [*kółka rolnicze*] in Galician villages to support and improve agricultural production, based on a model from the German partition. But when in 1882 the statutes of the *Towarzystwo Kółek Rolniczych* [TKR, Agrarian Circles' Association] were changed as a precondition for receiving funds from the Galician crown-land budget, the rights of village circles at the annual meetings were reduced and the majority of the board then consisted of large landowners.[35]

After their humble beginnings in the 1870s and 1880s, the number of local branches of civil-society organizations began to rise more noticeably from the 1890s, especially during the last decade before the First World War. The original educational purposes of the libraries and reading rooms were now increasingly supplemented by cooperatives and other structures with economic functions. After the turn of the century, when Ruthenian cooperatives developed rapidly, other Ruthenian national activities, for example, the establishment of private Ruthenian gymnasia, could draw on their financial resources. A large number of branches of the *Sich* and *Sokil* gymnastic associations were founded in villages during the last years before the war. The Ruthenian reading rooms in the villages were often also important centres for Ruthenian political activities, in particular for supporting Ruthenian candidates during elections.

While Ruthenian organizations covered the educational, economic, cultural and political needs of the rural population, the role of the Polish organizations was more ambivalent when it came to politics, especially in later years when there was rivalry between different political groups. Although they made clear contributions to education, improvements in agriculture and the village administration, they did not support the political mobilization of the peasants against the political predominance of the traditional elites.

One factor that strongly contributed to the development of the different organizations—partially starting from the 1880s, but most prominently after the turn of the century—was that an increasing number of peasant children, primarily the sons, were attending gymnasia, universities, teacher-training colleges and other institutions of higher learning. Here they acquired a strong sense of duty to work for their nation as well as to improve the living conditions in the villages.

On the eve of the First World War, thousands of local branches and circles of different Polish and Ruthenian organizations existed in the villages. By this time there were very few villages which did not have at least one of these organizations, while many villages had local branches of several organizations. These dragged the villages from their traditional isolation and integrated them through modern forms of organization and communication.[36]

The modern structures of organization and communication in rural areas were clearly divided along national lines, resulting in a civil society which was likewise divided.

---

35 Antoni Gurnicz, *Kółka rolnicze w Galicji. Studium społeczno-ekonomiczne*, Warszawa 1967, pp. 52–56; K. Struve, *Bauern und Nation*, pp. 148–154. On Stojałowski, see below.

36 For an overview of the development of Polish and Ruthenian organizational structures until the First World War, see K. Struve, *Bauern und Nation*, pp. 148–190.

None of the relevant organizations in rural Galicia were dual-national or non-national in character.[37]

The Public Sphere

The 1870s was also a period when the first lasting structures within the public sphere developed in rural areas in the form of weekly, fortnightly or monthly newspapers aimed at a peasant readership. The most important Ruthenian papers of the 1870s, *Russkaia Rada* and *Nauka*, have already been mentioned. *Russkaia Rada* began to appear in 1871 with the aim of informing the rural population about the political situation of the Ruthenians and mobilizing them for Ruthenian political aims. It was related to the foundation of the first Ruthenian (Russophile) political association of the same name a year before. However, like other Ruthenian and Polish newspapers for the rural population, *Russkaia Rada* also gave advice about improvements in agriculture, animal husbandry and the household. They provided information on the history of their nations and about contemporary political issues in Galicia, Austria and the rest of the world. They often included religious themes and warned against the danger of alcoholism. However, while the Ruthenian papers attempted to mobilize peasants in the support of Ruthenian candidates in elections, the first Polish publications for the rural population did not challenge the influence of the landlords and their traditional position of leadership, but advocated the "harmony of the classes" [*zgoda stanów*] and advised the peasants not to complain about their situation. In this respect, there was no major difference between the newspapers edited by Polish democrats and those with more conservative or religious editors.[38]

In the Ruthenian case, support for Ruthenian candidates during elections was also set in a Ruthenian national context in the newspapers for the peasants, as was the more general discourse about the different organizational forms for improvements in the villages. The newspapers provided information about the Ruthenian past, showed how improvements could be made through self-help and self-organization in the villages, and also presented political representation in parliaments as the struggle for national dignity and the recovery of the Ruthenians' former greatness and wealth. Therefore, active support for Ruthenian candidates during elections also appeared as a national duty, while voting for Polish candidates demonstrated a person's moral failing.[39]

37 Though none of them excluded members of a different nationality. In fact, Polish organizations such as the TKR and the early Polish educational associations saw themselves as Galician organizations and attempted to establish circles in Ruthenian villages. However, the organizational leaders were clearly Polish and they understood their philantropic activities as service to the nation. Ruthenian activists considered these activities to be attempts at Polonization.

38 K. Struve, *Bauern und Nation*, pp. 126–128.

39 This was similar in the Polish case, on the moral character of the discourse on reform in the villages, K. Stauter-Halsted, *The Nation in the village*, pp. 185–208.

However, the newspapers were important as a means of communication in both the Polish and Ruthenian cases. The more popular papers not only promoted messages from the intelligentsia activists and editors, but they also published readers' letters from the villages. A shared discourse between the editors and readers developed concerning an agenda for reform and change. When in later years Polish newspapers for the rural population also challenged the political hegemony of the traditional elites, as in the Ruthenian case, this discourse on reform and improvements also included politics and support for peasant candidates during elections. The letters contained descriptions of positive and negative examples from the villages. In this way, positive developments such as the foundation of reading rooms (mostly in the Ruthenian case) and later agrarian circles (in the Polish case), or other forms of local self-organization, served as examples for others. This was also true for village administration, political organization, and voting behaviour.[40]

Nevertheless, the public sphere in rural areas was also divided along national lines. There was no important newspaper for the rural population that was not clearly related to a national project.[41]

Peasants in Polish Politics

The Roman Catholic priest Stanisław Stojałowski was the first person from the Polish side to openly criticize the Polish elites' ignorance and fear of the peasantry, and the subterfuge they employed to prevent the peasants from expressing their political will. In 1875 he took over the editorship of the peasant newspapers *Wieniec* and *Pszczółka*, which appeared alternately every week. Over the next decades Stojałowski became a unique figure in Galicia's political landscape. He was one of the main protagonists of both Ultramontanism and Christian-social ideas in Galicia. He was a fierce critic of liberalism and its main supporters, the Polish democrats. But he also believed that the ordinary Catholic people were a bulwark against the evils of liberal modernity, and he became the most uncompromising defender of their political rights. At the same time, he was a Polish nationalist and attacked the Polish conservatives because of their accommodation with the Austrian state, their loyalism and their passivity when it came to the struggle for Polish independence. During the 1870s and the beginning of the 1880s, Stojałowski had some support from the Roman Catholic archbishop of L'viv, Franciszek Wierzchlejski. But he increasingly came into conflict with the Polish elites because of his critique of how they excluded peasants from politics and neglected their interests. Before the elections to the Galician diet in 1876, he advised his readers not to send peasants to parliament as their lack of education would prevent them from representing peasant interests successfully. But he called upon the Polish electoral committees to consider the opinions of the peasants when

40 J.-P. Himka, *Galician Villagers*, pp. 80–86; K. Struve, *Bauern und Nation*, pp. 133f.

41 During different periods, Polish activists and educational organizations also produced publications in Ukrainian. However, they mainly aimed to reduce the influence of Ruthenian organizations and parties.

proposing candidates. He also demanded that peasants should be included in the Polish electoral committees on district level and that the committees should organize meetings in villages. *Czas*, the newspaper of the most influential western Galician conservatives in Krakow, rejected Stojałowski's demands as "untimely" [*niewczesny*], but this rejection only increased his anger at "the obscurantism of the gentry".[42] Stojałowski criticized many of the gentry deputies from the fourth curia for their lack of interest in the problems of their voters and for their corrupt practices and pressure on the electorate. He explained to his peasant readers that they were no longer the subjects of the emperor or their landlords, but that they were now equal citizens of the state who should take their obligations seriously and not allow them to be bought.[43] Stojałowski's clear advocacy of peasants' civil rights and his critique of the Polish elites made his newspapers extremely popular and influential among Polish-speaking peasants during the 1880s and 1890s.[44]

It was only with the elections to the Galician diet in 1883 that Stojałowski explicitly broke with Polish national solidarity, suggesting to his readers that they should establish their own peasant electoral committees in those districts where the Polish committees did not involve peasants when selecting candidates. However, he made this proposal shortly before the election and he did not seem to be completely committed in this direction. Only before the next elections to the Galician diet in 1889 both Stojałowski and a group from the Polish democratic left, most prominently the editor of the L'viv daily *Kuryer Lwowski*,

---

42 See Stanisław STOJAŁOWSKI, *Liberalna blaga przedwyborcza i nowy program czynności przedwyborczych oraz słówko o kołtuństwie szlacheckim*, Lwów 1876. This pamphlet was addressed to the educated public. In his newspapers for the peasants, Stojałowski presented his critique more moderately.

43 See, for example, Wieniec no. 20, 21 September 1876, p. 1; K. STRUVE, *Bauern und Nation*, pp. 198f.

44 Unfortunately, there is still no comprehensive biography of this outstanding figure in Galician politics, see Franciszek KĄCKI, *Ks. Stanisław Stojałowski i jego działalność społeczno-polityczna*, vol. 1 1845–1890, Lwów 1937. A second volume has never been published. Andrzej KUDŁASZYK, *Ksiądz Stanisław Stojałowski. Studium historyczno-prawne*, Wrocław 1998, is mostly restricted to an analysis of his Christian-social writings. Sometimes in more general histories Stojałowski appears somewhat unjustly as a leading representative of antisemitism in Galicia. In fact, the whole Polish and Ruthenian discourse on village reform had a strong anti-Jewish tendency and aimed at excluding Jews from the rural economy; for a more extensive discussion see John-Paul HIMKA, *Ukrainian-Jewish Antagonism in the Galician Countryside During the Late Nineteenth Century*, in: Peter J. Potichnyj—Howard Aster (eds.), Ukrainian-Jewish Relations in Historical Perspective, Edmonton 1988, pp. 111–158; K. STRUVE, *Bauern und Nation*, pp. 384–433. In Stojałowski's case this was to a certain degree amplified by his Christian-social, anti-liberal views. However, in contrast to others from the Christian-social spectrum, antisemitism was never a central feature of his political views and was almost absent during his most radical phase in the 1890s. Only when he had been forced to moderate some of his position by a temporary excommunication in 1896 and, at the same time, when he lost influence to the more leftist *Stronnictwo Ludowe* did he instrumentalize antisemitic rhetoric against his opponents and, thereby, contributed to the instigation of the anti-Jewish riots of 1898; on this extensively, Tim BUCHEN, *Antisemitismus in Galizien. Agitation, Gewalt und Politik gegen Juden in der Habsburgermonarchie um 1900*, Berlin 2012; also Tim BUCHEN, *Religiöse Mobilisierung im Reich: Die imperialen Lebensläufe und politischen Karrieren von Joseph Bloch und Stanisław Stojałowski in der Habsburgermonarchie*, Geschichte und Gesellschaft 40, 2014, pp. 117–141.

Bolesław Wysłouch, called for the establishment of separate peasant electoral committees. A new weekly peasant newspaper, *Przyjaciel Ludu*, supported these committees.

Three years earlier in 1886, as editor of the L'viv journal *Przegląd Społeczny*, Wysłouch had published an article called *Szkice programowe*, outlining a political programme that he and others began to implement in 1889. This article wholeheartedly endorsed an ethnic concept of Polish national identity and declared the "people", the *lud*, to be the true foundation and guarantee of Polish national existence. It strongly rejected earlier political concepts which, in the tradition of the early-modern political concept of the Polish nation, emphasized the role of the gentry and intelligentsia. As the peasants were the true Polish nation, any hope for the resurrection of the Polish state could rest only with them. On the one hand, they had to be won over to become supporters of that aim, while on the other, all Polish national political groupings had to take into account peasant interests and their positive development.[45] This was a strong critique of both the conservative and democratic political elites who, in practical terms, had worked hard to exclude peasants from political participation during the previous decades. The *Szkice programowe* accused them of only pretending to act in the national interest, as they did not actively pursue the goal of national independence, they did not engage in improving conditions in the villages, and in fact worked to prevent the peasantry's active involvement in politics.

These ideas provided the foundation for the peasant party, the *Stronnictwo ludowe*, which came into being between the elections to the Galician diet in 1889 and 1895. In the years leading up to First World War, it contributed strongly to making Polish national identity an attractive concept for politically active peasants, as the claim that they were the fundamental part of the nation helped further their social, political and economic demands, as well as their practical emancipation in the sense that they could actually use their political rights.

In 1889 four peasants and one teacher were elected as candidates of separate peasant committees. However, the number of peasant committees and peasant candidates had been larger.[46] The real breakthrough for the peasant committees came with the elections to the Galician diet in 1895, when candidates from peasant committees were elected in 11 of 26 western Galician districts. In that year, Wysłouch's group, together with Stojałowski and his newspapers, were even more resolute in their support of the foundation of peasant committees. They also established a Central Pre-election Committee of the People's Party [*Centralny Komitet Przedwyborczy Stronnictwa Ludowego*] as a coordinating organization for the various peasant committees, and published a joint programme. This is considered to be the foundation of the Polish peasant party, the *Stronnictwo Ludowe*.[47]

45 The *Szkice programowe* was reprinted in Stanisław Lato—Witold Stankiewicz (eds.), *Programy stronnictw ludowych. Zbiór dokumentów*, Warszawa 1969, pp. 27–48. On Wysłouch, Peter Brock, *Nationalism and Populism in Partitioned Poland. Selected Essays*, London 1973, pp. 181–211; Andrzej Kudłaszyk, *Myśl społeczno-polityczna Bolesława Wysloucha 1855–1937*, Warszawa 1978.

46 One of the elected candidates soon resigned from his mandate, apparently under pressure from his landlord opponent, K. Struve, *Bauern und Nation*, pp. 220f..

47 K. Struve, *Bauern und Nation*, pp. 222–232; Ewa Maria Ożóg, *Powstanie Stronnictwa Ludowego*, in: Stanisław Dąbrowski (ed.), Działalność polityczna ruchu ludowego, Rzeszów 1996, pp. 23–32.

However, the encouragement and advice from Stojałowski's and Wysłouch's newspapers and their role reporting peasant activities in different parts of the crownland was only one factor in these electoral successes. There were two other important factors. One was the growing discontent among the peasants due to the fact that they were being represented in parliament by people whom they mistrusted. This was also the result of the peasants' increased understanding about the importance of representative bodies and their own rights. They learned about this through the newspapers, but also through practical experience in the villages and with district self-administration.[48]

The second factor was that from the mid-1880s clandestine youth groups linked to the conspirational *Liga Polska* emerged in gymnasia in smaller Galician cities. This was part of a new mobilization of the youth in the resumption of a more active struggle to regain Polish independence after the failure of the January uprising in 1863/64 and the subsequent predominance of positivism and loyalism. At this time, many peasant sons already attended the gymnasia in smaller towns. Not only did they try to acquire the villages for the Polish nation, but they also supported Stojałowski's and Wysłouch's efforts to encourage peasants to form their own electoral committees.[49]

The new *Stronnictwo Ludowe* that formed in 1895 changed its name to *Polskie Stronnictwo Ludowe* in 1903. It presented itself as the true national party because, as it claimed in its new main programme, it represented the real "core of the nation", the peasantry. Its conclusion was: "Therefore, any policy that is not concerned about [the peasantry's] living conditions is not a national policy."[50] Peasant activists also increasingly began to emphasize the peasants' patriotism and their central role in the nation. In 1903 the PSL declared April 4, the anniversary of the Battle of Racławice in 1794, as a *Święto Ludowe* [Peoples' Holiday]. The Battle of Racławice during the Kościuszko insurrection against the Russian army had been won due to a decisive attack by a peasant detachment with re-forged scythes, the famous *kosynierzy*, under the leadership of the peasant Bartosz

48 This element appeared most clearly in the western Galician region of Nowy Sącz. Here a group of wealthy and well-educated peasants had already challenged the political predominance of the conservatives in previous elections, but they were first successful in 1889 when Stanisław Potoczek won the mandate for the Galician diet. They cooperated with Stojałowski, but in 1892 separated from him and established their own party and newspaper. Only in 1908 did this group join the *Stronnictwo Ludowe*, Antoni Gurnicz, *O „równą miarkę" dla chłopów. Poglądy i działalność pierwszej chłopskiej organizacji politycznej w Polsce Związku Stronnictwa Chłopskiego 1893–1908*, Warszawa 1963; K. Struve, *Bauern und Nation*, pp. 205–217.

49 One of these activists was the peasant son Jan Stapiński, who at that time attended the gymnasium in Jasło, and who later became the leading politician of the *Stronnictwo Ludowe* before the First World War, see Jan Stapiński, *Pamiętnik*, ed. by Krzysztof Dunin-Wąsowicz, Warszawa 1959; K. Struve, *Bauern und Nation*, pp. 217–221.

50 S. Lato—W. Stankiewicz (eds.), *Programy*, p. 69.

Głowacki.[51] Re-enactments of the battle were occasionally staged in villages by peasants posing as *kosynierzy.*[52]

The universal male suffrage for the Reichsrat election in 1907 resulted in a major political reshuffle in Galicia. In western Galicia the PSL now won more seats than the conservatives. The western Galician Kraków conservatives were forced to share power with the PSL. As part of this "governing coalition" the peasant party acquired substantial political influence in Galicia and Vienna. Jan Stapiński, the PSL's leading politician at that time, was given the influential position of vice-president of the Polish club in the Reichsrat. In 1911 the PSL nominated Władysław Długosz as the Minister for Galicia in the Austrian government.[53]

During the last years before the First World War and during the war itself, the PSL tried to overcome the still widespread mistrust among the peasants concerning the goal of Polish independence by promoting the image of a democratic "peoples' Poland" (*Polska ludowa*), where the peasants would rule because of their large number, instead of the former "aristocratic Poland" [*Polska szlachecka*].[54] However, there still remained some mistrust among peasants concerning a Polish state. Self-identification among peasants according to religion, their social identity as peasants or as inhabitants of Galicia and the Austrian emperor's subjects, seems to have remained strong on the eve of the First World War, although as contemporary observers emphasized, there was now only a small number of peasants who rejected the description of Pole, attributing it only to landlords.[55]

Peasants and Ruthenian Politics

As has already been indicated above, the end of the 1870s and the beginning of the 1880s was also a period of important change for the Ruthenian movement. From the 1870s the Ukrainophile concept of Ruthenian identity had gained increasing support among the younger generation of the Ruthenian intelligentsia, primarily students of gymnasia and the L'viv university. For them the works of Taras Shevchenko and other Ukrainian writers, the *narod* and its language and culture, combined with more left-wing, socialist

51 On the Racławice myth among the Polish left, Franciszek ZIEJKA, *Złota legenda chłopów polskich*, Warszawa 1984.

52 On these and the use of other national celebrations by the peasant movement, J. MOLENDA, *Chłopi—naród—niepodległość*, pp. 134–215; Barbara JAKUBOWSKA, *Ruch ludowy wobec przeszłości narodowej (do 1939 r.)*, Warszawa 1995; see also K. STRUVE, *Bauern und Nation*, pp. 336–358; Keely STAUTER-HALSTED, *Rural Myth and the Modern Nation. Peasant Commemorations of Polish National Holidays, 1879–1910*, in: Maria Bucur—Nancy M. Wingfield (eds.), Staging the Past. The Politics of Commemoration in Habsburg Central Europe, West Lafayette 2001, pp. 153–177.

53 The new alliances and power also resulted in new tensions within the party, contributing to a split in 1913, Andrzej GARLICKI, *Powstanie Polskiego Stronnictwa Ludowego „Piast" 1913–1914*, Warszawa 1966.

54 J. MOLENDA, *Chłopi—naród—niepodległość*, pp. 216–240.

55 K. STRUVE, *Bauern und Nation*, pp. 358–361.

ideas, were the most important reference points for their political activities, rather than the Orthodox Church, the Russian language or the Czar and his empire.[56] In contrast to earlier times, the leading Ukrainophile activists in the 1880s belonged to the secular intelligentsia. They had been publishing the weekly newspaper *Bat'kivshchyna* for rural areas since 1867.[57]

From the 1880s more stable political organizational structures began to develop, including those of the peasants and the Ruthenian intelligentsia. During the 1880s and 1890s a number of regional Ruthenian political associations were founded, which usually also had peasant members. Some of them took the name *Sel'ians'ka rada* [Village Council], thereby emphasizing their roots in the villages. Political demands were presented and discussed at public political meetings in L'viv and in provincial towns with a strong participation of peasants. During these years a political programme developed which increasingly included peasant economic and social interests. In 1885 the Ukrainophiles registered their own crownland-wide political association under the name *Narodna Rada* [Peoples' Council]. In 1892 *Narodna Rada* published a basic political programme. The central elements of the programme were equality and the development of the Ruthenian nationality, on the one hand, and the peasants and their social and economic interests on the other.[58]

The elections to the Galician diet in 1889 also marked a turning point for the Ruthenians. For the first time their number of seats in the diet rose from eleven in 1883 to sixteen in 1889. There had been no peasants among the Ruthenian deputies in 1883, but there were two in 1889.[59] This was clearly the result of the increasing joint political activities and the development of stable organizations including both members of the Ruthenian intelligentsia and peasants over the previous years, as well as having peasants who were better educated and had a better understanding of the workings of state institutions.

The electoral success of 1889 was not repeated in the following elections to the Galician diet in 1895. The number of Ruthenian deputies fell to fourteen. However, this was mostly due to widespread interference by state officials, encouraged by Governor Kazimierz Badeni, and conflicts and divisions among the Ruthenian political activists after 1892 concerning cooperation with the Polish majority in the diet.[60] Nevertheless, a closer

56 John-Paul HIMKA, *Socialism in Galicia. The Emergence of Polish Social Democracy and Ukrainian Radicalism (1860–1890)*, Cambridge (MA) 1983, pp. 40ff.; Mykhailo PAVLYK, *Pro rus'ko-ukraïns'ki narodni chytalni*, in: Mykhailo PAVLYK, *Tvory*, Kyïv 1985, pp. 159–283, here pp. 275–283 (first published L'viv 1887).

57 Letters from the villages in *Batkivshchyna* in the middle of the 1880s are analysed in John-Paul Himka's important study *Galician villagers*.

58 K. STRUVE, *Bauern und Nation*, pp. 248–256.

59 On the elections of 1889, see Olena ARKUSHA, *Halyts'kyi seim. Vyborchi kampaniï 1889 i 1895 rr.*, L'viv 1996, pp. 61–83; Kost' LEVYTS'KYI, *Istoriia polityсznoï dumky halyts'kykh ukraïntsiv 1848–1914*, L'viv 1926, pp. 229–233.

60 Ihor CHORNOVOL, *Pol's'ko-ukraïns'ka uhoda 1890–1894 rr.*, L'viv 2000; K. LEVYTS'KYI, *Istoriia politychnoï dumky*, pp. 235–272.

analysis reveals how peasants and intelligentsia activists were becoming more strongly integrated into one political movement. While in previous decades the Ruthenian intelligentsia activists had tried to dissuade peasants from voting for other peasants as deputies, advising them instead to support candidates from the Ruthenian intelligentsia, in 1889 peasants appeared as the approved candidates of Ruthenian electoral committees in four districts. In 1895, peasants were the approved candidates in 19 of the 42 electoral districts where Ruthenian candidates stood for election.[61]

Another development in Ruthenian politics at the start of the 1890s was the appearance of the Radical Party. The origins of this party were in the socialist Ukrainophile intelligentsia. This party had significant influence in some regions, especially in Galicia's southeast, but also in the Sambir and Przemyśl regions, and they also had an active peasant membership. The party split in 1899 and some of their activists joined with the Ukrainophiles to form the "Ukrainian National Democratic Party" [*Ukraïns'ka Natsional'no-Demokratychna Partiia*, UNDP], which became the clearly dominant Ruthenian political grouping at the turn of the century.[62]

Both the influence of left-wing socialist ideas on the Ruthenian intelligentsia and the stronger integration of peasants contributed to the fact that peasant interests became an increasingly important part of the Ruthenian movement's political programme, especially for its Ukrainophile section. For example, in 1899 the UNDP demanded that the state purchase land from the estates and make it available to smallholders and the landless. In its 1913 programme, the party even suggested the compulsory purchase of estate land and its distribution among peasants as their property.[63] This is just one example of an obvious peasant interest becoming a demand of the main political organization of Ukrainian nationalism in Galicia. The improvement in the economic situation of the peasantry became of central interest to the Ukrainian nation.

The closer integration of peasants and intelligentsia activists, both in terms of their programmes and organization, resulted in the considerable strengthening of the Ruthenian movement, primarily its Ukrainian wing, until the eve of the First World War. This became apparent not only with the strong development and diversification of

---

61 K. Struve, *Bauern und Nation*, pp. 258f. In 1889 in most electoral districts Ukrainophiles and Russophiles cooperated and nominated one candidate. In 1895 Russophiles and opposition Ukrainophiles cooperated in most districts while pro-government Ukrainophiles nominated there own candidates. The above-mentioned numbers refer to the opposition Ruthenian candidates.

62 On the Radical Party during the 1890s, K. Jobst, *Zwischen Nationalismus und Internationalismus*, pp. 92ff; on the split and the foundation of the UNDP also, Vasyl' Rasevych, *Vynyknennia ta orhanizatsiini osnovy ukraïns'koï natsional'no-demokratychnoï partiï*, Visnyk L'vivs'koho Universytetu. Seriia istorychna 32, 1997, pp. 119–130; K. Levyts'kyi, *Istoriia politycznoï dumky*, pp. 324–332; a detailed discussion on political developments in the Sambir region around the turn of the century can be found in A. Zayarnyuk, *Framing the Ukrainian Peasantry*, pp. 177–374.

63 Stepan Baran, *Nasha prohrama i orhanizatsiia*, L'viv 1913, p. 12; K. Struve, *Bauern und Nation*, p. 282.

Ruthenian civil society, but also in the elections. In 1913, Ruthenian candidates won 32 seats in the Galician diet, more than at any election since 1861.[64]

Conclusion

In terms of the hypotheses and questions which have emerged from recent research discussions that were outlined at the start, the case of rural Galicia clearly suggests that increased nationalization of the society was not the result of a strong national identifications among the population, but consisted primarily in the structurization of civil society along national lines, i.e. the division of associations, co-operatives, political parties and other organizations into national segments. This was the result of the fact that all significant intelligentsia activities among the rural population had a national context. However, it was not nationalism but other more concrete offers and benefits that made these activities attractive to peasants. This may have been specific advice concerning improvements in agriculture or village administration, or they may have provided education, knowledge and also entertainment on a more general level (in the case of reading rooms and gymnastic associations). Political parties presented the peasants' concerns and interests in parliaments and in the public sphere. Indeed, the parties and organizations were only successful if they answered the specific needs and concerns of the peasant population. If they did not, they soon failed or trailed behind the others. The needs of the rural population were not national in nature, but were related to the economy, education, village administration and political representation. The deep national divisions in civil society were the result of the fact that no non-national or dual-national organizations existed to respond to the needs of the rural population in the above-mentioned areas. The idea of integrating peasants into modern society and politics on the non-national basis of peasant social identity and interests within an Austrian framework, which appeared as a possibility between 1848 and the 1870s, never materialized because there were no significant intelligentsia activities supporting it.

The legal reforms of the 1860s allowed for relatively broad political participation within different levels of government. However, legal reforms alone did not mean that the large section of society which now had political rights could effectively use them. Leaving village communities aside, any effective political participation and representation of peasants in parliaments at different levels required organization and a public sphere which was beyond the scope of the districts and small regions, and which allowed for the development of joint political programmes and activities. Before the turn of the century, and to a certain degree afterwards, the peasants were unable to develop and maintain such networks of organization and communication on their own, requiring the support of intelligentsia activists. They articulated peasant demands and interests in the language of nationalism.

64 K. Struve, *Bauern und Nation*, pp. 280f.

Peasants had to adjust to this national framework in order to facilitate cooperation and acquire support from the intelligentsia for their needs and goals. As has been indicated above, this was less problematic for the Ruthenian villagers, as it was easier for them to understand their mostly religiously defined Ruthenian identity as a national identity. In addition, declaring a separate national identity to the Poles meant to provide their demands with more weight because the neglect of the Ruthenian peasants' social interests and their status as equal Austrian citizens could then also be accused of suppressing the rights and dignity of an equal nation.

It was a larger and more difficult step for the peasants in western Galicia to identify with a Polish nationality that had traditionally been seen as the preserve of landlords and the educated classes. However, the peasants also began to understand that the redefined concept of Polish national identity which placed the peasants, the *lud*, at the centre—most obviously represented by the peasant party, the PSL—gave their demands additional weight because the improvement of peasants' lives and their equal political participation appeared here as a national concern. On that basis, in the Polish case it also became possible to view the ruling Galician conservatives' policy regarding peasant interests and rural affairs as a failure in terms of the Polish national interest. Reference to national identity gave extra weight to the peasants' political and economic demands within the public sphere.

Overall, it can be stated that the Galician case clearly shows that it would be an oversimplification to explain the influence of nationalism (and its limits) as simply the work of the nationalists (or their failure) at the turn of the century. More importantly, nationalism had acquired a structuring function in civil society as a prerequisite for the effective political participation of those broad sections of society which had received political rights in the 1860s and later.

Bibliography

Olena ARKUSHA, *Halyts'kyi seim. Vyborchi kampaniï 1889 i 1895 rr.* [The Galician Diet. Electoral Campaigns in 1889 and 1895], L'viv 1996.

Stepan BARAN, *Nasha prohrama i orhanizatsiia* [Our Programme and Organisation], L'viv 1913.

Jakub S. BENEŠ, *Workers and Nationalism. Czech and German Social Democracy in Habsburg Austria, 1890–1918*, Oxford 2017.

Harald BINDER, *Galizien in Wien. Parteien, Wahlen, Fraktionen im Übergang zur Massenpolitik*, Wien 2005.

James BJORK, *Neither German nor Pole. Catholicism and National Indifference in a Central European Borderland*, Ann Arbor 2008.

Emil BRIX, *Die Umgangssprachen in Altösterreich zwischen Agitation und Assimilation. Die Sprachenstatistik in den zisleithanischen Volkszählungen 1880 bis 1910*, Wien 1982.

Peter BROCK, *Nationalism and Populism in Partitioned Poland. Selected Essays*, London 1973.

Rogers BRUBAKER, *Ethnicity without Groups*, Cambridge (MA) 2004.

Tim BUCHEN, *Antisemitismus in Galizien. Agitation, Gewalt und Politik gegen Juden in der Habsburgermonarchie um 1900*, Berlin 2012.

Tim BUCHEN, *Religiöse Mobilisierung im Reich: Die imperialen Lebensläufe und politischen Karrieren von Joseph Bloch und Stanisław Stojałowski in der Habsburgermonarchie*, Geschichte und Gesellschaft 40, 2014, pp. 117–141.

Józef BUSZKO, *Polacy w parlamencie austriackim 1848–1918* [Poles in the Austrian Parliament 1848-1918], Warszawa 1996.

Ihor CHORNOVOL, *Pol's'ko-ukraïns'ka uhoda 1890–1894 rr.* [The Polish-Ukrainian Agreement 1890-1895], L'viv 2000.

Ihor CHORNOVOL, *Ukraïns'ka fraktsiia halyts'koho kraiovoho sejmu 1861–1901 r.* [The Ukrainian Faction of the Galician Crownland Diet 1861-1901], L'viv 2002.

Gary B. COHEN, *Nationalist Politics and Dynamics of State and Civil Society in the Habsburg Monarchy, 1867–1914*, Central European History 40, 2007, pp. 241–278.

Gary B. COHEN, *The Politics of Ethnic Survival: Germans in Prague, 1861–1914*, Princeton 1981.

Laurence COLE, *Differentiation or Indifference? Changing Perspectives on National Identification in the Austrian Half of the Habsburg Monarchy*, in: Maarten van Ginderachter—Marnix Beyen (eds.), Nationhood from Below: Europe in the Long Nineteenth Century, Basingstoke 2012, pp. 96–119.

Krzysztof K. DASZYK—Tomasz KARGOL—Tomasz SZUBERT (eds.), *Rok 1846 w Krakowie i Galicji. Odniesienia, interpretacje, pamięc* [The Year 1846 in Cracow and Galicia. References, Interpretations, Memory], Kraków 2016.

Andrzej GARLICKI, *Powstanie Polskiego Stronnictwa Ludowego „Piast" 1913–1914* [The Formation of the Polish People's Party „Piast"], Warszawa 1966.

Maarten VAN GINDERACHTER—Jon Fox (eds.), *National Indifference and the History of Nationalism in Modern Europe*, London 2019.

Stanisław GRODZISKI, *Sejm Krajowy galicyjski 1861–1914* [The Galician Crownland Diet 1861–1914], vol. 1, Warszawa 1993.

Konstanty GRZYBOWSKI, *Galicja 1848–1914. Historia ustroju politycznego na tle historii ustroju Austrii* [Galicia 1848-1914. A History of its Political System before the Background of Austria's Political System], Kraków 1959.

Antoni GURNICZ, *Kółka rolnicze w Galicji. Studium społeczno-ekonomiczne* [Agrarian Circles in Galicia. A Social-Economic Study], Warszawa 1967.

Antoni GURNICZ, *O „równą miarkę" dla chłopów. Poglądy i działalność pierwszej chłopskiej organizacji politycznej w Polsce Związku Stronnictwa Chłopskiego 1893–1908* [For the „Equal Measure" for the Peasants. Views and Activities of the First Political Peasant Organisation in Poland „Związek Stronnictwa Chłopskiego" 1893–1908], Warszawa 1963.

John-Paul HIMKA, *The Construction of Nationality in Galician Rus': Icarian Flights in Almost All Directions*, in: Ronald Grigor Suny—Michael D. Kennedy (eds.), Intellectuals and the Articulation of the Nation, Ann Arbor 1999, pp. 109–164.

John-Paul HIMKA, *Galician Villagers and the Ukrainian National Movement in the Nineteenth Century*, London 1988.

John-Paul HIMKA, *Religion and Nationality in Western Ukraine. The Greek Catholic Church and the Ruthenian National Movement in Galicia, 1867–1900*, Montreal 1999.

John-Paul HIMKA, *Socialism in Galicia. The Emergence of Polish Social Democracy and Ukrainian Radicalism (1860–1890)*, Cambridge (MA) 1983.

John-Paul HIMKA, *Ukrainian-Jewish Antagonism in the Galician Countryside During the Late Nineteenth Century*, in: Peter J. Potichnyj—Howard Aster (eds.), Ukrainian-Jewish Relations in Historical Perspective, Edmonton 1988, pp. 111–158.

Barbara JAKUBOWSKA, *Ruch ludowy wobec przeszłości narodowej (do 1939 r.)* [The Peasant Movement and the Nation's Past (until 1939)], Warszawa 1995.

Kerstin S. JOBST, *Zwischen Nationalismus und Internationalismus. Die polnische und ukrainische Sozialdemokratie in Galizien von 1890 bis 1914. Ein Beitrag zur Nationalitätenfrage im Habsburgerreich*, Hamburg 1996.

Pieter M. JUDSON, *Guardians of Nations. Activists of the Language Frontiers of Imperial Austria*, Cambridge (MA) 2006.

Pieter M. JUDSON, *The Habsburg Empire. A New History*, Cambridge (MA) 2016.

Franciszek KĄCKI, *Ks. Stanisław Stojałowski i jego działalność społeczno-polityczna* [Rev. Stanisław Stojałowski and his Social and Political Activities], vol. 1, 1845–1890, Lwów 1937.

Dem Kaiserstaate Österreich gewidmet von einem seiner Bewohner, Teschen 1861.

Klemens KAPS, *Ungleiche Entwicklung in Zentraleuropa. Galizien zwischen überregionaler Arbeitsteilung und imperialer Politik, 1772–1914*, Wien 2015.

Stefan KIENIEWICZ, *Pomiędzy Stadionem a Goslarem. Sprawa włościańska w Galicji w 1848 r.* [Between Stadion and Goslar. The Peasant Question in Galicia in 1848], Wrocław 1980.

Stefan KIENIEWICZ, *Ruch chłopski w Galicji w 1846 roku* [The Peasant Movement in Galicia in 1846], Wrocław 1951.

Jeremy KING, *Budweisers into Czechs and Germans. A local history of Bohemian politics, 1848–1948*, Princeton 2002.

Andrzej KUDŁASZYK, *Ksiądz Stanisław Stojałowski. Studium historyczno-prawne* [Reverend Stanisław Stojałowski. A Historical and Legal Study], Wrocław 1998.

Andrzej KUDŁASZYK, *Myśl społeczno-polityczna Bolesława Wysłoucha 1855–1937* [The Social and Political Ideas of Bolesław Wysłouch 1855–1937], Warszawa 1978.

Stanisław LATO—Witold STANKIEWICZ (eds.), *Programy stronnictw ludowych. Zbiór dokumentów* [Programmes of the Peasant Parties. A Collection of Documents], Warszawa 1969.

Kost' LEVYTS'KYI, *Istoriia politycznoï dumky halyts'kykh ukraïntsiv 1848–1914* [A History of the Political Ideas of the Galician Ukrainians, 1848–1914], L'viv 1926.

Paul Robert MAGOCSI, *The Kachkovs'kyi Society and the National Revival in Nineteenth Century East Galicia*, Harvard Ukrainian Studies 15, 1991, pp. 48–87.

Rudolf A. MARK, *Galizien unter österreichischer Herrschaft. Verwaltung—Kirche—Bevölkerung*, Marburg 1994.

Christoph Freiherr MARSCHALL VON BIEBERSTEIN, *Freiheit in der Unfreiheit. Die nationale Autonomie der Polen in Galizien nach dem österreichisch-ungarischen Ausgleich von 1867*, Wiesbaden 1993.

Jan MOLENDA, *Chłopi—naród –niepodległość. Kształtowanie się postaw narodowych i obywatelskich chłopów w Galicji i Królestwie Polskim w przededniu odrodzenia Polski* [Peasants—Nation—Independence. The Formation of National and Civic Attitudes among Peasants in Galicia and the Kingdom of Poland on the eve of Poland's Rebirth], Warszawa 1999.

Michael Moser, *New Contributions to the History of the Ukrainian Language*, Toronto 2016

Ewa Maria OŻÓG, *Powstanie Stronnictwa Ludowego* [The Foundation of the People's Party], in: Stanisław Dąbrowski (ed.), Działalność polityczna ruchu ludowego [The Political Activities of the People's Movement], Rzeszów 1996, pp. 23–32.

Svjatoslav PACHOLKIV, *Emanzipation durch Bildung. Entwicklung und gesellschaftliche Rolle der ukrainischen Intelligenz im habsburgischen Galizien (1890–1914)*, Wien 2002.

Stepan PERS'KYI, *Populiarna istoriia tovarystva "Prosvita" u L'vovi* [A Popular History of the „Prosvita" Association in L'viv], L'viv 1932.

Mykhailo PAVLYK, *Tvory* [Works], Kyïv 1985.

Józef PUTEK, *Pierwszy wstępy włościaństwa polskiego 1848–1861* [The First Steps of the Polish Peasantry 1848–1861], Kraków n. d. [1933].

Vasyl' RASEVYCH, *Vynyknennia ta orhanizatsiini osnovy ukraïns'koï natsional'no-demokratychnoï partiï* [The Emergence and Organizational Base of the Ukrainian National-Democratic Party], Visnyk L'vivs'koho Universytetu. Seriia istorychna 32, 1997, pp. 119–130.

Roman ROSDOLSKY, *Die Bauernabgeordneten im konstituierenden österreichischen Reichstag 1848–1849*, Wien 1976.

Roman ROSDOLSKY, *Untertan und Staat in Galizien. Die Reformen unter Maria Theresia und Joseph II.*, Mainz 1992.

Magdalena SEMCZYSZYN, *Galicyjskie wybory. Działalność Centralnego Komitetu Wyborczego w Galicji Wschodniej w latach 1867–1906* [Galician Elections. The Activities of the Central Electoral Committee in Eastern Galicia, 1867–1906], Warszawa 2014.

Ostap SEREDA, *"My tu ne pryishly na smikh": uchast' skhidnohalyc'kykh selian u seimovykh vyborakh ta zasidanniakh u L'vovi (60-I roky XIX st.)* [„We have not come here for fun": the Participation of Eastern Galician Villagers in Diet Elections and Sessions in L'viv (1860s of the 19th century)], in: Kazimierz Karolczak (ed.): L'viv. Misto—suspil'stvo—kultura/Lwów. Miasto—społeczeństwo—kultura [L'viv. City—Society—Culture], vol. 4, Kraków 2002, pp. 165–186.

Thomas W. SIMONS, *The Peasant Revolt of 1846 in Galicia: Recent Polish Historiography*, Slavic Review 30, 1971, pp. 795–817.

Krzysztof ŚLUSAREK, *Uwłaszczenie chłopów w Galicji zachodniej* [Reform of Peasant Property Rights in Western Galicia], Kraków 2002.

Jan STAPIŃSKI, *Pamiętnik* [Memoirs], ed. by Krzysztof Dunin-Wąsowicz, Warszawa 1959.

Keely STAUTER-HALSTED, *The Nation in the Village. The Genesis of Peasant National Identity in Austrian Poland, 1848–1914*, Ithaca 2001.

Keely STAUTER-HALSTED, *Rural Myth and the Modern Nation. Peasant Commemorations of Polish National Holidays, 1879–1910*, in: Maria Bucur—Nancy M. Wingfield (eds.), Staging the Past. The Politics of Commemoration in Habsburg Central Europe, West Lafayette 2001, pp. 153–177.

Stanisław STOJAŁOWSKI, *Liberalna blaga przedwyborcza i nowy program czynności przedwyborczych oraz słówko o kołtuństwie szlacheckim* [The Liberal Pre-electoral Plague and a New Programme of Pre-electoral Activities as well as a Word about Gentry Obscurantism], Lwów 1876.

Kai STRUVE, *Bauern und Nation in Galizien. Über Zugehorigkeit und soziale Emanzipation im 19. Jahrhundert*, Göttingen 2005.

Kai STRUVE, *Górny Śląsk na przełomie XIX i XX w.—nacjonalizacja społeczeństwa w perspektywie porównawczej* [Upper Silesia at the Turn of the19th and 20th Cenuries—Nationalization of Society in a Comparative Perspective], in: Sebastian Rosenbaum (ed.): Górnoślązacy. Problemy społeczności pogranicza w XX wieku [Upper Silesians. Problems of a Borderland Community in the 20th Century], Katowice 2014, pp. 16–36.

Kai STRUVE, *Politische Mobilisierung und nationale Identifikation. Die Wahlbeteiligung der Landbevölkerung in Galizien 1861–1911*, in: Zeitschrift für Ostmitteleuropaforschung 54, 2005, pp. 377–398.

Stefan SUCHONEK, *Poseł Jan Siwiec (Karta z dziejów ruchu ludowego w Galicji)* [Deputy Jan Siwiec (A Page from the History of the Peasant Movement in Galicia], in: Henryk Barycz—Jan Hulewicz (eds.), Studia z dziejów kultury polskiej [Studies on the History of Polish Culture], Warszawa 1949, pp. 539–562.

Józef SZOCKI, *Literatura popularna dla ludu na przykładzie Wydawnictwa Ludowego 1882–1920* [Popular Literature on the Example of Wydawnictwo Ludowe 1882–1920], Kraków 1994.

Ryszard TERLECKI, *Oświata dorosłych i popularyzacja nauki w Galicji w okresie autonomii* [Adult Education and the Popularization of Knowledge in Galicia during the Period of Autonomy], Wrocław 1990.

Anna Veronika WENDLAND, *Die Russophilen in Galizien. Ukrainische Konservative zwischen Österreich und Rußland 1848–1915*, Wien 2001.

Tara ZAHRA, *Imagined Noncommunities. National Indifference as a Category of Analysis*, Slavic Review 69, 2010, pp. 93–119.

Tara ZAHRA, *Kidnapped Souls. National indifference and the battle for children in the Bohemian lands, 1900–1948*, Ithaca 2008.

Andriy ZAYARNYUK, *Framing the Ukrainian Peasantry in Habsburg Galicia, 1846–1914*, Edmonton 2013.

Franciszek ZIEJKA, *Złota legenda chłopów polskich* [The Golden Legend of the Polish Peasants], Warszawa 1984.

Civil Society in Polish Cooperatives in the Province of Posen before the First World War

Torsten Lorenz

Abstract

The relationship between cooperatives and civil society has rarely been investigated by historians. However, there was great potential from their governing principles, their internal organisation and their functioning for the emergence and development of civil society and civil practices. Using the example of Polish cooperatives in the Prussian province of Posen (Poznania/Wielkopolska) before the First World War, this article makes an attempt at a preliminary evaluation of this relationship. The result is ambivalent: On the one hand, the leadership of the Polish cooperative movement succeeded in its efforts at community building, integrating along ethnic divisions and even educating Polish peasants towards more self-conscience and autonomy. This, however, came at the cost of increasing ethnic segregation and paternalistic leadership in cooperatives on a regional as well as local level.

In 1907, the German economist Ludwig Bernhard published the first edition of his book *The Polish Question. The Polish Community in the Prussian State.*[1] This extensive study met with great public interest because of the continuing intensification of the German-Polish nationality struggle. It was commented on by economists and politicians on both sides, and even the highest authorities of the Prussian provinces of Posen (Poznań/Wielkopolska) and West Prussia obtained information from Bernhard's work.[2] It quickly became the standard work on the Polish cooperative system in the provinces of Posen and West Prussia and was published in two further editions.

In his study, Bernhard examined in detail the system of Polish cooperatives and farmers' associations, its formation from the middle of the 19th century, its structure and actors, as well as the credit policy of the Polish *Volksbanks* [*banki ludowe*], which occupied a central position within this system. Bernhard's core thesis is that, with the help

1 Ludwig Bernhard, *Die Polenfrage. Das polnische Gemeinwesen im preußischen Staat*, Leipzig 1910.

2 See e. g. Oberpräsident to Ministry of Trade, Posen, 7. 12. 1907, Geheimes Staatsarchiv Preußischer Kulturbesitz, Berlin-Dahlem (GStA), I. HA, Rep. 151, I C, Finanzministerium 10285: Erwerbs- und Wirtschaftsgenossenschaften in den Ostmarken, 1905–1910.

of peasant associations and cooperatives, the Polish intelligentsia not only succeeded in addressing and organizing large sections of the Polish population, but also in mobilizing them for the national movement and establishing a kind of Polish cooperative republic in the Prussian-German state—the "community" that the economist addressed in the title of his book. For Bernhard, cooperatives were thus a tool for the socialization of the Polish population in the Prussian eastern provinces, an assumption which my following remarks will confirm. But were they a contribution to the emergence of a civil society? I would like to explore this question using the example of the Polish cooperative system in the Prussian province of Posen [*Wielkopolska*] before the First World War.

Firstly, on the basis of more recent research, I will outline the development of the cooperative system in East Central Europe. One decisive influencing factor with regard to the functioning of civil society, according to the central argument, was modern nationalism. Subsequently, I will try to determine its civil-society potential at a more abstract level. I will then juxtapose the theory with the reality in a specific case. I will examine separately the integrative and disintegrative tendencies of the Polish cooperative system in the province of Posen: on the one hand, mobilization and socialization, on the other, national disintegration and paternalistic leadership structure. The picture presented is decidedly ambivalent: the elites of the Polish cooperative movement succeeded in organizing large parts of the Polish population in the Prussian province of Posen, in mobilizing them nationally, and in forming nationally conscious elites in the economy and local administration, who continued to perform important functions even after the foundation of the Polish state in 1918. The price for this, however, was considerable: the national division within the cooperative system and its national political instrumentalization not only further enhanced a social line of conflict, but the paternalistic style of leadership, which was a basic prerequisite for fulfilling the national political function, could not be reconciled with civic values and democracy.

The Development of Cooperatives in East Central Europe until the First World War

The modern cooperatives were founded in the middle of the 19th century.[3] The fathers of the cooperative movement, from the founders of the Rochdale Society of Equitable Pioneers (founded in 1844) to Hermann Schulze-Delitzsch (1808–1883) and Friedrich Wilhelm Raiffeisen (1818–1888), strove to improve the living conditions of social groups that were disadvantaged in the transformation to a bourgeois society, thereby attempting

3 A more detailed discussion on East Central European cooperative history with a focus on the relationship to national movements can be found in Torsten Lorenz, *Introduction: Cooperatives in Ethnic Conflicts*, in: Torsten Lorenz (ed.), Cooperatives in Ethnic Conflicts. Eastern Europe in the 19th and Early 20th Century, Berlin 2006, pp. 9–44.

to address an important social issue.[4] While the social image and utopia of the cooperative pioneers often differed greatly and ranged from socialist to Christian-conservative to market-liberal ideas, they had one basic idea in common: to provide small agricultural and commercial producers who were marginalized or threatened by marginalization, as well as simple consumers, with opportunities for economic development by bundling purchasing power and market potential and coordinating their economic activities, and integrating them into the emerging capitalist market economy.[5] Their real achievement in integrating small producers and consumers into the overall economy made the cooperatives a success story.

The cooperative idea also found supporters in East Central Europe at an early stage. The proximity to the kingdom of Saxony, where Schulze-Delitzsch founded his first "associations", was partly responsible for the fact that his ideas were taken up by activists from the Czech national movement in Bohemia as early as the 1850s.[6] No less significant was the fact that hopes for political change had been dashed with the revolution of 1848 and the subsequent shift of political activities to social, economic and cultural spheres (the term "organic work" became popular in the Polish lands). When the reaction phase came to an end at the turn of the 1860s and the association system experienced an upswing, the first modern cooperatives in East Central Europe also emerged sporadically.[7] But it was only between the beginning of the 1870s and the middle of the 1890s (in Bohemia, development began a decade earlier) that the cooperative system developed into a broader movement.[8] In this first phase, a sustained wave of associations swept across large parts of East Central Europe and numerous cooperatives emerged; from Bohemia via the Polish provinces of Prussia to the north-eastern provinces of the Habsburg Monarchy and the Russian Baltic Sea provinces.[9] Most of them were credit cooperatives, which played an important role in the nascent industrialization in Bohemia and accompanied

4 Johnston BIRCHALL, *The International Co-operative Movement*, Manchester 1997, pp. 1–34; reliable though affirmative of the cooperative movement is Helmut FAUST, *History of the cooperative movement. Origin and Path of the Cooperative Movement in the German Language Area*, Frankfurt am Main 1977.

5 Holm SUNDHAUSSEN, *Einführung. Zur Bedeutung der Genossenschaften in Vergangenheit und Gegenwart Osteuropas*, in: Erwin Oberländer et al., Genossenschaften in Osteuropa. Alternative zur Planwirtschaft?, Wiesbaden 1993, pp. 5–12, here p. 6.

6 Catherine ALBRECHT, *Nationalism in the Cooperative Movement in Bohemia before 1914*, in: T. Lorenz (ed.), Cooperatives in Ethnic Conflicts, pp. 215–227, here 216f.; the influence of Schulze, who in the 1850s served as a transferred judge in Wreschen (Września) in the province of Posen, is comparable; see L. BERNHARD, *Die Polenfrage*, p. 100.

7 Stefan-Ludwig HOFFMANN, *Geselligkeit und Demokratie. Vereine und zivile Gesellschaft im transnationalen Vergleich 1750–1914*, Göttingen 2003, pp. 60–73.

8 T. LORENZ, *Introduction*, pp. 22–23.

9 For an introduction, see the national studies in T. LORENZ (ed.), *Cooperatives in Ethnic Conflicts* (the literature mentioned in the selective bibliography for this volume, pp. 343–357), and the contributions in Erwin OBERLÄNDER et al., *Genossenschaften in Osteuropa. Alternative zur Planwirtschaft?*, Wiesbaden 1993.

the capitalist transformation of agriculture in the more agrarian regions of East Central Europe.[10] In addition to financial transactions, other economic tasks were also increasingly being brought together and cooperatives for crafts and agriculture were formed, as well as sales cooperatives, especially dairy cooperatives; finally, consumer associations were formed where an urban proletariat was established.[11] The cooperatives experienced a real boom in the second phase around the middle of the 1890s, when such self-help organizations were founded in more distant areas. It is characteristic of these years that, in addition to the number of cooperative associations, the intensity of national conflicts in East Central Europe also increased, and most of the cooperatives of the national minorities entered into a close, symbiotic relationship with the national movements.[12] The question of whether and to what extent there was a causal connection with the intensification of national conflicts in East Central Europe cannot be conclusively answered on the basis of the available research results. On the one hand, the number of cooperatives grew in areas such as *Wielkopolska*, Bohemia and Transylvania, and special forms of conflict developed, such as parcelling cooperatives, as a result of the national struggle shifting from the cultural to the economic sphere.[13] On the other hand, the number of cooperatives also grew rapidly in Germany and the predominantly German countries of the Habsburg Monarchy.[14] A cautious interpretation will, therefore, attribute the upswing in the cooperative system primarily to the growth of the association system as a whole.[15]

Therefore, before the First World War, local initiatives grew into an ever denser network of cooperative enterprises. It is certainly no exaggeration to say that it was a common structural feature of all European countries. Over time, the decentralized cooperative system formed associations at regional and national level because, on the one hand, further concentration was required in order to further increase supply and demand power, and on the other, the laws enacted in response to the rapid development of the cooperative system prescribed regular revisions.[16] It is noteworthy that, in contrast to the cooperatives which were initially formed from members of certain social groups and were by no means ethnically homogeneous later on, the cooperative associations in East Central Europe

10 For the development of credit cooperatives in Bohemia see C. ALBRECHT, *Nationalism in the Cooperative Movement in Bohemia*, and Jan HÁJEK, *Záložny a spořitelny—pilíře českého peněžnictví*, in: Jan Hájek—Vlastislav Lacina, Od úvěrních družstev k bankovním koncernům, Praha 1999, pp. 121–158.

11 T. LORENZ, *Introduction*, pp. 28–29.

12 T. LORENZ, *Introduction*, pp. 22-29.

13 L. BERNHARD, *Die Polenfrage*, pp. 329–330.

14 Ernst BRUCKMÜLLER, *Landwirtschaftliche Organisationen und gesellschaftliche Modernisierung: Vereine, Genossenschaften und politische Mobilisierung der Landwirtschaft Österreichs vom Vormärz bis 1914*, Salzburg 1977, p. 156.

15 On this see S.-L. HOFFMANN, *Geselligkeit und Demokratie*, pp. 74–77.

16 On the function of association formations from an economic perspective, see Timothy W. GUINNANE, *Regional Organizations in the German Cooperative Banking System in the Late 19th Century*, Research in Economics 51, 1997, pp. 251–274.

were almost without exception formed on an ethnic basis and thus embodied the pursuit of national political autonomy and national economic self-sufficiency from the outset.[17]

The pioneers of the national movements soon recognized the enormous development potential offered by the cooperatives to their movement. Cooperative work was therefore a welcome field of activity not only for the clergy, which pursued moral goals (especially in the case of Catholics after the issuing of the *Rerum novarum* papal encyclical in 1891), but also for the increasingly numerous members of the secular intelligentsia of the national minorities, who often did not find employment in the civil service.[18] The network of cooperatives made it possible to reach the populations in even more distant regions, to contribute to the formation of a self-sufficient national economy through economic development, to create publicity through the cooperative press, and to pursue popular enlightenment through educational means—all under national auspices.[19] Numerous examples also prove that the leaders of the cooperative movement were to a large extent identical to the heads of national organizations and parties at both a regional and local level.[20] In some cases, cooperatives became the economic basis of the national movements and an actor in the national struggles. The question is to what extent this development was conducive or detrimental to the formation of civil society's structures, values and patterns of behaviour. On the one hand, cooperatives became a vehicle for national political mobilization and national social integration; on the other, they had a disintegrative effect on society as a whole because they contributed towards divisions along national lines.

In addition to the special role of the intelligentsia, the growth of the cooperative system was also the consequence of the state's good will towards it. Unlike many associations, cooperatives were not under general suspicion, they did not pursue political goals and were not directed against the existing order. As a tool of socio-economic modernization, they were almost always subsidized by the state; for example, by establishing central coffers such as the "Prussian Treasury" or by directly receiving state subsidies.[21] However, this could also be used to intervene in business decisions and to exert discriminatory pressure, which is why the Schulze-Delitzsch Association, unlike its Raiffeisen counterpart, consistently refused to accept state subsidies.

17 T. LORENZ, *Introduction*, p. 22.

18 On the role of the clergy in the Polish and Ukrainian self-help movement in Galicia, see Kai STRUVE, *Peasant Emancipation and National Integration. Agrarian Circles, Village Reading Rooms, and Cooperatives in Galicia*, in: T. Lorenz (ed.), Cooperatives in Ethnic Conflict, pp. 229–250; on the role of the Catholic clergy in Slovenia, Žarko LAZAREVIĆ, *National and Economic Features of Slovene Cooperatives*, in: T. Lorenz (ed.), Cooperatives in Ethnic Conflicts, pp. 251–262.

19 Alexander DILLON, *The Forgotten Movement: Cooperatives and Cooperative Networks in Ukraine and Imperial Russia*, Harvard Ukrainian Studies 23, 1999, no. 1–2, pp. 129–143.

20 This principle of personal union, already described by L. BERNHARD, *Die Polenfrage*, p. 154, brought together the cultural and economic institutions of the national movements throughout East Central Europe. Further evidence can be found in T. LORENZ, *Introduction*, p. 26.

21 This was especially the case in the Habsburg Monarchy, see E. BRUCKMÜLLER, *Landwirtschaftliche Organisationen und gesellschaftliche Modernisierung*, pp. 131–133.

As a result, at the turn of the 20th century the activities of the cooperatives became increasingly blurred between economic tasks and national political instrumentalization. They found themselves caught in a triangle of conflict between the state, the majority nation and the national minorities. While they were a tool in the pursuit of economic emancipation or even national independence for the minorities, for the majority they often served to protect "national property", for example by creating credit cooperatives whose sole purpose was to protect "threatened" property from being transferred to "foreign" hands through loans.[22] For its part, the state increasingly tried to influence the business and composition of the members of cooperatives. Therefore, cooperatives became increasingly ethnically homogeneous and a subject as well as object in the East Central European national struggles of the late-19th and early-20th centuries—a fact that could hardly remain without consequences for the civil-society potential of cooperatives.

The Civil-Society Potential of Cooperatives

The relationship between cooperatives and civil society (or the democratic approaches that may be identified as such in relation to East Central Europe) seems ambivalent:[23] On the one hand, the cooperative system in Europe developed as part of the broad stream of the association movement (it was certainly no coincidence that Hermann Schulze-Delitzsch still called his first cooperatives "associations"), and since the "passion for associations" also began to encompass the petty bourgeois, peasant and proletarian classes, the cooperatives moved towards democratic principles, social self-organization and solidarity in solving everyday economic problems. On the other hand, cooperatives were nothing more than economic enterprises that could only justify their existence in the emerging capitalist economic order if they achieved market success. The cooperatives thus stood in an area of tension between the state, the market, the family, and civil society—between the latter and the market—and they also had other intersections with the state (policy of promoting the cooperative system) and the family (family economic organization of many enterprises).[24]

The frequently ambivalent positions of the cooperatives were partly a consequence of the historical development outlined above, and partly due to the programmatic writings

22 Catherine Albrecht, *Economic Nationalism among German Bohemians*, Nationalities Papers 24, 1996, pp. 17–30, here pp. 21–22.

23 As far as I know, this relationship has not yet been addressed. S.-L. Hoffmann, *Geselligkeit und Demokratie*, for example, does not mention the cooperatives at all in his otherwise good overview.

24 In defining civil society as an "in-between" area, I am using the definition of Jürgen Kocka, *Zivilgesellschaft als historisches Problem*, in: Christoph Conrad et al. (eds.), Europäische Zivilgesellschaft zwischen Ost und West. Begriff, Geschichte, Chancen, Frankfurt am Main 2000, pp. 13–39, here p. 21; Wilhelm Jäger, *Der Genossenschaftsbegriff als Problem der Theorie und Ordnungspolitik*, in: Erwin Oberländer—Hans Lemberg—Holm Sundhaussen (eds.), Genossenschaften in Osteuropa. Alternative zur Planwirtschaft?, Wiesbaden 1993, pp. 13–22; as well as the contributions in Eduard Mändle—Walter Svoboda (eds.), *Genossenschafts-Lexikon*, Wiesbaden 1992.

of the cooperative pioneers and the cooperative laws which determined the place of the cooperatives in the economic order. Starting from the assumption that cooperatives had an economic and social function in history, the economist and cooperative researcher Georg Draheim developed the concept of the "dual nature" of cooperatives at the beginning of the 1950s.[25] According to Draheim, cooperatives are joint enterprises supported by their members, which are subject to the "rule of the accounting pen" and thus function according to rational economic principles. However, Draheim also states that cooperatives are associations of individuals, not impersonal associations of capital (such as public limited companies).[26] The central position of the person and not the capital brought in by him has important consequences for the cooperative's goals: its performance is measured not only by market success but also by the fulfilment of social goals, such as the integration of the cooperative community (i.e. partial reintegration in response to the disintegration of the capitalist age). Nevertheless, cooperatives remain dependent on economic success: Cooperatives which continually fail to achieve market success disappear from the market and are thus unable to achieve their social goals. Conversely, economic performance depends on the fulfilment of social goals: Only a community built on civil-society resources such as trust, responsibility and participation is capable of successfully managing a cooperative in the long term. Market success and integration are, therefore, closely linked.[27]

However, the achievement of a positive balance between economic and social performance first requires the creation and then exploitation of the three civil-society potentials of trust, responsibility and participation mentioned above. The principle of cooperative democracy, which is constitutive for the cooperative movement, serves this purpose. The principle of democracy is formally anchored: the supreme decision-making body of the cooperative is the general assembly of all its members, which must be consulted on any fundamental decisions on business policy. All members are represented at the general meeting according to the principle of "one man, one vote", i.e. one vote each, irrespective of the number of business shares.[28] In societies where the participation of the individual was predetermined by income or assets based on the old liberal principle, the egalitarian cooperative organization possessed considerable democratic potential. The purpose of the principle of democracy is to strengthen the participation of the individual cooperative member in the joint enterprise's decision-making and to increase the feeling of responsibility towards a common cause ("checks" such as the principle of joint liability for the debts of the cooperative contribute to this in another way). The creation of the resource of trust, on the other hand, is achieved by the transparency of the decisions of the board of directors, which represents trust at the general assembly vis-à-vis the members. In this way, another civil society resource—the public—is created at the same time.

---

25 Georg DRAHEIM, *Die Genossenschaft als Unternehmungstyp*, Göttingen 1952, p. 1.

26 G. DRAHEIM, *Die Genossenschaft als Unternehmungstyp*, pp. 16–18.

27 See e.g. Timothy GUINNANE, *Cooperatives as Information Machines: German Rural Credit Cooperatives, 1883–1914*, The Journal of Economic History 61, 2001, pp. 366–389.

28 Eduard MÄNDLE, *Demokratische Mehrheitsregel in Genossenschaften*, in: E. Mändle—W. Svoboda (eds.), Genossenschafts-Lexikon, pp. 120–121.

The cooperatives thus have considerable civil-society potential, both in history and in cooperative theory. In the following I would like to present the most important developments in the Polish cooperative system in *Wielkopolska* before the First World War and then consider the civil-society aspect of cooperatives.

Economy and Society in the Prussian Province of Posen

The society of the province of Posen crossed into the bourgeois era with a complex combination of economic, social and ethno-religious conflicts, which since the middle of the 19th century have increasingly been interpreted as national in nature. These lines of conflict had a decisive influence on the development of the *Wielkopolska* cooperative system. The dominant class in *Wielkopolska*'s economy—the landowning aristocracy—was mostly Catholic-Polish, less often Protestant-German, and the urban population was to a considerable extent Jewish and Protestant-German; the rural population was almost exclusively Catholic-Polish. Religious and national allegiances usually coincided: Catholic usually meant "Polish", Protestant usually "German".[29] According to official statistics, around the year 1910 the population of the province consisted of 38% Germans (including 2–3% Jews) and 61% Poles.[30] Due to the history of migration, the proportion of the German population was higher in the western and northern peripheral areas than in the centre and east of the province.

After it had lost its well-developed cloth-making industry in some cities in the 1820s due to emigration to Congress Poland, *Wielkopolska* experienced reagrarization. The repercussions of the Prussian reforms, from the liberation of the peasants to the introduction of freedom of trade and the abolition of guild obligations, created the legal conditions for commercial-industrial development and the emergence of capitalist markets, but could not prevent the province from becoming an agricultural hinterland in the rapidly industrializing regions of west and central Germany. There was no notable industrial development, with only a few large industrial enterprises in existence. Trade and commerce were organized on a small scale, serving mostly the local population and seldom opening up to larger markets. Capital poverty was an obstacle to development in all sectors of the economy of *Wielkopolska*.[31]

The establishment of cooperatives was a way of helping small businesses to get off the ground in the eastern provinces, even more so than in the more western regions of Germany: Although each cooperative member had to participate with a share in the business, the legal form of an open partnership offered the possibility of keeping the share

29 As an introduction see my work Torsten LORENZ, *Von Birnbaum nach Międzychód. Bürgergesellschaft und Nationalitätenkampf in Großpolen bis zum Zweiten Weltkrieg*, Berlin 2005, with the most important literature.

30 Czesław ŁUCZAK (ed.), *Dzieje Wielkopolski*, vol. 2, Poznań 1973, p. 363.

31 Czesław ŁUCZAK, *Dzieje gospodarcze Wielkopolski w okresie zaborów (1815–1918)*, Poznań 2001, p. 71.

arbitrarily small. In this way, members of less wealthy classes could also join a cooperative and benefit from its range of goods and services.

While mortgage loans were mostly provided by mortgage banks, the increasingly dense network of cooperative banks provided trade and agriculture with operational loans and promoted the transition to more intensive land management.[32] The purchasing and sales cooperatives, like the bank cooperatives, freed the small producers from their dependence on credit usurers or traders who paid only poor prices and demanded excessive amounts for the items offered. In a region such as *Wielkopolska*, this inevitably had national implications, as the money lenders and traders were often Jews, while the producers were Poles or Germans. The founding of a cooperative was, therefore, often seen as a national emancipatory move, in addition to the pursuit of economic and social emancipation.

National Divisions in Cooperatives

The first cooperatives which were established in the province of Posen at the beginning of the 1860s—mostly municipal advance funds based on the principles of Schulze-Delitzsch—were multinational and had both German and Polish members. However, disputes soon arose about the language of business and negotiation in some of them, and so in some cities with a majority Polish population the nationally conscious Poles began to establish "their own" parallel cooperatives.[33] The national principle was also constitutive for the foundation of the Polish Association of Commercial and Agricultural Cooperatives (*Związek Spółek Zarobkowych i Gospodarczych*) in 1871. It was founded as a central association for 29 Polish cooperatives from the provinces of Posen, West Prussia and Silesia.[34] The separational tendency of the Polish minority, which had made itself felt since the 1830s in the burgeoning association system, was also reflected in the cooperative system.[35]

Nevertheless, the membership of individual cooperatives (with a few exceptions, mostly where a district had an almost exclusively Polish population) was never completely homogeneous. The sources show that at the end of the 19th century, between five and ten percent, and in some cases up to 15%, of the members of the cooperatives considered "Polish" were Germans; there was a similar situation in the "German" cooperatives.[36]

32 More information on the credit problem in the province of Poznan: Torsten LORENZ—Uwe MÜLLER, *National Segregation and Mass Mobilization: Polish Cooperatives in the Posen Province before the First World War*, in: T. Lorenz (ed.), Cooperatives in Ethnic Conflicts, pp. 183–200.

33 L. BERNHARD, *Die Polenfrage*, pp. 102–103.

34 C. ŁUCZAK, *Dzieje gospodarcze Wielkopolski*, p. 75.

35 On the development of national segregation in associations, T. LORENZ, *Von Birnbaum nach Międzychód*.

36 See the numerous reports by district councillors from the districts of the administrative district Bromberg, in GStA, XIV. HA, Rep. 30, Regierung Bromberg 729: Die polnischen Erwerbs- und Wirtschaftsgenossenschaften 1896–1909, vol. 1. The national allocation of a cooperative was mostly done by the business language as well as the affiliation to the Polish or German association.

However, this also proves that the principle of "each to his own" increasingly determined economic activity at that time. Nevertheless, the principle might weaken due to economic opportunism; i.e. if the conditions in a foreign ethnic cooperative were more favourable, if "one's own" did not exist, or if the member was indifferent to the national question.[37]

Until the second half of the 1880s, the Polish cooperatives in the Prussian eastern provinces primarily pursued their own mission, namely to promote the economic activity of their members. They provided them with operating loans, which enabled them to modernize their agricultural or craft enterprises, and they were given capital at favourable interest rates. Others sold agricultural commodities, stored grain or provided milk from the members' farms. This changed with the settlement laws of 1886 and the struggle for land.[38] The settlement policy, which aimed to weaken the Polish aristocracy in Polish society, became an opportunity for the Poles to establish resistance institutions such as the *Landbank* [*Bank Ziemski*] and parcelling cooperatives, which sought to transfer the property of Polish aristocrats into the hands of Polish peasants. Cooperatives thus began to play an active role in the emerging economic national struggle, and it was only a matter of time before the cooperative banks also intervened. When the economic national struggle began to affect the cities in the 1890s, it was often Polish *Volksbanks* that made it possible for Polish buyers to acquire prestigious real estate.[39]

This active role in the national struggle, however, required sizeable mobilization, for it was only through this that such a concentration of working capital was possible to finance nationally prestigious projects in addition to the usual lending business. A necessary prerequisite was the development of a middle class and a middle-class peasantry (the shares in the Polish cooperatives which had been organized according to the Schulze-Delitzsch model were relatively high), who had made considerable progress in the seemingly quiet 1880s.[40]

---

37 The phenomenon of economic nationalism mentioned here was the focus of a research project from 2002 to 2005 which resulted in, e.g. T. LORENZ (ed.), *Cooperatives in Ethnic Conflicts*; Eduard KUBŮ—Helga SCHULTZ (eds.), *Wirtschaftsnationalismus als Entwicklungsstrategie ostmitteleuropäischer Eliten*, Prag 2004; Eduard KUBŮ—Helga SCHULTZ (eds.), *History and Culture of Economic Nationalism in East Central Europe*, Berlin 2006. On the economic struggle in Poznania see Rudolf JAWORSKI, *Handel und Gewerbe im Nationalitätenkampf. Studien zur Wirtschaftsgesinnung der Polen in der Provinz Posen (1871–1914)*, Göttingen 1986.

38 On the settlement policy, see the controversial contributions by Uwe MÜLLER, *Modernisierung oder Diskriminierung? Siedlungspolitik in den preußischen Ostprovinzen zwischen nationalitäten- und agrarpolitischen Zielen*, in: Uwe Müller (ed.), Ausgebeutet oder alimentiert? Regionale Wirtschaftspolitik und nationale Minderheiten in Ostmitteleuropa (1871–1939), Berlin 2006, pp. 141–165, and Stefan KOWAL, *Die ökonomischen Auswirkungen der Nationalitätenpolitik im preußischen Teilungsgebiet Polens (1871–1918)*, in: ibid., pp. 167–178.

39 See e.g. "Regierungspräsident Bromberg to Oberpräsident of Posen province", Bromberg, 8. 1. 1903, GStA, XIV. HA, Rep. 30, no. 729 (note 36), vol. 1.

40 R. JAWORSKI, *Handel und Gewerbe im Nationalitätenkampf*, passim; Stefan KOWAL, *Społeczeństwo Wielkopolski i Pomorza Nadwiślańskiego w latach 1871–1914. Przemiany demograficzne i społeczno-zawodowe*, Poznań 1982, passim.

In order to mobilize capital, the Polish cooperatives used quite different means: the *Volksbanks* consistently pursued a policy of high interest rates. Their interest rates on savings were usually about 1,5% above the discount rate of the Reichsbank and also exceeded the interest rates paid by competitors—German cooperative banks, savings banks and commercial banks.[41] In addition, the Polish *Volksbanks* paid very attractive dividends on the business shares acquired by members: in 1908 they averaged around 6%, the highest rate being 10%.[42] Conversely, the correspondingly higher interest rates charged by the Polish *Volksbanks* for loans were not an obstacle for many people to borrow: the procedure for granting loans in the *Volksbanks* was regarded as unbureaucratic, the examination of guarantors and securities as lax.[43] The fact that these conditions also attracted German customers merely indicates that the Polish *Volksbanks* had succeeded in gaining a market advantage over their competitors. However, some councillors reported that mortgage loans were only granted to Germans when it was expected that the borrower would not be able to pay off his debts.[44] The Polish *Volksbanks* also proved to be flexible: there were numerous reports that the heads of Polish cooperative banks advised potential borrowers to primarily cover their needs with the state mortgage banks in order to have sufficient funds at their disposal when it was time to purchase properties of "national importance" or to grant operating loans to Polish businessmen.[45]

The business policy of the Polish *Volksbanks* was complemented by widespread propaganda to invest savings deposits in Polish *Volksbanks*. Catholic clergymen promoted the *Volksbanks* in church services, at rallies, or as chairmen of the increasingly numerous peasant associations (*Kółka rolnicze*).[46] The trust and authority enjoyed by the clergy were thus projected onto the national financial institutions. A boycott of "German" institutions had been in place from the mid-1890s: in the spring of 1901, for example, the Posen police chief reported that Polish savers had withdrawn their deposits in large numbers from a branch of the *Kreissparkasse* Bromberg (Bydgoszcz) and invested them in Polish *Volksbanks*. As a result, the savings deposits of the branch had declined within one year

41 "Regierungspräsident Bromberg to Oberpräsident of Posen province", Bromberg, 8. 1. 1903, GStA, XIV. HA, Rep. 30, no. 729 (note 36), vol. 1; see also Henryk Sitarek, *Rola kredytu w rozwoju gospodarki Wielkopolski na przełomie XIX i XX wieku. Bank Związku Spółek Zarobkowych w Poznaniu 1885–1918*, Warszawa 1977.

42 *IV. Sonderausgabe des Gesamtüberblicks über die polnische Tagesliteratur*, Heft II: Rechenschaftsberichte für das Jahr 1908, Posen 1909, Teil III: Jahresberichte der dem Verbande der Erwerbs- und Wirtschaftsgenossenschaften—Związek Spółek Zarobkowych—angeschlossenen Erwerbsgenossenschaften und Banken, usw.

43 "Regierungspräsident Bromberg to Oberpräsident of Posen province", Bromberg, 8. 1. 1903, GStA, XIV. HA, Rep. 30, no. 729 (note 36), vol. 1.

44 "Landrat Mogilno to Regierungspräsident Bromberg, Mogilno", 27. 12. 1902, GStA, XIV. HA, Rep. 30, no. 729 (note 36), vol. 1.

45 "Landrat Wongrowitz to Regierungspräsident Bromberg", Wongrowitz, 11. 6. 1908, GStA, XIV. HA, Rep. 30, no. 729 (note 36), vol. 3.

46 Archiwum Państwowe w Poznaniu, Polskie partie polityczne, organizacje, stowarzyszenia i związki z lat 1841–1953, 146: Kółko rolnicze w Chrzypsku, p. 38, note from 24. 2. 1907.

from 23,071 to 6,604 Reichsmark.[47] The Polish boycott reached a climax in late summer 1903, when all Prussian state officials were ordered, under threat of disciplinary action, to no longer have dealings with the Polish *Volksbank*.[48]

The history of the Polish cooperative banks in the province of Posen shows that, despite all their progress, the separation in economic life was only partial. It was only the free capital market, and thus mostly "German" funds, that enabled Polish cooperatives to play an important role in the struggle of the nationalities. This was due to the prudent business policy of both the overall management of the Polish cooperative system and the heads of the individual cooperatives.

National Mobilization in the Polish Cooperative System

Nevertheless, the history of the Polish cooperative system was by no means "one success after another".[49] It reflected the social problems in Polish society in the first three decades following the system's foundation. The formation of the intelligentsia and bourgeoisie progressed slowly until the 1880s, and there was a lack of professionally trained personnel capable of leading the cooperatives. As a result, many cooperative enterprises encountered difficulties during the turbulent economic period of the "founder's crash" in the second half of the 1870s and had to cease their business operations.[50] Nevertheless, the impression of stagnation from the end of the 1870s is misleading (see Table 1):

47 "Polizeipräsident to Oberpräsident", Posen, 17. 5. 1901, GStA, XIV. HA, Rep. 30, no. 729 (note 36), vol. 1.

48 GStA, XIV. HA, Rep. 30, no. 729 (note 36), vol. 1, passim.

49 Lech TRZECIAKOWSKI, *Wielkopolski program samomodernizacji—kształtowanie się nowoczesnego społeczeństwa*, in: Lech Trzeciakowski—Krzysztof Makowski (eds.), Samomodernizacja społeczeństw w XIX wieku. Irlandczycy, Czesi, Polacy, Poznań 1999, pp. 65–105, here p. 90.

50 L. BERNHARD, *Die Polenfrage*, p. 131. The cooperative system in Bohemia underwent a similar development, see Catherine ALBRECHT, *Nationalism in the Cooperative Movement in Bohemia*, pp. 222–223.

Table 1: Development of the Polish Association of Commercial and Economic Cooperatives (Związek Spółek Zarobkowych i Gospodarczych) in the Province of Posen[51]

Year	Cooperatives	Members	Members per cooperative
1873	43	7,660	178
1878	73	14,508	199
1883	63	18,343	291
1888	61	24,173	396
1893	84	28,815	343
1898	114	41,950	368
1903	141	67,241	477
1908	234	105,793	452

Indeed, while the number of individual cooperatives (usually bank cooperatives) affiliated to the Polish Association of Acquisition and Agricultural Cooperatives decreased, the number of members steadily increased. It was, therefore, more of a process of selection and contraction, during which the economically weaker cooperatives disappeared from the market, while the stronger ones expanded their businesses and recruited new members. At the same time, the figures can be interpreted as a cautiously positive development in trade and agriculture, as they point to the increasing economic activity of the Polish population, which now came to the cooperatives with loan applications or savings deposits. The growth process of the Polish cooperative system accelerated from the 1880s to the 1890s and the start of the 1900s. The figures in Table 1, which show a wave of start-ups from then, are an indication of this. In the first decade of the 20th century, the cooperatives covered a very broad strata of the Polish population in *Wielkopolska*. By the end of the decade, some 8% of Poles in the province of Posen already belonged to a Polish cooperative.[52] The cooperative system thus became a mass phenomenon at the very time when the Polish national movement entered its political phase.

The year 1893 was a crucial year for the national and cooperative movement. It marked the end of the rule of the aristocrat-dominated Polish club in the *Landtag* and *Reichstag*, and the transference of the initiative into the hands of the intelligentsia and bourgeoisie. The activities of the Polish elites thus shifted to the province and began to include the local level, i.e. the level at which cooperative activities also developed. In 1893, the clergyman Piotr Wawrzyniak took over the leadership of the Central Cooperative Association. In the following years, he travelled tirelessly across the province of Posen, promoting the

51 *IV. Sonderausgabe des Gesamtüberblicks über die polnische Tagesliteratur*, Heft 2 (note 42); own calculations.

52 Calculated on the basis of the figures in Richard Blanke, *Orphans of Versailles. The Germans in Western Poland 1918–1939*, Lexington 1993, p. 245.

cooperative movement and capitalist values such as efficiency and thrift.[53] Wawrzyniak skilfully mixed general economic and nationalist ideas by encouraging his listeners to invest their savings in the Polish Volksbank. In many places Wawrzyniak took the initiative to found cooperatives, alerting the suspicions of the authorities who rightly assumed that his actions were in consultation with the management of the association and local activists of the national movement: The district administrator from Wawrzyniak's hometown of Mogilno highlighted the activities of the Catholic clergy, while his colleague from Filehne (Wieleń) reported that applications for new cooperatives were received "by village".[54] The enlargement of the Polish cooperative system in the 1890s was, therefore, not the result of initiatives by local groups interested in establishing cooperatives for economic reasons, but more the result of the combined activity of the management of the associations and the local intelligentsia.

The year 1893 also saw the populist movement of the editor-in-chief of the national Polish newspaper *Orędownik*, Roman Szymański, launch an attack on agricultural associations and attempt to seize power in municipal craftsmen's associations and cooperatives. The radical Polish press became full of reports of alleged incompetence and embezzlement by the boards of Polish cooperatives.[55] At the same time, populist activists attempted to persuade the cooperative general assemblies to elect their supporters from the bourgeoisie and intelligentsia onto the boards of directors and supervisory boards. Wawrzyniak's allies in the leadership of the Polish cooperative system usually succeeded in fending off takeover attempts, but at the cost of the progressive politicization and radicalization of the cooperative organizations. After Wawrzyniak himself stood at the Prussian state parliament elections of 1894, the heads of the individual cooperatives (now mostly bourgeois and intellectual) began to become increasingly involved in the Polish electoral committees. As a result of this activity their political views became more radical, but at the same time political action was moderate and gradual. This led to the development of the principle of a "personal union", which was typical of the relationship between the cooperative movement and the national movement: both operated on a strict division of labour externally, but were closely linked by the people who led the cooperatives.[56]

Therefore, at the turn of the century, the cooperative system became the first institution with a broad social base in the Polish population of the province of Posen. Its steadily increasing membership proves that more and more Poles were ready to improve their own economic situation by joining a growing cooperative community and that Polish society was becoming increasingly democratic. The mass basis gave legitimacy to the leadership's activities and made the cooperatives the most important institution of "organic work", an ideology which led the Poles of the Prussian Eastern provinces to catch up in terms

53 Czesław Łuczak, *Ks. Piotr Wawrzyniak (1849–1910)*, Poznań 2000.

54 "Landrat Filehne to Regierungspräsident Bromberg", Filehne, 5. 12. 1902, GStA, XIV. HA, Rep. 30, no. 729 (note 36), vol. 1; "Landrat to Regierungspräsident", Mogilno, 27. 12. 1902, ibid.

55 L. Bernhard, *Die Polenfrage*, pp. 249–250.

56 "Landrat Wongrowitz to Regierungspräsident Bromberg", 11. 6. 1908, GStA, XIV. HA, Rep. 30, no. 729, (note 36), vol. 3.

of economic development and education, bringing the issue of political independence back onto the political agenda at a later date.[57] However, this focus on ethnicity limited the pursuit of democratization and self-responsibility from the outset: both ended where their own national group stopped, and the leadership of the Polish national movement placed national unity and leadership above democracy and self-responsibility. This became increasingly clear with the intensification of the national struggle in the 1890s.

The Leadership of the Polish Cooperative System

While the closure of the system in the 1860s served primarily to ward off "foreign" state influence, the Polish cooperative system became an active participant in the national struggle in the late 1880s. The management of the Polish Cooperative Association believed that both objectives required the merger of all Polish cooperatives and tightly centralized administration. The clerical-aristocratic elites which led the cooperative system at a provincial level also set the direction for individual cooperatives and installed a leadership structure which was less than transparent, marked by nepotism and a paternalistic-authoritarian style of leadership.

Two important figures in the Polish cooperative system in the province of Posen were the Catholic priests Augustyn Szamarzewski and Piotr Wawrzyniak, who helped shape it and were largely responsible for its success. Szamarzewski, who took part in the January Uprising of 1863, assumed the leadership of the relatively new cooperative association in 1872. As its "patron" he travelled around the province and founded 14 cooperatives in 1873 alone. With a mixture of persuasion, calls for national solidarity and some gentle pressure, Szamarzewski persuaded the majority of Polish cooperatives which had remained outside the association to report regularly on their business activities or to join his association.[58] In 1875, only about 30% of Polish cooperatives belonged to the Association of Commercial and Agricultural Cooperatives. By 1888, this figure had risen to about 94%.[59] In this way, Szamarzewski moulded the association into a similar form to that of the Polish national cooperative system, while also becoming the undisputed leader of the organization.

However, the aforementioned Piotr Wawrzyniak became an outstanding figure within the Polish cooperative system. What Szamarzewski had achieved only informally and partially, Wawrzyniak, who was first elected deputy chairman in 1887 and then chairman

57 Maciej Janowski, *Gab es in Polen eine Zivilgesellschaft?*, in: Arnd Bauerkämper (ed.), Die Praxis der Zivilgesellschaft. Akteure, Handeln und Strukturen im internationalen Vergleich, Frankfurt am Main 2003, pp. 293–316, here p. 300, interprets Polish "organic work" as a Polish version of civil society.

58 L. Bernhard, *Die Polenfrage*, pp. 105–106.

59 L. Bernhard, *Die Polenfrage*, pp. 105–106; Leo Wegener, *Der wirtschaftliche Kampf der Deutschen mit den Polen um die Provinz Posen*, Posen 1903, p. 173. According to Wegener, the figures for the cooperatives remaining outside the Polish federation are, however, uncertain, as not all of the Polish cooperatives reported to the federation or had it carry out audits.

of the Polish federation in 1891, achieved on a grander scale.[60] In 1892 during the "era of reconciliation", following a lengthy process, the Prussian minister of trade granted the federation the right of revision, giving the Polish cooperative federation the powers it would use in subsequent years. The right to audit meant that not only cooperatives affiliated to the association were largely protected from the appointment of state auditors and thus from official control and intervention. In addition, the revision law created a legally uniform Polish association of Polish cooperatives from the provinces of Posen and West Prussia, giving the leadership an important tool for disciplining associated cooperatives. The revision law allowed access to the business and its correspondence, and thus the opportunity to exert pressure on the management of the primary cooperatives.[61] Wawrzyniak's position as trustee of the Polish Association Bank [*Bank Związku Spółek Zarobkowych i Gospodarskich*], Bank of the Association of Commercial and Agricultural Cooperatives and the practice of granting credit only to those cooperatives he considered "creditworthy" gave him considerable power.[62] Having also cemented his position in the power struggles within his association in 1897, Wawrzyniak had practically unlimited power in his oligarchically structured organization. He used this position to consolidate the association and discipline affiliated individual cooperatives until his death in 1910.

At the local level, cooperative elites and power relations were almost the mirror image of those at the regional level: here, too, the Catholic priests dominated the cooperative boards and supervisory boards, although their position in the village was more a reflection of their social position, education and administrative tasks in the parishes. The Prussian authorities closely followed the development of the Polish cooperatives and attributed their increase to the activities of the Polish clergy, whose social commitment had increased since the *Rerum novarum* papal social encyclical of May 1891.[63] In early 1903, for example, the president of the Bydgoszcz government wrote to the chief president of the province of Posen: "The souls [cooperatives, T.L.] of the Catholic clergy are everywhere, especially those who have distinguished themselves elsewhere as leaders of the national Polish movement, Polish lawyers, landowners, etc."[64] A look at the local cooperative leaders also confirms the impression of the leading role of the Catholic clergy. In 1915, there were three priests at the Association Day among the representatives of the five Polish cooperatives from the Birnbaum district (Międzychód). Alongside them, a landowner, two merchants and a doctor travelled to Posen to attend the meeting of the Polish Cooperative Association. Five years previously these men were among the founding

60 C. Łuczak, *Ks. Piotr Wawrzyniak*, p. 27.

61 L. Bernhard, *Die Polenfrage*, p. 139.

62 L. Bernhard, *Die Polenfrage*, p. 225.

63 Marek Chamot, *Polska myśl chrześcijańsko-społeczna w zaborze pruskim w latach 1890–1918*, Toruń 1991, pp. 20–21.

64 "Regierungspräsident Bromberg to Oberpräsident of Posen province", Bromberg, 8. 1. 1903, GStA, XIV. HA, Rep. 30, no. 729 (note 36), vol. 1.

members of three Polish cooperatives in the cities of Birnbaum and Zirke (Sieraków).[65] Therefore, the change in the elite that had become apparent in the Polish national movement from the 1890s could also be noticed in the local cooperative leadership: the aristocratic elite, which had initiated the establishment of the first Polish cooperative in the Birnbaum district in 1903, for example, was being increasingly displaced by the intelligentsia and experts from the bourgeoisie.[66]

Notwithstanding this constant socio-structural change within the cooperative leadership, its leadership style hardly changed—not least because of the national political enslavement of the cooperative system: decisions were made in small groups and the leadership remained paternalistic, sometimes authoritarian. Reports show how the leaders of the associations and local executive boards put pressure on association congresses and general assemblies, manipulating decisions for their own benefit and thus for the benefit of the Polish national movement.[67] Therefore, on the eve of the First World War, nationalism and democracy were increasingly at odds with each other within Polish cooperatives.

Conclusion

Even the beginnings of *Wielkopolska*'s cooperative system were marked by national division: nationally conscious Poles established parallel cooperatives because they felt cheated by German board members, or because they could not present their ideas at general assemblies, with the result that they soon founded their own independent associations. As the economy also began to be affected by national conflicts at the end of the 1880s, the Polish cooperatives also became actively involved in them. The Polish cooperative system was closely linked to the Polish national movement in the province of Posen and was its communication channel, mobilization base and economic backbone. The national principle was constitutive for the Polish cooperative system in the province of Posen and clearly distinguished it from its counterparts in the western regions of Europe.

With regard to the Polish cooperative system's contribution to civil society, the picture is correspondingly ambivalent: its leadership succeeded in organizing a considerable part of the Polish population in *Wielkopolska* by helping them to help themselves and to integrate them into them community. The local cooperative activists—initially often landowners from the nobility, latterly mainly Catholic priests, entrepreneurs and

---

65 "Protokół Sejmiku Związku Spółek Zarobkowych i Gospodarczych odbytego w dniach 27 i 28 września 1915 r. w Poznaniu", GStA, XIV. HA, Rep. 30: Regierung Bromberg, no. 730: Die polnischen Erwerbs- und Wirtschaftsgenossenschaften 1904–; Archiwum Państwowe w Poznaniu, Sąd Powiatowy Międzychód, no. 168: Bank Ludowy 1915–; analysis and overview of the clergy in the leadership of Polish cooperatives see L. BERNHARD, *Die Polenfrage*, pp. 372–400.

66 On the change to the elites in the Polish national movement before the First World War, see Szczepan WIERZCHOSŁAWSKI, *Elity polskiego ruchu narodowego w Poznańskiem i w Prusach Zachodnich w latach 1850–1914*, Toruń 1992; on cooperatives in rural Birnbaum before the First World War see ibid., pp. 184–189.

67 GStA, XIV. HA, Rep. 30, no. 729, (note 36), vol. 3, passim.

merchants—provided help in economic emergencies and expanded education, thus promoting nationalism amongst the peasantry and petty bourgeois by creating trust in national institutions. In addition, cooperative activities were a way of forming elites: there are numerous examples of peasant activists who acquired knowledge and skills by assuming responsibility in cooperatives and peasant associations (which also performed cooperative tasks), and who, after gaining state independence, held leading positions in local administrations and in local trade unions or party groups.[68]

At the same time, national social integration was quite detrimental to social integration as a whole because it promoted a new line of conflict. In addition, the emphasis on national solidarity had serious consequences for the leadership style of the Polish cooperative system: in the provinces and at a local level, the management of the cooperative was in the hands of a small, closely linked management group of about a dozen men who dominated the executive and supervisory boards. Their leadership style ranged from paternalistic to authoritarian and opposition was barely tolerated. Examples show that the decision-making process was often opaque, there was manipulation of the general assemblies, and critics were pushed out of the cooperatives.

As a result, the main characteristic of the Polish cooperative system in the province of Posen—its national function—became both a blessing and a curse with regard to the creation of civil-society structures and behaviour. Although civil society and cooperatives grew due to national social integration, this was often at the expense of internal cooperative democracy.

Bibliography

Catherine ALBRECHT, *Economic Nationalism among German Bohemians*, Nationalities Papers 24, 1996, pp. 17–30.

Catherine ALBRECHT, *Nationalism in the Cooperative Movement in Bohemia before 1914*, in: T. Lorenz (ed.), Cooperatives in Ethnic Conflicts, pp. 215–227.

Ludwig BERNHARD, *Die Polenfrage. Das polnische Gemeinwesen im preußischen Staat*, Leipzig 1910.

Johnston BIRCHALL, *The International Co-operative Movement*, Manchester 1997.

Richard BLANKE, *Orphans of Versailles. The Germans in Western Poland 1918–1939*, Lexington 1993.

Ernst BRUCKMÜLLER, *Landwirtschaftliche Organisationen und gesellschaftliche Modernisierung: Vereine, Genossenschaften und politische Mobilisierung der Landwirtschaft Österreichs vom Vormärz bis 1914*, Salzburg 1977.

Marek CHAMOT, *Polska myśl chrześcijańsko-społeczna w zaborze pruskim w latach 1890–1918* [Polish Christian-Social ideas in the Prussian partition in the years 1890–1918], Toruń 1991.

68 T. LORENZ, *Von Birnbaum nach Międzychód*, p. 184.

Alexander DILLON, *The Forgotten Movement: Cooperatives and Cooperative Networks in Ukraine and Imperial Russia*, Harvard Ukrainian Studies 23, 1999, no. 1–2, pp. 129–143.

Georg DRAHEIM, *Die Genossenschaft als Unternehmungstyp*, Göttingen 1952.

Helmut FAUST, *History of the cooperative movement. Origin and Path of the Cooperative Movement in the German Language Area*, Frankfurt am Main 1977.

Timothy W. GUINNANE, *Cooperatives as Information Machines: German Rural Credit Cooperatives, 1883–1914*, The Journal of Economic History 61, 2001, pp. 366–389.

Timothy W. GUINNANE, *Regional Organizations in the German Cooperative Banking System in the Late 19th Century*, Research in Economics 51, 1997, pp. 251–274.

Jan HÁJEK, *Záložny a spořitelny—pilíře českého peněžnictví* [Credit cooperatives and savings banks—the pillars of Czech banking], in: Jan Hájek—Vlastislav Lacina, Od úvěrních družstev k bankovním koncernům [From Credit cooperatives to banking corporations], Praha 1999, pp. 121–158.

Stefan-Ludwig HOFFMANN, *Geselligkeit und Demokratie. Vereine und zivile Gesellschaft im transnationalen Vergleich 1750-1914*, Göttingen 2003.

Wilhelm JÄGER, *Der Genossenschaftsbegriff als Problem der Theorie und Ordnungspolitik*, in: Erwin Oberländer—Hans Lemberg—Holm Sundhaussen (eds.), Genossenschaften in Osteuropa. Alternative zur Planwirtschaft?, Wiesbaden 1993, pp. 13–22.

Maciej JANOWSKI, *Gab es in Polen eine Zivilgesellschaft?*, in: Arnd Bauerkämper (ed.), Die Praxis der Zivilgesellschaft. Akteure, Handeln und Strukturen im internationalen Vergleich, Frankfurt am Main 2003, pp. 293–316.

Rudolf JAWORSKI, *Handel und Gewerbe im Nationalitätenkampf. Studien zur Wirtschaftsgesinnung der Polen in der Provinz Posen (1871–1914)*, Göttingen 1986.

Jürgen KOCKA, *Zivilgesellschaft als historisches Problem*, in: Christoph Conrad et al. (eds.), Europäische Zivilgesellschaft zwischen Ost und West. Begriff, Geschichte, Chancen, Frankfurt am Main 2000, pp. 13–39.

Stefan KOWAL, *Die ökonomischen Auswirkungen der Nationalitätenpolitik im preußischen Teilungsgebiet Polens (1871–1918)*, in: Uwe Müller (ed.), Ausgebeutet oder alimentiert? Regionale Wirtschaftspolitik und nationale Minderheiten in Ostmitteleuropa (1871–1939), Berlin 2006, pp. 167–178.

Stefan KOWAL, *Społeczeństwo Wielkopolski i Pomorza Nadwiślańskiego w latach 1871–1914. Przemiany demograficzne i społeczno-zawodowe* [The society of *Wielkopolska* and Pomerania in the years 1871-1914. Demographic and social-occupational change], Poznań 1982.

Eduard KUBŮ—Helga SCHULTZ (eds.), *History and Culture of Economic Nationalism in East Central Europe*, Berlin 2006.

Eduard KUBŮ—Helga SCHULTZ (eds.), *Wirtschaftsnationalismus als Entwicklungsstrategie ostmitteleuropäischer Eliten*, Prag 2004.

Žarko LAZAREVIĆ, *National and Economic Features of Slovene Cooperatives*, in: Torsten Lorenz (ed.), Cooperatives in Ethnic Conflicts. Eastern Europe in the 19th and Early 20th Century, Berlin 2006, pp. 251–262.

Torsten LORENZ, *Introduction: Cooperatives in Ethnic Conflicts*, in: Torsten Lorenz (ed.), Cooperatives in Ethnic Conflicts. Eastern Europe in the 19th and Early 20th Century, Berlin 2006, pp. 9–44.

Torsten LORENZ, *Von Birnbaum nach Międzychód. Bürgergesellschaft und Nationalitätenkampf in Großpolen bis zum Zweiten Weltkrieg*, Berlin 2005.

Torsten LORENZ—Uwe MÜLLER, *National Segregation and Mass Mobilization: Polish Cooperatives in the Posen Province before the First World War*, in: Torsten Lorenz (ed.), Cooperatives in Ethnic Conflicts. Eastern Europe in the 19th and Early 20th Century, Berlin 2006, pp. 183–200.

Czesław ŁUCZAK, *Dzieje gospodarcze Wielkopolski w okresie zaborów (1815–1918)* [The economic history of *Wielkopolska* in the time of the partitions (1815-1918)], Poznań 2001.

Czesław ŁUCZAK (ed.), *Dzieje Wielkopolski* [The history of *Wielkopolska*], vol. 2, Poznań 1973.

Czesław ŁUCZAK, *Ks. Piotr Wawrzyniak (1849–1910)*, Poznań 2000.

Eduard MÄNDLE, *Demokratische Mehrheitsregel in Genossenschaften*, in: E. Mändle—W. Svoboda (eds.), Genossenschafts-Lexikon, pp. 120–121.

Eduard MÄNDLE—Walter SVOBODA (eds.), *Genossenschafts-Lexikon*, Wiesbaden 1992.

Uwe MÜLLER, *Modernisierung oder Diskriminierung? Siedlungspolitik in den preußischen Ostprovinzen zwischen nationalitäten- und agrarpolitischen Zielen*, in: Uwe Müller (ed.), Ausgebeutet oder alimentiert? Regionale Wirtschaftspolitik und nationale Minderheiten in Ostmitteleuropa (1871–1939), Berlin 2006, pp. 141–165.

Erwin OBERLÄNDER et al., *Genossenschaften in Osteuropa. Alternative zur Planwirtschaft?*, Wiesbaden 1993.

Henryk SITAREK, *Rola kredytu w rozwoju gospodarki Wielkopolski na przełomie XIX i XX wieku. Bank Związku Spółek Zarobkowych w Poznaniu 1885–1918* [The role of credit in the development of the economy of *Wielkopolska* at the turn of the 19th and 20th century. The Bank of the Association of Commercial and Agricultural Cooperatives in Poznań 1885–1918], Warszawa 1977.

Kai STRUVE, *Peasant Emancipation and National Integration. Agrarian Circles, Village Reading Rooms, and Cooperatives in Galicia*, in: Torsten Lorenz (ed.), Cooperatives in Ethnic Conflicts. Eastern Europe in the 19th and Early 20th Century, Berlin 2006, pp. 229–250.

Holm SUNDHAUSSEN, *Einführung. Zur Bedeutung der Genossenschaften in Vergangenheit und Gegenwart Osteuropas*, in: Erwin Oberländer et al., Genossenschaften in Osteuropa. Alternative zur Planwirtschaft?, Wiesbaden 1993, pp. 5–12.

Leo WEGENER, *Der wirtschaftliche Kampf der Deutschen mit den Polen um die Provinz Posen*, Posen 1903.

Szczepan WIERZCHOSŁAWSKI, *Elity polskiego ruchu narodowego w Poznańskiem i w Prusach Zachodnich w latach 1850–1914* [The elites of the Polish national movement in Poznania and West Prussia in the years 1850–1914], Toruń 1992.

Lech TRZECIAKOWSKI, *Wielkopolski program samomodernizacji—kształtowanie się nowoczesnego społeczeństwa* [*Wielkopolska*'s program of self-modernization—the development of a modern society], in: Lech Trzeciakowski—Krzysztof Makowski (eds.), Samomodernizacja społeczeństw w XIX wieku. Irlandczycy, Czesi, Polacy [The self-modernization of societies in the 19th century. Irishmen, Czechs, Poles], Poznań 1999, pp. 65–105.

Farmers as New Citizens and Members of the Czech Nation: Agricultural Associations and the Transformation of Local Societies in Rural Bohemia*

YUKO KIRYU

Abstract

The development of civil society has been a major issue in Czech historiography. However, relatively little is known about the associated modernization process as it applies to rural Bohemia. The objective of this study is to clarify the rural modernization process through its connection to the principles of civil society by examining the development of agricultural associations during the 1850s and 1860s in Bohemia. This paper discusses the expansion of agricultural associations and attempts to answer two questions. Firstly, how did this process relate to the transformation of local practices and societies that were previously based on the estate system? Secondly, how did Czech national and liberal discourses function during this process?

The development of civil society has been a major issue in Czech historiography.[1] However, relatively little is known about the associated modernization process as it applies to rural Bohemia, with most relevant studies having focused on the urban milieu.

This lack of information can partly be ascribed to the fact that studies on the political and social changes in rural Bohemia during the second half of the "long" 19th century have centred on the development of the agrarian movement, which culminated with the founding of the Czech Agrarian Party [*Česká strana agrární*] in 1899. Most previous studies have focused on the status or estate [*stavovský*] aspect of this issue. Therefore, the

---

* This article is a revised and shorter version of the study which was originally published in Japanese: *1850–60 nenndai Bohemia ni okeru Nōgyōkyōkai to Chiikishakai: Nōmin, Kokumin, Kōkyōken* [Agricultural Associations in Bohemia: Farmers, the Nation and the ‚Public Sphere'], Seiyō-shigaku [The Studies in Western History], 2007, no. 226, pp. 91–111.

1 Rudolf KUČERA, *Občanská společnost. Koncept a jeho historizace*, Dějiny—Teorie—Kritika 2007, no. 2, p. 219. As Kučera's article shows, many studies analysed the history of 19th century Bohemia from the perspective of building civil society. Otto Urban's pioneering work offered a significant theoretical starting point in this way: Otto URBAN, *Kapitalismus a česká společnost*, Praha 1978.

current body of literature primarily discusses how farmers established independent political organizations, thus breaking away from the Czech liberals.[2] Scholars have emphasised the "anti-liberal" tendencies of farmers by focusing on this confrontation. These research trends at least partly explain why so few studies have analysed how the modernization process occurred in rural areas through its connection with the principles of civil society.

Table 1: Number of Agricultural Associations in Bohemia, 1856–1890

Year	1856	1871	1875	1880	1890
Number	9 (18 branches)	93	132	245	1064

Moriz von STUBENRAUCH, *Statistische Darstellung des Vereinswesens im Kaiserthume Österreich*, Wien 1857, pp. 192–209; Statistisches Jahrbuch 1871(1872), pp. 460–465; 1875(1878), p. 24; 1880 (1881), p. 24; Das landwirtschaftliche Genossenschaftswesen und die sonstige landwirtschaftliche Interessenvertretung. Zu 710 und 711 der Beilagen zu den stenographischen Protokollen des Abgeordnetenhauses des Reichsrates, 9. Session 1893, pp. 87–91.

However, rural Bohemia was not completely isolated from the modernization process; on the contrary, the number of Bohemian agricultural associations significantly increased during the second half of the 19th century (Table 1). It is well known that the associations which began to spread in European countries during the 18th century advocated new principles designed to undermine the estate system and facilitate the emergence of a civic public sphere.[3] This suggests a need to examine the rural modernization process through its connection to the principles of civil society.

2 For information on the agrarian movement, see Otakar FRANKENBERGER, *Antonín Švehla v dějinách československé strany agrární*, Praha 1931; Václav CHUNDELA, *Stanislav Kubr, zakladatel české strany agrární, sedlák a politik*, Praha 1933; *Počátky agrárního hnutí v Prokůpkově kraji*, Kutná Hora 1936; Mořic MICHÁLEK, *Zemědělští buditelé*, Praha 1937; Jan NOŽIČKA, *Jan Antonín Prokůpek, apoštol hospodářského pokroku a národní svornosti*, Praha 1939; Jurij KŘÍŽEK, *Krise cukrovarnictví v českých zemích v osmdesátých letech minulého století a její význam pro vzrůst rolnického hnutí*, Československý časopis historický 4, 1956, pp. 270–298; 5, 1957, pp. 417–447, 473–506; 6, 1958, pp. 46–59; Jan HAVRÁNEK, *Die ökonomische und politische Lage der Bauernschaft in den böhmischen Ländern in den letzten Jahrzehnten des 19. Jahrhunderts*, Jahrbuch für Wirtschaftsgeschichte, 1966, no. 2, pp. 96–136; Jan HAVRÁNEK—Josef PETRÁŇ, *Rolnické hnutí v českých zemích v letech 1775–1918*, Československý časopis historický 17, 1969, pp. 863–886; Peter HEUMOS, *Agrarische Interessen und nationale Politik in Böhmen 1848–1889*, Wiesbaden 1979; Tomáš VOJTĚCH, *Mladočeši a boj o politickou moc v Čechách*, Praha 1980; Jiří ŠOUŠA—Daniel N. MILER—Mary H. SAMAL (eds.), *Politická a stavovská zemědělská hnutí ve 20. Století*, Uherské Hradiště 2000; Jiří ŠOUŠA—Daniel N. MILER—Mary H. SAMAL (eds.), *K úloze a významu agrárního hnutí v českých a československých dějinách*, Praha 2001.

3 Jürgen HABERMAS, *Strukturwandel der Öffentlichkeit*, Frankfurt a. M. 1962; Thomas NIPPERDEY, *Verein als soziale Struktur in Deutschland im späten 18. und frühen 19. Jahrhundert*, in: Hartmut Boockmann (ed.), Geschichtswissenschaft und Vereinswesen im 19. Jahrhundert, Göttingen 1972, pp. 1–44; Wolfgang HARDTWIG, *Strukturmerkmale und Entwicklungstendenzen des Vereinswesens*

The objective of this study was to clarify this process by examining the development of agricultural associations during the 1850s and 1860s.[4] In Bohemia, hereditary subjection [*Erbuntertänigkeit*] was abolished during the revolution of 1848/1849. The decades following this revolution were key periods for the development of rural Bohemian society. It is also necessary to consider Otto Urban's pioneering work when analysing the construction of civil society. Urban argued that the process was accompanied by the transformation of local societies, which constituted the former "feudal society" in addition to forming the modern Czech nation.[5]

This paper discusses the expansion of agricultural associations in Bohemia and attempts to answer two questions. Firstly, how did this process relate to the transformation of local practices and societies that were previously based on the estate system? Secondly, how did Czech national and liberal discourses function during this process?

An examination of these issues will help clarify the process of nationalization and the politicization of Bohemian villagers in the context of the modernization process in connection with the principles of civil society. This is a diversion from previous studies on the subject, which have primarily focused on other aspects.[6] An investigation of this type will also facilitate the integration of rural Bohemian history into the overall narrative, including issues dealing with the Habsburg monarchy; the development of civil society is now a major aspect in historiography concerning this monarchy, to which the *Bürgertumsforschung* has contributed significantly since the 1980s.[7]

---

in Deutschland 1789–1848, Historische Zeitschrift, Beiheft 9, 1984, pp. 11–50; Stefan-Ludwig HOFFMANN, *Geselligkeit und Demokratie*, Göttingen 2003.

4 Most previous studies on agricultural associations focused on institutional aspects, but did not examine them from the perspective of building civil society. Jaroslav KABEŠ, *Počátky hospodářských spolků v Čechách (1848–1855)*, Časopis pro dějiny venkova, 1936, pp. 135–143; Josef NOŽIČKA, *Počátky rolnického spolčování*, Časopis pro dějiny venkova 1939, pp. 30–42, 82–91; Miloslav VOLF, *Organizace a působení Vlastenecko-hospodářské společnosti*, Praha 1961; Miloslav VOLF, *Organizační vývoj Vlastenecko-hospodářské společnosti*, Vědecké Práce Československého zemědělského muzea 1967, pp. 67–81; Antonín VERBÍK, *Zemědělské instituce v letech 1848–1900 v českých zemích*, Vědecké práce Zemědělského muzea 1979, pp. 143–162; P. HEUMOS, *Agrarische Interessen und nationale Politik in Böhmen*. A few valuable exceptions are found in the works of František Kutnar and Christoph Stölzl. Kutnar provided important insight into agricultural associations in the context of social transformation after the abolition of hereditary subjection; this account provides a useful starting point for further analysis. However, his understanding of the nation requires revision when considering the recent development of studies on the nation and nationalism from a constructive perspective. Franatišek KUTNAR, *Pokusy o sociálně politickou aktivitu rolnictva v Čechách za Bachova absolutismu*, Sborník historický 1971, pp. 71–84; Christoph STÖLZL, *Die Ära Bach in Böhmen*, München 1971.

5 O. URBAN, *Kapitalismus a česká společnost*.

6 Previous studies on the agrarian movement have typically explained the politicization process from a socioeconomic perspective.

7 For example, Helmut RUMPLER—Peter URBANITSCH (eds.), *Die Habsburgermonarchie 1848–1918*, vol. 8, *Die Politische Öffentlichkeit und Zivilgesellschaft*. Part 1, *Vereine, Parteien und Interessenverbände als Träger der politischen Partizipation*; Part 2, *Die Presse als Faktor der politischen Mobilisierung*, Wien, 2006.

Due to limited documentation, the following analysis focuses on the development of agricultural associations in the Boleslav [*Boleslavský*] and Prague [*Pražský*] prefectures [*kraje*].[8]

The Foundation of Agricultural Associations

The abolition of hereditary subjection during the revolution of 1848/49 initiated the spread of Bohemian agricultural associations. This not only abolished the corvée, which was a burden to peasant farmers, but also emancipated them from subject [*Untertan*] status. Educating farmers thus became an important item of the agenda. The Viennese government sought new measures to promote agricultural production under these circumstances and centred on professional education for the peasantry. In Bohemia, Czech liberals eagerly tackled this issue. They envisioned a modern Czech nation comprised of equal and independent citizens capable of upholding the *raison d'état*. Part of this platform involved stressing the need for the enlightenment of farmers.[9] Although their intentions were different, both the government and Czech liberals considered associations a major means of achieving this concept.[10]

However, the revolution was supressed. The government attempted to restrict the social and political activities of its inhabitants, including those involved in association life. It only permitted the establishment of agricultural associations as branches of the Patriotic-Economic Society in the Kingdom of Bohemia [*k.k. Patriotisch-ökonomische Gesellschaft im Königreiche Böhmen*] in Prague.[11] This was established in 1769 on the initiative of the Theresian regime to promote agriculture. Until the mid-19th century, this largely consisted of nobles, state and patrimonial officials, and specialists.[12] By promoting the establishment of branch associations of this society in which nobles and their employees maintained influence, the government attempted to achieve the enlightenment of farmers without encouraging political radicalization.[13] Branch agricultural associations

8 These neighbouring prefectures were fertile agricultural regions in which farmers with relatively large farmlands cultivated grain crops and sugar beets. Jaroslav Purš, *Die Entwicklung des Kapitalismus in der Landwirtschaft der böhmischen Länder in der Zeit von 1849–1879*, Jahrbuch für Wirtschaftsgeschichte 3, 1963, p. 76. On the structure of landownership in Bohemia, ibid., p. 95.

9 On the overlap of liberal and Czech national thought, see František Kutnar, *Obrozenské vlastenectví a nacionalismus*, Praha 2003, Chapter 7.

10 Yuko Kiryu, *Kodym's Newspaper and the Creation of a Rural Public Sphere in Bohemia*, Český časopis historický 115, 2017, pp. 413–414.

11 Agricultural associations that were established by individual initiatives until then were disbanded. F. Kutnar, *Pokusy o sociálně politickou aktivitu rolnictva*, p. 75.

12 National Archive, Prague (NA), fond Vlastenecko-hospodářská společnost (VHS), book no. 41, Stand der k. k. patriotisch-ökonomischen Gesellschaft im Königreich Böhmen 1840; book no. 42, Stand der k. k. patriotisch-ökonomischen Gesellschaft im Königreich Böhmen 1840–1849.

13 On branch establishment, see J. Kabeš, *Počátky hospodářských spolků v Čechách*, pp. 137–143.

were then established by members of the Patriotic-Economic Society (Table 2).[14] However, the members mainly consisted of nobles, manor employees, intellectuals, and city elites; farmer participation was limited.[15] Such participation did not increase until the mid-to-late 1850s.[16]

Table 2: Agricultural Associations in Bohemia, 1849–1853

Prefecture	Year of founda-tion	Location of associations	Occupation of chairs	Number of members		
				1851	1852	1853
Prague prefecture	1851	Praha	Nobleman	30	30	41
	1850	Louny	Administrator of manor	73	88	88
	1851	Příbram	Pharmacist	-	108	106
	1851	Dobřichovice	-	34	-	-
Budějovice prefecture	1851	Budějovice	Nobleman	287	296	350
	1851	Sedlčany	Administrator of manor	60	52	45
Pardubice prefecture	1851	Pardubice	Nobleman	163	-	-
	1851	Kolín	Nobleman	113	127	133
Jičín prefecture	1851	Jičín	Nobleman	110	106	103
	1851	Ml. Boleslav	District captain	63	71	105
	1851	Mnichovo Hradiště	-	93	91	-

14 According to the draft guidelines of the Patriotic-Economic Society, which were approved in 1850, prefectural associations [*Kreisverein*] were to be established in every prefectural capital and, if necessary, it was also possible to establish some sectional associations [*Kreisverein-Sectionen*] in one prefecture. Both prefectural and sectional associations were granted the right to found district associations [*Bezirksvereine*]. However, the government gradually began to restrict the activities of the Patriotic-Economic Society. Finally, only 13 prefectural associations were permitted to survive and other branches were dissolved. NA, VHS, box 221, Entwurf der Grundzüge für die Errichtung der Kreis- und Bezirks-vereine; A. Verbík, *Zemědělské instituce*, p. 150.

15 NA, VHS, box 277, "Ersuchschreiben der patr.- ökonm. Gesellschaft (PÖG) an die Herren: Erwein Grafen Nostitz, Adolf Grafen von Ledebouz und Ludwig Karel Edler von Nadherny", 4. 12. 1849; "Dankschrift der PÖG an die Herren Kreispräsidenten zu Pardubitz, Jičín, Eger, Böhmischen-Leippa", Pilsen und Budweis, 13. 7. 1851; Týdenník, 1851, pp. 382–384.

16 F. Kutnar, *Pokusy o sociálně politickou aktivitu rolnictva*, p. 75.

Prefecture	Year of foundation	Location of associations	Occupation of chairs	Number of members		
				1851	1852	1853
Česká Lípa prefecture	1851	Česká Lípa	Nobleman	68	204	-
	1849	Třebenice	Official	-	41	50
	1852	Liberec	Administrator of manor	-	103	145
	1852	Šluknov	-	-	43	-
Cheb prefecture	1851	Cheb	Owner of manor	68	67	66
	1851	Kadaň	Nobleman	24	-	-
	1851	Žatec	Nobleman	53	60	-
Plzeň prefecture	1851	Plzeň	Nobleman	97	123	132

National Archive, VHS, Book no. 60, "Seznam hospodářských spolků a jednot v zemi"

The next chapter discusses the Boleslav prefecture and clarifies how farmers participated in agricultural associations. How did this process relate to the transformation of local practices and societies that were previously based on the estate system?

Farmer Participation in Agricultural Associations: the Boleslav Prefecture

The Boleslav prefectural branch was founded in 1851 to promote agriculture in Mladá Boleslav.[17] Membership was characterised by two factors. Firstly, there were many honorary members, while secondly, manor employees [*Wirtschaftsbeamte*] comprised the largest group, although landowners [*Grundbesitzer*] including farmers also participated (Table 3). The first chair was A. Klusaczek/Klusáček, a district captain [*Bezirkshauptmann*]. He was replaced by the aristocrat Hugo von Thurn-Taxis in 1855. A contemporary journal article indicates that only the German language was used at that time.[18] These combined factors reveal that the association inherited many traditional features from the Patriotic-Economic Society in Prague.[19] It thus did not reflect the peasantry.

17 This association was founded as a branch of the Jičín prefectural agricultural association. It became the Boleslav prefectural agricultural association after the establishment of the Boleslav prefecture in 1855. NA, VHS, book no. 60, "Seznam hospodářských spolků a jednot v zemi". In this paper, we consistently refer to it as the Boleslav prefectural agricultural association.

18 Pokrok hopodářský, 1862, pp. 284–285.

19 One of the society's main tasks was to spread agricultural knowledge through publishing. At first this focused on German publications for specialists; it was not until 1838 that journals were published for ordinary people in German and Czech. Nevertheless, publications intended for

Table 3: Social Structure of the Members of the Boleslav Prefectural Agricultural Association in 1854

	Total	Ordinary members	Honorary members
Manor employees (*Wirtschaftsbeamte*)	45	34	11
Landowners (*Grundbesitzer*)	18	18	0
Clergymen	11	10	1
Burghers	11*	9	2
Officials	9	3	6
Nobles	7	4	3
Doctors	4	1	3
Millers	4	4	0
Owners of farms (*Gutsbesitzer*)	3	1	2
Horticulturists	3	3	0
Teacher	1	1	0
Pharmacist	1	1	0
Brewer	1	1	0
Merchant	1	1	0
Factory owner	1	1	0
Builder (*Baumeister*)	1	1	0
Others	2	1	1
Unknown	1	1	0
Total	124	95	29

National Archive, VHS, no. 1144, box 229, "Alphabetisches Verzeichniss der bei dem Jungbunzlauer land- und forstwirthschaftlichen Verein wirkenden und Ehrenmitglieder"

* Two were mayors.

specialists continued to be published in German. Karel Bednařík, *Časopisy a kalendáře vydávané Vlastenecko-hospodářskou společností v Praze*, Praha 1977.

Jan Krouský, a farmer from Katusice near Mladá Boleslav, played a key role in increasing farmer participation in the Boleslav prefectural agricultural association. He met the famous patriot [*vlastenec*] Karel Alois Vinařický in the 1830s before becoming a member of the *Matice česká* in 1839, the purpose of which was to support publishing in Czech.[20] By circulating Czech publications, Krouský promoted local enlightenment and extended the network of patriots.[21] He was also interested in agricultural improvements and had already joined the Boleslav prefectural agricultural association.[22]

Krouský demanded that the Boleslav prefectural agricultural association accept the use of the Czech language to increase farmer involvement. He argued the following: "[The use of German] prevented not directly, but indirectly, the participation of the common Bohemian/Czech [*pouhý Čech*] at its meetings. It took away from him the opportunity to refine his opinions and benefit from the fruits of agricultural science. They were indispensable for our age and came to be beneficial only when they became the property of the whole [*veškerenstvo*], not exclusively for certain classes."[23] The association eventually accepted the use of the Czech language in 1857.[24] In that same year, Krouský appealed to regional farmers to participate in the agricultural association. He believed that the association related "mainly to our agricultural interests" and was a means of providing education. He stated that "progress consisted in education, and the welfare of the nation consisted in progress". Krouský appealed to them with the following statement: "Let us acknowledge the value of our estate, let us have a passionate love for our occupation and let us participate in public life with this love, away from our shyness and unformed views, and join in the association."[25]

Local authorities reported that farmer participation in the Boleslav association increased radically after this appeal. They stated: "As for Krouský's activities for the Czech elements [*czechische Elemente*] in the Boleslav association, more than 70 Czech farmers [*czechische Landleute*] joined it. All these people live in Krouský's neighbourhood across the river Iser and this area seems to be the base for the Czech coteries in this region. When the Czech party [*czechische Partei*] began to send the youth to the association through Krouský, its membership only numbered 140. Considering this fact, the former will no doubt soon achieve dominance in the association."[26] Other local authority reports additionally state that Thurn-Taxis resigned as chair due to "annoyance at the new members

20 On Krouský's biography, see Jan Šafránek, *Život a působení Jana Krouského*, Kolín 1878.

21 Yuko Kiryu, *Bohemian Patriots and Their Network in the First Half of the Nineteenth*, Suravukenkyu, vol. 61, 2014, pp. 83–107. On network of Bohemian patriots general, see Miroslav Hroch, *Social Preconditions of National Revival in Europe*, Cambridge 1985.

22 District Archive Mladá Boleslav (SOkA MB), fond Krouských, no. 8 III/3, "Stanovy lesnického a hospodářského spolku v Mladé Boleslavi", 1851.

23 Josef V. Šimák, *Dopisování Jana Krouského a jeho přátel*, Praha 1932, p. 215.

24 Jan Šafránek, *Život a působení Jana Krouského*, p. 34.

25 J. V. Šimák, *Dopisování Jana Krouského*, pp. 216–217.

26 NA, fond Presidium Českého místodržitelství (PM) 1855–1859, 8/5/9/3, box 496, "Bunzlauer Bezirksvorstand an Kreisamt-Präsidium", 2. 1. 1858.

who joined as a result of Krouský's campaigning"; he complained that they would "be dominant in it and threaten its further development".[27]

These local authorities' reports show that they perceived this radical growth in farmer participation as an expansion of "Czech party" power through campaigning. However, the diary of the peasant Jan E. Konopas, who lived in Sudoměř, a neighbouring village to Katusice, reveals other aspects to this process. Konopas wrote about a conversation between himself and Jan Goldbach, who was an ally of Krouský and a member of the Boleslav association.[28] Konopas wrote the following: "I asked Goldbach about the agricultural association in Mladá Boleslav, because I had heard that most of the discussions there were incomprehensible, which I complained about, and all the residents in our neighbourhood—especially the peasantry—ought to go there to listen [to the discussions]. However, [the attempt to let them participate] did not succeed then. [I said that] the agricultural association was <u>only for the lords [*jen pro pány*]</u> and that farmers would not want to join it unless it became <u>ours [*náš*]</u>. Goldbach replied that it would soon be <u>ours,</u> which satisfied me [underlining by author]."[29] According to this diary, both used non-national categories in their discussion of the matter, i.e. they used categories such as "we" and "the lords". Here, the term "lords" can be assumed to have primarily referred to nobles and their employees in the rural context.[30]

Krouský's appeal mentioned above also presented the association's language issue as a class matter: "[the fruit of agricultural science] came to be beneficial only when it became the property of everyone, not exclusively for <u>certain classes</u> [underlining by author]."[31] The fact that nobles and patrimonial officials conventionally used German in public spaces regardless of their native language explains the background to this statement.[32]

The above sentence and the conversation between Konopas and Goldbach demonstrate that the social relationship between "us" and the "lords", as derived from hereditary subjection, had not lost its influence after its abolition. On the other hand, new practices and demands developed for farmers in the Boleslav prefecture during that time.

Firstly, both Krouský's leadership and the emerging network of literate farmers like Goldbach and Konopas played an important role in increasing farmer participation in the agricultural association. The official report cited above pointed out that new farmer members lived "in Krouský's neighbourhood", thus emphasising the influence of his campaigning.[33] However, we should not accept this report literally. Instead, we should

---

27 NA, PM 1855–59, 8/5/9/3, box 496, "Bunzlauer Kreisvorstand an Statthalterei-Präsidium", 26. 1. 1858.

28 SOkA MB, fond Krouských, inv. no. 8 III/3, "Stanovy lesnického a hospodářského spolku v Mladé Boleslavi", 1851.

29 František Zuman, *Jan Evangelista Konopas, písmák v Sudoměři a jeho deník*, Časopis pro dějiny venkova 1941, p. 37.

30 František Kutnar, *František Jan Vavák*, Praha 1941, s. 108.

31 J. V. Šimák, *Dopisování Jana Krouského*, p. 215.

32 Posel z Prahy, 1857, no. 9, pp. 316–317.

33 NA, fond Presidium Českého místodržitelství (PM) 1855–1859, 8/5/9/3, box 496, "Bunzlauer Bezirksvorstand an Kreisamt-Präsidium", 2. 1. 1858.

recall that Krouský promoted local education and extended the network of patriots by circulating Czech publications. Konopas belonged to the readers' network around Krouský, while Goldbach was a member of the *Matice česká*.[34] The above conversation was conducted when they borrowed books from each other.[35] Konopas, who was a dedicated reader and correspondent of the *Hospodářské noviny* [Agricultural Newspaper] edited by Czech liberal Filip Stanislav Kodym, joined the Boleslav association after Krouský's appeal and had already participated in its meetings by 1857.[36] These facts suggest that the network of farmers cultivated new reading habits and contributed to a radical growth in farmer participation in the Boleslav association.

Secondly, both Krouský's efforts and the existence of the farmers who responded positively to his call demonstrate a growing desire to improve their status and increase participation in social life to achieve equality with other social groups. The agricultural association offered a place to realize these aspirations.

The national discourse associated with liberal principles appears to have contributed to the legitimation of the desires of the farmers. In 1857, a letter concerning the reform of the Boleslav prefectural agricultural association was published in a journal entitled *Posel z Prahy* (Messenger from Prague), which was edited by the Czech liberal František Šimáček. As noted above, Czech liberals regarded farmers as both new citizens and members of the nation; they insisted that they were able to contribute to national prosperity along with other social groups in the associations.[37] Šimáček also supported the reform of the Boleslav association, arguing the following: "A lord as well as a person who is not a lord [*pán, nepán*] are all neighbours and no one has greater rights in life nor before the law, unless he contributes to the community or the whole [*celek*] by his intellect or achievements."[38] As mentioned earlier, Krouský demanded that the Czech language be introduced into the association by arguing that the benefits of agricultural science should be "the property of everyone [*veškerenstvo*], not exclusively of certain classes". He further presented participation in the Boleslav association as a contribution to the nation.[39] Therefore, both national and liberal discourses offered a way for farmers to legitimize their aspirations.

Farmer participation in the Boleslav association increased as a result of these measures. In 1859, Josef Volšan, a leaseholder who was close to Krouský, assumed the position of chair; Czech then became the main language used during association meetings.[40] During the 1860s, the famous Czech liberals Rudolf Thurn-Taxis and Karel Mattuš became

34 František Zuman, *Jan Evangelista Konopas*, Časopis pro dějiny venkova 1940, p. 215; 1941, pp. 32, 37–38; Jan Šafránek, *Z doby národního rána českého*, Časopis pro dějiny venkova 1917, p. 186.

35 F. Zuman, *Jan Evangelista Konopas*, 1941, s. 37.

36 Hospodářské noviny 1856, pp. 191, 301–302, 399–400; 1857, pp. 210, 387; NA, PM 1855–1859, 8/5/9/3, box 496, "Bunzlauer Kreisvorstand an Statthalterei-Präsidium", 26. 1. 1858.

37 For example, Pokrok hospodářský, 1862, p. 202.

38 Posel z Prahy, 1857, č. 9, p. 316.

39 Josef V. Šimák, *Dopisování Jana Krouského a jeho přátel*, p. 215.

40 However, those who were not proficient in Czech were permitted to use German. Ferdinand Strejček, *Jak se probouzela Mladá Boleslav*, Mladá Boleslav 1929, p. 192.

association chairs, which provided them with an important venue in which to conduct their activities.[41]

To summarize, the government promoted the foundation of agricultural associations as branches of the Patriotic-Economic Society to achieve farmer enlightenment without resulting in political radicalization. However, Boleslav's prefectural history indicates that the foundation of an agricultural association as a new institution resulted in actions contrary to the regime's expectations. Farmers attempted to challenge the dominance of the "lords", transform the association into "theirs", and achieve equal participation in social life through national and liberal discourses for legitimation. An emerging network of farmers who cultivated the practice of reading supported this process. These farmers were eager to take part in social life as equal members. While the social relationships from the era of hereditary subjection did not lose their influence after its abolition, the agricultural association offered a new place for famers to socialize. This made it possible to transform social relations based on the status system.

Agricultural Associations in Bohemia during the 1860s

1. The Social Structure of Agricultural Associations

Increased farmer participation in agricultural associations was reported in other regions during the late 1850s, albeit not as radical as in the Boleslav prefecture.[42] In 1861, it was possible to establish agricultural associations at both prefectural and district levels. Member recruitment was promoted by municipal mayors and the clergy.[43] Membership substantially increased when compared to numbers from the early 1850s (Table 4).

Table 4: Agricultural Associations in Bohemia in 1862

Name	Number of district branches	Number of members
Boleslav association [*Boleslavská jednota*]	7	931
Budějovice association [*Budějovická jednota*]	0	228
Čáslav association [*Čáslavská jednota*]	4	388
Cheb association [*Chebská jednota*]	0	91
Chrudim association [*Chrudimská jednota*]	7	641
Jičín association [*Jičínská jednota*]	0	120

41 Boleslavan, 1862–1863, p. 198; "Denní zprávy z M. Boleslavi", Národní listy, 28. 11. 1864.

42 NA, PM 1855-59, 8/5/2/9, box 495, "Chef der Prager obersten Polizeibehörde an Statthalterei", 10. 3. 1858; J. Nožička, *Jan Antonín Prokůpek*, p. 40.

43 Boleslavan, 1862, p. 156, 197; "Dopisy z Kuklen", Národní listy, 9. 1. 1862.

Name	Number of district branches	Number of members
Hradec association [*Hradecká jednota*]	5	863
Liberec association [*Liberecká jednota*]	0	179
Litoměřice association [*Litoměřická jednota*]	9	671
Písek association [*Písecká jednota*]	9	638
Plzeň association [*Plzeňská jednota*]	6	1014
Prague association [*Pražská jednota*]	20	2186
Žátec association [*Žátecká jednota*]	12	771

Pokrok hospodářský, 1863, s. 332

Did this growth in membership affect the social structure? Because there are no available documents pertaining to the Boleslav association, it is important to analyse the social structure of the Prague prefectural association. This is because the Prague and Boleslav prefectures were adjacent and thus contained similar agricultural features. In Prague, farmers left other social groups and began to constitute the core membership (Table 5). However, this did not mean that other social groups were totally driven away. Instead, membership was comprised of various social groups, including urban dwellers and intellectuals. It can, therefore, be said that the agricultural association created a new community beyond the boundaries of occupation, social status, and city or village location.

Table 5: Social Structure of the Members of the Prague Prefectural Agricultural Association in 1862

Agriculture 893 Farmers, 198 Administrators of manors [*hospodářští úředníci*] 66 Agriculturalists [*hospodáři*], 53 Owners of farms [*statkáři*], 42 Leaseholders 39 Foresters, 31 Owners of manors, 12 Horticulturists 15 Others
Agricultural industry 87 Millers, 29 Brewers
Industry 20 Artisans, 20 Industrialists, 5 Managers of mining industries
Trade 27 Merchants, 23 Retailers
Executives of municipalities 126 Mayors of municipalities (24 mayors were clearly from cities) 10 Municipal councillors
City dwellers 155 Burghers, 13 Office workers

Intellectuals 116 Teachers, 71 Clergymen, 23 Doctors, 16 Lawyers, 13 Notaries, 9 Professors 9 Teachers of secondary schools, 6 Engineers, 8 Others
Officials 57 Officials (52 were k.k. Officials)
Others 21 Publicans, 23 Others, 15 Unknown
Total 2251

National Archive, PM 1860–1870, 8/5/11, box 849, "Seznam údů hospodářského spolku kraje pražského koncem roku 1862".

It is noteworthy that prominent Czech liberals such as Julius Grégr, Antonín Otakar Zeithammer, Filip Stanislav Kodym, Jan Palacký, Rudolf Thurn-Taxis, and František Šimáček also belonged to the Prague prefectural agricultural association.[44] Reports made by the authorities and records from meetings indicate that the association offered an important place for Czech liberals to conduct their activities.[45] This is similar in composition to the Boleslav association.

2. *Agricultural Association Activities and Local Societies*

What activities did agricultural associations engage in during the 1860s? Many members summed this up with the statement "Our motto is progress", which was used at meetings.[46]Agricultural associations thus set "progress" as their goal. With this as their objective, they believed that education was a primary means for promotion and carried out the following activities: 1) meetings, 2) agricultural exhibitions, 3) library foundations, 4) agricultural school foundations, 5) the establishment of savings banks and agricultural enterprises.[47]

Education was considered both a major means of developing agriculture and a method for improving members as citizens of the nation. This is evident in the following statement: "Education awakes civic virtue, national awareness, and a love of the public spirit in us."[48] This sentiment also explains the high importance of rule-based discussions at association meetings. These discussions were expected to promote agriculture based

44 Pokrok hospodářský, 1862, pp. 54–56.

45 For example, NA, PM 1855-59, 8/5/2/9, box 495, "Chef der Prager obersten Polizeibehörde an Statthalterei", 10. 3. 1858; Pokrok hospodářský 1862, pp. 38–40.

46 For example, Pokrok hospodářský, 1862, pp. 39, 414.

47 SOkA MB, fond Krouských, inv. no. 8 III/3; "Jednací řád filiálních spolků spojených s cís. k. vlastenskou hosp. společností v král. Českém. Pro hospodářský filiální spolek kraje Boleslavského", 1860; Pokrok hospodářský, 1862, pp. 39, 128, 414; 1863, p. 120.

48 Pokrok hospodářský, 1862, p. 39.

on "science", while teaching members how to engage in public discourse as citizens, as follows: "Agricultural associations became the school for the public life of a peasant, he learns how to act publicly, to speak clearly and without fear and prepares a better future for our precious fatherland."[49] The meeting debates were initially led by city notables and intellectuals, while the "passive attitude" of farmers was sometimes pointed out.[50] However, farmers began to acquire public discussion skills and increasingly participated in debates.[51]

Agricultural association activities were assumed to encourage the interaction between members of various backgrounds while fostering a certain common cultural identity.[52] Dinners were usually held after meetings and were sometimes combined with other leisure activities, including theatrical performances, dances, and concerts. A certain stylization is evident in these gatherings. For instance, members began and ended each meeting with the cheer "Vivat [*Sláva*]!" and also engaged in singing.[53] All association activities fostered a common cultural identity among members. Reports also state that association meetings allowed banners to be displayed in "national colours" while endorsing "national dance" and "national songs" such as *Kde domov můj* [Where is my home].[54] Czech national symbols were invented by Czech liberals who envisioned a modern Czech nation comprised of equal and independent citizens who would embody and popularize the concept.[55] These national symbols were also adopted by agricultural associations in which members of different status gathered as equals and contributed to shaping a new cultural identity.

Above all, the major achievement of agricultural associations was the creation of a new forum for "public" discussion at district and prefectural levels.[56] The importance of such a forum should be emphasised because similar social and political activities were restricted until 1867 despite promulgation of the October Diploma and the February Patent. Association members attended meetings not only to discuss agricultural production, but a whole range of issues, including education, municipal community administration, financial institutions, public security, and paupers. Members continually emphasized that agricultural associations provided a forum in which the idea of "equality"

49 Pokrok hospodářský, 1862, pp. 100–101.

50 For example, Pokrok hospodářský, 1864, p. 236.

51 J. Nožička, *Počátky rolnického spolčování*, p. 37; Boleslavan, 1861–1862, pp. 52, 245 et passim.

52 NA, PM 1860-1870, 8/5/11/1, box 849, "Chrudimer Bezirksvorstand an Statthalterei", 14. 3. 1864; "Melniker Bezirksamt an Statthalterei-Präsidium", 7. 9. 1961; Pokrok hospodářský, 1862, pp. 203, 211, 398–400; 1863, s. 324; Boleslavan, 1861–1862, s. 237.

53 NA, PM 1860–1870, 8/5/11/1, box 849, "Prager Kreisamt an Statthalterei-Präsidium", 9. 7. 1862; "Prager Kreisamt an Statthalterei-Präsidium", 24. 9. 1862; Pokrok hospodářský, 1862, s. 40, 203, 241; Boleslavan, 1861–1862, s. 277.

54 NA, PM 1860–1870, 8/5/11/1, box 849, "Prager KA an SHP", 9. 7. 1862; "Prager KA an SHP", 24. 9. 1862; Pokrok hospodářský, 1862, pp. 203, 241, 400; Boleslavan, 1861–1862, p. 277 et passim.

55 Taku Shinohara, *A New Trend in the Czech Historiography: On Self-Representation of the Czech Nation in the 19th Century*, Tōoshi-kenkyu (The Journal of East European Studies) 1997, pp. 15–22.

56 Pokrok hospodářský, 1862, p. 210.

was realized, i.e., that they were not contributing to the interests of certain individuals or groups, but to the "public good" and the "nation" as a whole.[57] By legitimising their "publicness" in this way and sometimes opposing the regime, members created a new forum for discussion in rural Bohemia.[58]

3. *Farmers' Political Practices*

Although agricultural associations were prohibited from directly engaging in political activities, they functioned as important channels through which farmers could influence politics at various levels. After the convocation of the Bohemian Diet in 1861, agricultural associations occasionally sent petitions addressing agricultural problems, including those involving land consolidation, shooting, land taxes, servant laws, and the contribution fund [*kontribučenské sýpky*].[59] This was an attempt to influence the political decision-making process.

Furthermore, the Czech liberal Karel Mattuš demonstrated that agricultural associations functioned as a kind of vote-gathering base for Czech liberals, who did not possess a firm organizational basis. He stated the following: "The representatives of the rural municipalities, who came to know me through the activities in the agricultural associations in particular, elected me as a member of the district board in their curia."[60]

The personal networks and experiences acquired through these agricultural association activities were also assumed to offer an avenue for furthering the political careers of farmers. For example, five out of eight members of the Bělá district board were elected in the curia for rural municipalities in 1868; they also served as committee members for the Bělá district agricultural association.[61] Moreover, some farmers successfully advanced their political careers and were elected to the Bohemian Diet. This success was based on association activities and the district boards.[62] Therefore, agricultural associations created a new local political structure resulting in self-governing institutions. Farmers also participated here, thus acquiring new political behaviour.

Conclusions

After hereditary subjection was abolished in 1848/1849, the government promoted the foundation of branch associations of the Patriotic-Economic Society to achieve farmer

57 Pokrok hospodářský, 1862, p. 210; 1865, p. 308; Hospodářské noviny, 1865, p. 308.

58 Boleslavan, 1861–62, pp.198, 213.

59 Boleslavan, 1865–66, pp. 2, 6, 73; Pokrok hospodářský, 1862, pp. 55, 71 et passim.

60 Karel Mattuš, *Paměti*, Praha 1921, s. 45.

61 SOkA MB, fond Okresní zastupitelstvo Bělá, box 7, "Výtah z protokolu sepsaného při valném zasedání okresního zastupitelstva bělského", 23. 7. 1868; *Boleslavan*, 1865–1866, p. 70.

62 Josef Husák—Rudolf Schránil (eds.), *Sněm království Českého 1861–1911. Personalie*, Praha 1911.

enlightenment under the influence of nobles and their employees. However, the history of the Boleslav prefecture shows that this attempt resulted in new behaviour among farmers, who cultivated the practice of reading and were eager to achieve equal participation in social life. These farmers attempted to challenge the dominance of the "lords", transform the association into "theirs", and realize equal participation in social life through national and liberal discourses designed for legitimation.

These agricultural associations substantially expanded during the 1860s, an increase accompanied by a transformation in their social composition. Their major achievement was the construction of a new forum for "public" discussion at both district and prefectural levels. Here, all estates were expected to participate "equally", while contributing to the "public good" and the "nation" as a whole. By so doing they helped spread new liberal and national principles while creating a new local political structure. Farmers also participated in agricultural association activities, thus changing their practices.

The above analysis clearly shows how Bohemian farmers perceived liberal and national principles in the context of rural areas where they lived and internalised them. It is, therefore, inappropriate to presuppose "illiberal" tendencies in Bohemian farmers. However, many previous studies on the agrarian movement have done so. It is well known that the rise of the agrarian movement was accompanied by the spread of agricultural associations. The new laws of 1867 liberalized foundations and association activities while legalizing political associations. This also facilitated the specialization of associations and probably caused a shift in agricultural association functions as they existed in local society. However, this does not mean that they lost their original character. This paper's findings suggest it is necessary to analyse the development of the agrarian movement in the context of an expanding public sphere. This should also consider the spread of new liberal and national principles, which accompanied the transformation of local practices and societies. Such an approach will provide new clarity to the confrontation between farmers and Czech liberals. This will contribute to a better understanding of the social transformation experienced in the Habsburg monarchy during the "long" 19th century, while also magnifying the peasant political movement in general modern history.

Bibliography

Karel BEDNAŘÍK, *Časopisy a kalendáře vydávané Vlastenecko-hospodářskou společností v Praze* [The Periodicals and Calendars Published by Patriotic-Economic Society in Prague], Praha 1977.

Václav CHUNDELA, *Stanislav Kubr, zakladatel české strany agrární, sedlák a politik* [Stanislav Kubr. The Founder of the Czech Agrarian Party, Farmer, and Politician], Praha 1933.

Otakar FRANKENBERGER, *Antonín Švehla v dějinách československé strany agrární* [Antonín Švehla in the History of the Czechoslovak Agrarian Party], Praha 1931.

Jürgen HABERMAS, *Strukturwandel der Öffentlichkeit*, Frankfurt a. M. 1962.

Wolfgang HARDTWIG, *Strukturmerkmale und Entwicklungstendenzen des Vereinswesens in Deutschland 1789–1848*, Historische Zeitschrift, Beiheft 9, 1984, pp. 11–50.

Jan HAVRÁNEK, *Die ökonomische und politische Lage der Bauernschaft in den böhmischen Ländern in den letzten Jahrzehnten des 19. Jahrhunderts*, Jahrbuch für Wirtschaftsgeschichte, 1966, no. 2, pp. 96–136.

Jan HAVRÁNEK—Josef PETRÁŇ, *Rolnické hnutí v českých zemích v letech 1775–1918* [The Peasant Movement in the Bohemian Lands], Československý časopis historický 17, 1969, pp. 863–886.

Peter HEUMOS, *Agrarische Interessen und nationale Politik in Böhmen 1848–1889*, Wiesbaden 1979.

Stefan-Ludwig HOFFMANN, *Geselligkeit und Demokratie*, Göttingen 2003.

Miroslav HROCH, *Social Preconditions of National Revival in Europe*, Cambridge 1985.

Josef HUSÁK—Rudolf SCHRÁNIL (eds.), *Sněm království Českého 1861–1911. Personalie* [The Bohemian Diet], Praha 1911.

Jaroslav KABEŠ, *Počátky hospodářských spolků v Čechách (1848–1855)* [The Beginnings of Agricultural Associations in Bohemia], Časopis pro dějiny venkova 1936, pp. 135–143.

Yuko KIRYU, *Bohemian Patriots and Their Network in the First Half of the Nineteenth*, Suravu-kenkyu, vol. 61, 2014, pp. 83–107.

Yuko KIRYU, *Kodym's Newspaper and the Creation of a Rural Public Sphere in Bohemia*, Český časopis historický 115, 2017, pp. 413–414.

Jurij KŘÍŽEK, *Krise cukrovarnictví v českých zemích v osmdesátých letech minulého století a její význam pro vzrůst rolnického hnutí* [The Crisis of Sugar Industry in the Bohemian Lands and Its Significance for the Development of Peasant Movement], Československý časopis historický 4, 1956, pp. 270–298; 5, 1957, pp. 417–447, 473–506; 6, 1958, pp. 46–59.

Rudolf KUČERA, *Občanská společnost. Koncept a jeho historizace*, Dějiny—Teorie—Kritika 2007, no. 2, pp. 219–231.

František KUTNAR, *František Jan Vavák*, Praha 1941.

František KUTNAR, *Obrozenské vlastenectví a nacionalismus* [The Revivalist Patriotism and Nationalism], Praha 2003.

Franatišek KUTNAR, *Pokusy o sociálně politickou aktivitu rolnictva v Čechách za Bachova absolutismu* [Attempts on the Socio-Political Activity of the Peasantry in Bohemia under Bach's Absolutism], Sborník historický 1971, pp. 71–84.

Karel MATTUŠ, *Paměti* [Memoirs], Praha 1921.

Mořic MICHÁLEK, *Zemědělští buditelé* [The Agrarian Awakeners], Praha 1937.

Thomas NIPPERDEY, *Verein als soziale Struktur in Deutschland im späten 18. und frühen 19. Jahrhundert*, in: Hartmut Boockmann (ed.), Geschichtswissenschaft und Vereinswesen im 19. Jahrhundert, Göttingen 1972, pp. 1–44.

Jan NOŽIČKA, *Jan Antonín Prokůpek, apoštol hospodářského pokroku a národní svornosti* [Jan Antonín Prokůpek, an Apostle of the Agricultural Progess and National Concordance], Praha 1939.

Josef NOŽIČKA, *Počátky rolnického spolčování* [The Beginnings of the Peasant Association], Časopis pro dějiny venkova 1939, pp. 30–42, 82–91.

Počátky agrárního hnutí v Prokůpkově kraji [The Beginnings of the Agrarian Movement in the Prokůpek's Region], Kutná Hora 1936.

Jaroslav PURŠ, *Die Entwicklung des Kapitalismus in der Landwirtschaft der böhmischen Länder in der Zeit von 1849–1879*, Jahrbuch für Wirtschaftsgeschichte 3, 1963, pp. 31-96.

Helmut RUMPLER—Peter URBANITSCH (eds.), *Die Habsburgermonarchie 1848–1918*, vol. 8, *Die Politische Öffentlichkeit und Zivilgesellschaft*. Part 1, *Vereine, Parteien und Interessenverbände als Träger der politischen Partizipation*; Part 2, *Die Presse als Faktor der politischen Mobilisierung*, Wien, 2006.

Taku SHINOHARA, *A New Trend in the Czech Historiography: On Self-Representation of the Czech Nation in the 19th Century*, Tōoshi-kenkyu (The Journal of East European Studies) 1997, pp. 15–22.

Christoph STÖLZL, *Die Ära Bach in Böhmen*, München 1971.

Ferdinand STREJČEK, *Jak se probouzela Mladá Boleslav* [How Did Mladá Boleslav awaken], Mladá Boleslav 1929.

Jan ŠAFRÁNEK, *Život a působení Jana Krouského* [The Life and Activities of Jan Krouský], Kolín 1878.

Josef V. ŠIMÁK, *Dopisování Jana Krouského a jeho přátel*, Praha 1932.

Jiří ŠOUŠA—Daniel N. MILER—Mary H. SAMAL (eds.), *K úloze a významu agrárního hnutí v českých a československých dějinách* [On the Role and Significance of Agrarian Movement in Czech and Czechoslovak History], Praha 2001

Jiří ŠOUŠA—Daniel N. MILER—Mary H. SAMAL (eds.), *Politická a stavovská zemědělská hnutí ve 20. století* [The Political and Agrarian Movements in 20th century], Uherské Hradiště 2000.

Otto URBAN, *Kapitalismus a česká společnost* [The Capitalism and Czech Society], Praha 1978.

Antonín VERBÍK, *Zemědělské instituce v letech 1848–1900 v českých zemích* [The Agricultural Institutions in Bohemian Lands], Vědecké práce Zemědělského muzea 1979, pp. 143–162.

Tomáš VOJTĚCH, *Mladočeši a boj o politickou moc v Čechách* [The Young Czechs and the Struggle for Political Power in Bohemia], Praha 1980.

Miloslav VOLF, *Organizace a působení Vlastenecko-hospodářské společnosti* [The Organization and Activities of Patriotic-Economic Society, Praha 1961.

Miloslav VOLF, *Organizační vývoj Vlastenecko-hospodářské společnosti* [The Organizational Development of the Patriotic-Economic Society], Vědecké Práce Československého zemědělského muzea 1967, pp. 67–81.

František ZUMAN, *Jan Evangelista Konopas, písmák v Sudoměři a jeho deník* [Jan Evangelista Konopas, the peasant writer in Sudoměř and his diary], Časopis pro dějiny venkova 1940, pp. 142–155, 205–218;1941, pp. 25–39.

The Countryside between the State, Nation and Civil Society: External Impulses and Local Initiatives*

Pavel Kladiwa

Abstract

This paper examines a period at the turn of the 20th century when the wave of social and economic changes was also felt in poor and peripheral regions such as Wallachia in the eastern part of Moravia. This followed on from the abolition of serfdom, the revolutions in industry, transport and agricultural, the rise of civil society, and the development of the education system. This paper follows the state's attempts at modernization, manifested mainly in the education system which underwent fundamental changes, and also initiatives from civil society. Nationalist ideology and civic activism were brought to rural life from the towns, mainly through the activities of the members of the intelligentsia who had migrated there and set down roots, but partially also based on local initiatives. The cooperative system and associations were a distinctive feature of the social modernization and political mobilization of the rural environment. Politicization had begun at the end of the 19th century in connection with extending the right to vote, and in the ethnically homogeneous Czech-speaking areas this was characterized mainly by the conflict between the clerical and progressive (anti-clerical) camps.

The last half a century of the existence of the Habsburg Monarchy was a period of great social change. It witnessed the building of a modern civil society, based on civil rights and capitalist relations, and on the arrival of industrialization and national emancipation. Czech historiography has already produced a number of monographs and studies concerning these processes. It has, therefore, mapped the overall social development of the Czech society quite well, albeit not as well from the perspective of society in the Bohemian lands. The impact and circumstances of great social changes are studied within the context of the entire Bohemian lands (i.e. basically from the perspective of the centre), or, alternatively, within the context of urban society.

* This study was produced as part of the Czech Science Foundation (GAČR) grant no. 17-02986S: The transformation and social activation of rural areas in Moravia and Austrian Silesia 1861–1914.

Czech historiography, however, lacks a synthesizing presentation of the social processes capturing the rural milieu in more detail. It requires more detailed studies about the establishment of associations and cooperatives in the countryside, about the agents of social change (mainly the social group of the intelligentsia), about the activity of the parish priests and their relations with other leading figures of the local milieu, about the composition and activity of municipal governments, the transfer of "high politics" into the local milieu (meetings before provincial and parliamentary elections), and about the growth of administrative activity (the state penetrating the local milieu).[1] From the aspect of the reconstruction of the bi-directionality of communication ties, it is worthwhile observing a specific region comprehensively, i.e. not a single village in isolation, but the village milieu and its ties to the local centres (district court, district office, electoral district).

Studies from abroad focusing on the development of the civil and national society with respect to rural areas can serve as inspiration.[2] They tend to emphasise that:

a. The response of rural communities to modernizing impulses from elsewhere is a multi-layered phenomenon, combining acceptance of these impulses with their adaptation to local conditions.
b. The nation is also (perhaps primarily) viewed as a social contract, i.e. a contract between the local milieu and the centre. During the integration of the rural regions, specific modernization measures had become interconnected with national goals. The attitude of the country folk towards various offers of integration from both the state and the opposition was formed from pragmatic reasons and consideration of the "utility value". The nation was not a value in itself, but gained attractiveness only in connection with specific promises concerning the present and future. One decisive contribution to the integration process was the extension of the franchise.[3]
c. National/civil identity as a concept of self-perception grows in importance among an increasing number of rural people only after the isolation of rural communities has been alleviated by the organizational and communication structures of civil society. For this reason, it is important to trace the emergence of structures enabling national communication and organization (newspapers, educational and agricultural associations, other clubs and associations, political parties).

---

1 In this respect it is possible to follow up the successful research conducted by Masaryk University in Brno. See Lukáš Fasora—Jiří Hanuš—Jiří Malíř (eds.), *Sekularizace venkovského prostoru v 19. století*, Brno 2009; Stanislav Balík et al., *Český antiklerikalismus. Zdroje, témata a podoba českého antiklerikalismu v letech 1848–1938*, Praha 2015. Norbert Franz writes about the "Durchstaatlichung des letzten Dorfes": Norbert Franz, *Durchstaatlichung und Ausweitung der Kommunalaufgaben im 19. Jahrhundert. Tätigkeitsfeld und Handlungsspielräume ausgewählter französischer und luxemburgischer Landgemeinden im mikrohistorischen Vergleich (1805–1890)*, Trier 2006.

2 For a detailed characteristic of a selected bibliography see Pavel Kladiwa, *The Transformation and Social Activation of Rural Areas. The Bohemian Lands in 1861–1914 (A Preliminary outline of the issue)*, Moderní dějiny/Modern History 26, 2018, no. 1, pp. 1–29.

3 Ruth Dörner, *Staat und Nation im Dorf*, München 2006, pp. 327, 331, 332.

The pivotal ideas are politicization and modernization. The basis of wide-ranging and long-term societal modernization lay in the integration of individuals and social groups into supra-regional and "over-class" structures as the result of building a centralized, bureaucratically administered state, mainly at the cost of traditional social, local and religious ties. The process of politicization can be compared to the increasing participation of the population in public events and to their identification with certain political ideas, parties or figures. Both these processes were accompanied by a rise in nationalism.

Important economic, social and cultural changes, which were related to the abolition of servitude, industrialization, urbanization, the introduction of constitutionality and school reforms, significantly affected and gradually transformed the way of life even in the countryside. The state's regulating and modernizing activity played a fundamental role in this, as the state, through its regulations and decrees, reacted to the needs of the period and initiated the changes which first noticeably manifested themselves in the urban milieu, but which also increasingly found their way into the countryside.

The phenomenon of social change was further related to two mutually connected, though not identical, types of activities. Throughout the second half of the 19th century, increasingly stronger national agitation gradually and with growing intensity manifested itself even in rural areas, dragging the countryside into national life, or, at least, into the national discourse. Additionally, after breaking free from subservience to the manorial lords and establishing municipal governments, and as a consequence of the development of community life and, in the late 19th century, even political life (the extension of political rights), local self-initiatives and civil society also started to develop. Here civil society is meant in the German term *Zivilgesellschaft*, where active participation in the community itself is the basic principle of socio-civic behavioural patterns. A typical feature of civil society is the supersession of individual interests, resulting in various forms of societal groupings.[4]

While state intervention was a completely external impulse which local society could do little to influence (perhaps only in the final pre-war years in the form of interpellations and other activities of "its" deputies), the other two types of activity already had local roots. Both the national and civic ideology were imported to the rural milieu from the urban milieu, mainly due to the activities of the incoming members of the intelligentsia (teachers, solicitors, clerks, doctors, clergymen), which subsequently took root and became grounded in local initiatives.

In order to study this issue it is essential to follow the communication and organizational structures through which the civic (modernization) and national discourse established themselves in the rural milieu, as well as how this discourse was perceived and adapted content-wise in a peripheral milieu.

4 Rudolf Kučera, *Civil Society. The Concept and Its Historicisation*, Dějiny—Teorie—Kritika 2007, no. 2, pp. 219–231, here pp. 223, 226.

Wallachia (a region in East Moravia close to the Slovak border) is a region which is particularly suitable for research into the transformation of the rural milieu in the second half of the 19th and the early 20th century due to its particularity. It was a submontane, agrarian, economically backward and, as far as transport was concerned, remote (railway construction came late) area, characterized by villages and an extensive land register. Apart from agriculture, Wallachia's traditional economy was mainly based on the wealth of the forests, sheep breeding and glass-making. Most of the inhabitants still made a living through various kinds of cottage industries. There were only a few larger plants in the region (glassworks in Vsetín, Krásno nad Bečvou, Velké Karlovice and Nový Hrozenkov, the Thonet factory in Vsetín).[5] As far as urban centres were concerned, Vsetín developed faster than traditional Valašské Meziříčí, as it had more industry and thus more inhabitants—in 1910 its population was 7,584, while in Valašské Meziříčí it was only 3,583. However, Valašské Meziříčí remained the cultural and social centre of the region, the seat of the district governor's office (it was only in 1909 that the Vsetín political district separated from it), and it also had a grammar school from 1871.

Religion played an important role in Wallachia and the secularization process advanced here much more slowly than in industrial regions. Evidence of this is the political importance of the Catholic parties, which dominated both in the rural electoral districts and in the general elections in 1907 and 1911, i.e. after the introduction of the general, direct and equal right to vote for men. In terms of religion, Wallachia had the largest representation of non-Catholics per head of population, even outstripping Bohemia. In 1890 the judicial district of Vsetín had a population of 32,664, of which 16,297 were Catholics, 8,224 Lutherans, 7,749 Calvinists and 387 Jews.[6]

The main problems the region had to deal with in the fifty years preceding the First World War were social and economic backwardness, poverty, a lack of job opportunities (resulting in migration, even overseas), alcoholism, usury, indebtedness, a lack of information, a lack of education and social naivety. Therefore, any activities which tried to raise the region economically, socially and culturally were all the more meritorious for it, and these are precisely the activities that my paper will examine.

The State as the Main Initiator of Change, especially in the Education System

The state was the main initiator of change in rural areas through acts, regulations and the activities of bodies such as the district governor's office, the district doctor, district vet, district civil engineer and, naturally, also through the education system. A relatively large group of educated state officials worked at the central district governor's office (41 people in Vsetín in 1910), through which the state functioned as a modernizing agent (mainly in matters of education, healthcare, veterinary services and building regulations). Even

5 Ladislav Baletka, *Vsetín. Město a čas*, Vsetín 2008, pp. 102–107.

6 Matouš Václavek, *Vlastivěda moravská. 2. Místopis, Vsatský okres*, Brno 1902, p. 2.

the municipal governments in villages were compelled to communicate regularly with the state authorities and the district school board. In the first three months of 1910 the municipality of Velké Karlovice received a total of 626 items of official correspondence, i.e. approximately 7 items a day.

In addition to schools, the state mainly supervised the inspection of cattle before slaughter, the presence of a vet at any necessary slaughtering and at markets in general, the issuing of cattle passports, ensuring cattle markets met the standards of hygiene, etc. The state had already tried to impose other infrastructural changes in rural towns. For instance, in 1861 the district governor's office ordered the local government in Vsetín to pave the pathways in front of houses and in squares, and to provide street lighting. However, due to the financial expense for the repairs of dams damaged by floods, both the paving and the lighting were temporarily postponed.

The most important manifestation of state discipline in the countryside was the general system of education. The state powers realized that a lack of education was the main obstacle to progress, in particular complete illiteracy. The situation in peripheral Wallachia was especially bad. In 1890 the level of illiteracy in the judicial district of Valašské Meziříčí was 26% and in the neighbouring district of Vsetín as high as 34.5%, while the average for all of Moravia was only 6.9%. Throughout the entire 19th century, school attendance remained irregular and was neglected in favour of child labour. It even proved difficult to travel to school from some of the remote submontane settlements. In the mid-1870s, more than 60% of children in Velké Karlovice neglected their classes (the attendance sheet directly stated that the reason was the long distance to school and a lack of space in the school), 40% of pupils in Hovězí, 32% in Nový Hrozenkov, 22% in Zašová and 17% in Vsetín.[7] In October 1878, on a district-wide level, the absence rate reached 10% in the judicial district of Valašské Meziříčí and 23% in the district of Vsetín; this was 9% and 43% in September 1880 in the same districts respectively, and finally 8% and 20% in October 1887.[8] School absence was not the same throughout the whole school year as it fluctuated based on the employment of children in agricultural work. In the school year 1882/1883 the annual absence-rate average for the first grade in Hovězí was 51.5%; however, in February and March the absence rate was "only" 21% and 27% respectively, while in May it was 71%, in June 69% and in July 68%. The situation was even worse for the second grade. The annual absence-rate average reached 77% (December 41%, February 35%, May and June 94%, July 96%).[9]

In the following years it was necessary, firstly, to make the network of schools denser and, secondly, to make parents send their children regularly to them. In September 1878 there were 14 schools in the judicial district of Vsetín; ten years later there were 20 schools in 18 municipalities (two schools in both Hovězí and Nový Hrozenkov; Velké Karlovice

7 State District Archive in Vsetín (SOkA Vsetín), collection Okresní úřad [District Office] Valašské Meziříčí (OÚ VM), box 159, a survey regarding the state of the education system in 1875–1876.

8 SOkA Vsetín, collection Okresní školní výbor [District School Committee] (OŠV) Valašské Meziříčí, box 6.

9 Ibid.

still belonged to another district at that time).[10] In 1910 there were 41 *Volksschulen* in the district of Vsetín (now including Velké Karlovice).[11] The increase in the number of schools in Wallachia was much higher than the average for all of Moravia (according to statistical data, the number of public *Volksschulen* in Moravia increased from 2,055 in the school year 1883/84 to 2,688 in the school year 1912/13, i.e. by 31%), which demonstrates the entirely unsatisfactory position to start with. However, the large areas of some Wallachian municipalities, typical of submontane regions, meant that despite this increase, some children still had to walk far to get to school. In 1909 in Velké Karlovice 24% of pupils from the school *U Kostela* had to walk a distance greater than four kilometres to get to their classes, in the school in the Lesková valley it was 15%, in the school in the Miloňov valley 14%, and in the Podťaté valley 31%.[12]

In 1896, 164 male and female teachers, 2 catechists and 21 industrial teachers worked in the political district of Valašské Meziříčí.[13]

The local school boards sent attendance sheets with absence without leave to the district school board, which subsequently penalised the parents with a fine. In November 1878 the Ministry of Culture and Education notified all district school boards that poor school attendance was to be penalised, which had not always been carried out. For this reason it ordered all district school boards to submit children's attendance sheets and penalties for absences without leave, and an explanation was demanded in the cases where the penalty was dropped.[14]

However, when submitting attendance sheets, teachers not only fought parents but also the local school board, which was under considerable influence from local representatives.[15] The local government often did not want to penalise the parents; it might have been afraid of losing votes or it simply shared the parents' opinion about the pointlessness of school. The relationship between the local population and the government and the teacher was, therefore, often far from idyllic. A significant section of the rural population did not understand the point of education (the truth being that for parents struggling to make ends meet in the poverty of the countryside, they needed their children as extra labour. Their negative attitude to school was, from their point of view, more of a reflection of the "bloody reality" than disinterest or apathy) and would be angry with teachers for penalizing them for their children's absence and who were trying to teach their children some discipline.

---

10 Ibid.

11 SOkA Vsetín, OŠV Vsetín, box 10, sign. 57-3.

12 SOkA Vsetín, OŠV Valašské Meziříčí, box 9.

13 Jan Petrus, *Statistika hejtmanství valašskomeziříčského*, Holešov 1896, p. 22.

14 SOkA Vsetín, OŠV Valašské Meziříčí, box 6.

15 The members of the local school board included the mayor of the municipality as its chairman, the headmaster or administrator of the school (if there was more than one school in the area, then the oldest one), representatives of religious associations and members elected by local representatives for three years.

I will offer three examples. In 1890, a teacher called Jan Vojtek in Velká Lhota was involved in a dispute with Marie Melicharčíková, whose son had been sent home from school for not coming appropriately dressed. His mother soon came running to the school and started berating the teacher, who ordered her out of the school. Subsequently she made a complaint about him to the municipal committee. The teacher described the meeting as follows: "Afterwards the committee meeting continued, and only when some members got drunk on spirits did they finally return to the first point [i.e. the complaint about the teacher], and the deputy chairman of the local school board, Fabián, being drunk, started to berate the teacher in front of the whole assembly. Even the chairman of the local school board seconded him, at the same time complaining about the order of things, claiming that I should not punish pupils so much for their poor school attendance, that I had to forgive them sometimes as well, that the law was not made for villages but for towns, and that he would introduce a new regulation replacing the old one (...). Seeing their vulgar behaviour, the administrator of the school [i.e. the teacher Vojtek] took his leave. However, at home he was once again disturbed by the deputy chairman shouting on his way home from the pub, who bellowed under the windows of my flat, using the abusive words..."[16]

In Seninka, the teacher Václav Věchet also had problems with the local administration. In January 1891 the local school board complained about him to the district school board, claiming he did not teach the children any discipline. Věchet denied this, characterizing himself as a conscientious teacher. In his own words, he only had a problem with children whose attendance was poor. They arrived, were cheeky and could not be disciplined, so as a result, they often did not come to school. When the teacher complained about their parents to the local school board, the board exempted them from paying the fine on the grounds of poverty. The teacher also complained that the local school board forbade him from airing the classroom in winter.[17]

In 1910, a teacher called Josef Dobiáš from Jablůnka commented quite succinctly on the complaints about his alleged excessive strictness: "By striving to the utmost to achieve positive results in the lessons, I was forced to act more strictly, mainly with the children from the clearings, who, with their poor attendance and, in the stated cases, moral depravity, ruined and held back the lessons. That such children, who are used to complete freedom and a lack of discipline at home, do not like going to school is understandable, as the forced discipline at school is unpleasant for them. All members of staff can testify that instead of supporting the teachers the parents in Jablůnka even oppose and berate them, making all their hard work even more difficult..."[18]

On important development for raising the level of education in the region was the establishment of a grammar school in Valašské Meziříčí in 1871, meaning a relatively large group of teachers (there were 22 in 1883) came to the town, who participated very

16 SOkA Vsetín, OŠV Valašské Meziříčí, box 98, inventory no. 228.
17 Ibid.
18 SOkA Vsetín, OŠV Vsetín, box 72, sign. 62f-2.

actively in the social and cultural life. Without them, for example, the establishment of the Museum Association in Valašské Meziříčí would have been unthinkable.

The establishment of the Winter Agricultural School in Rožnov in 1897 was extremely important for the practical development of the economy. Its long-standing headmaster, Emanuel Vencl, became a well-known and respected figure, who gave lectures all over Wallachia. He acquainted farmers with new developments in arable farming and animal husbandry, and also explained to them how to apply for state or provincial subsidies.

Civil Society Taking Root in Rural Areas: Associations and Local Government, Clericalism versus Progressivism, the Politicization of the Milieu

Civil society is mainly a matter of civic initiatives and people's activity. It would hardly have had a chance to develop amongst the former serfs if it were not for the initiative of those few individuals who were educated and, therefore, also had insight into and knowledge of the social changes which had taken place in more developed areas. These people were mainly the teachers, parish priests and clerks from large estates, while in towns there were also solicitors, professors and others who played a key role in these initiatives. Let us look at a few specific examples.

In 1900, four solicitors, three doctors, a notary, a vet, twenty-three teachers and four catechists, plus, of course, clergymen worked in the largest town of the region, Vsetín.[19] In Nový Hrozenkov the changes were initiated mainly by Edmund Hawerland, a doctor working at the local glassworks. He was instrumental in building schools in Vranča and Stanovnice and in the expansion of the school "*U Kostela*".[20] In Hovězí, there were two important figures: the parish priest Jan Daněk and the local large-estate administrator Jan Bernard, who was very active organizing educational lectures for the local Agricultural Association.[21] He highlighted how necessary it was to educate the peasants. In Velké Karlovice people of high standing in local society included the teacher František Šivic, the forester Rudolf Zahrada, the parish priest Jan Nepustil, and, most importantly, Salomon Reich. In the period 1877–1899, Reich (1817–1900) was the mayor of the municipality. He supported the establishment of schools (for example, he financed the entire interior furnishing of the new school building by the church from 1879), the post office and telephone station. In 1842 he and his brother Samuel rented Františka's Glassworks and in 1862 they built and rented a new glassworks, the Mariánské Glassworks in Léskové. In addition, they also built houses for factory workers. In 1888 the Reichs bought both glassworks from Count Rudolf Kinský.

---

19 Richard Pavlík, *Kronika města Vsetína z let 1850–1960*, Vsetín 1960, pp. 240, 267.

20 Silvestr Kazmíř, *Nový Hrozenkov. Poohlédnutí za historií rázovité valašské dědiny 1649–2009*, Nový Hrozenkov 2009, p. 245.

21 Jan Bernard, *Přednášky konané v hospodářském spolku na Hovězí, a konečný návrh na zřízení rolnické školy v okresu*, Brno 1886.

A distinctive feature of the social modernization and political mobilization of rural areas was the cooperative system and associations. Credit unions (cheap and accessible loans were vital) and agricultural associations played an important role. In Wallachia, Raiffeisenkas were established in the late 19th century, mainly owing to the initiative of the local clergymen: in Halenkov (1896, chaplain Jan Vévoda), in Jablůnka (1896, Evangelical vicar J. Drobný), in Poličná (1897, teacher Vojtěch Chlebovský), in Hovězí (1899, parish priest J. Daněk and teacher J. Dokulil), in Vsetín (chaplain Fr. Světlík, under the name of the Zádruha Savings and Credit Association) and in Nový Hrozenkov.

In the countryside, the most important and, as far as the membership was concerned, the most numerous were agricultural associations. In 1897 the Agricultural Union for the District of Valašské Meziříčí in Zašová had 347 members, the Agricultural and Industrial Association for Vsetín district, with its headquarters in Vsetín, had 183 members, the "Přemysl", Agricultural Association for the District of Vsetín in Jablůnka had 517 members, and the Hovězí Agricultural Association with its headquarters in Hovězí also had 517 members.[22] In 1897 the prominent members of the latter association were the factory owner and mayor of Velké Karlovice, Salomon Reich; the imperial deputy for Uherský Brod, Ignac Seichert; the doctor Vilém Soeser from Velké Karlovice; the solicitor Alois Mikyška from Valašské Meziříčí; the provincial deputy Antonín Hůlka; the parish priest from Pržno, P. Prostějovský; the head teacher from Liptál, Max Pilát; the head teacher Dagobert Berg from Halenkov, the parish priest P. Procházka from Halenkov, the head teacher Jan Dokulil and four other teachers from Hovězí; the parish priest Jan Daněk and the Evangelical parish priest Gustav Říčan from Hovězí, as well as a number of prominent figures from Vsetín, e.g. the provincial deputy Karel Bubela; the parish priest and dean Augustin Žádník; the school headmaster Matouš Václavek and several teachers; the district judge Jan Pazderka; from Nový Hrozenkov e.g. the doctor Edmund Hawerland; the head teachers Antonín Diblík and František Růžička; and the parish priest Jan Štěpán, etc.[23]

From Vsetín, those engaged in the Agricultural and Industrial Association for Vsetín district included the mayor Josef Černocký, the provincial deputy Karel Bubela, the *Stadtschule* teacher Klement David, the specialist teacher František Hladný, the imperial royal judicial councillor Jan Pazderka, the vet Jan Raubüchl, the doctor František Sova, the chaplain Antonín Solař, the glassworks director Adolf Schönbeck, the headmasters Matouš Václavek and Josef Zlámal, and the dean Augustin Žádník. From Johanová, Polanka and Roketnice, the members of the association included the mayor and the teacher, while the mayor and the teacher as well as other people were from Seninka and Leskovec. In 1897 the association held 7 committee and 8 public meetings, which also included 13 lectures. The meetings took place in the town as well as the neighbouring villages. The association established a fruit-tree nursery, an artificial-fertiliser storage

---

22 Josef Adam et al., *Velké Karlovice 1714–2014*, Velké Karlovice 2014, pp. 34, 129, 130; SOkA Vsetín, OÚ VM, box. 428, sign. N-1.

23 Ibid.

facility (where the fertiliser was sold at factory prices) and a cooperative for the local insurance of cattle.[24]

According to the annual report from 1897, the Agricultural Union for the District of Valašské Meziříčí in Zašová organized lectures in Krhová, Lešná and Choryně, established two cooperatives for breeding bulls in Lešná and Choryně, and maintained a fruit-tree nursery and a garden nursery in Zašová. In 1902, the District Agricultural Union in Vsetín (established in 1900 by the merger of the associations in Vsetín, Hovězí and Jablůnka) held five public meetings with ten lectures in different parts of the district, organized a forage crop and cattle course and launched the drainage of the land in Vsetín (which was completed in 1903). Agricultural associations also encouraged peasants to fertilize meadows.

According to the Catholic *Noviny z Pod-Radhoště* [Newspaper from Below Radhošť], the main objective of the co-op store in Halenkov, established by the local Raiffeisenka in the early 20th century, was to free people from subjection to Jewish merchants.[25] Judging by the period sources, the socially naive population running into debt, which was connected to alcoholism, was indeed a serious problem in Wallachia. The negative effect of Jewish innkeepers on the indebtedness of households, often ending in the seizure of property, was criticised by the headmaster of the *Stadtschulen* in Vsetín, Matouš Václavek.[26] However, it is difficult, if not impossible, to statistically document what percentage of usurers were made up of Jews. On the other hand, the share of Jewish innkeepers is easily traceable, based on the concessions granted.

There also existed other types of associations in the Wallachian countryside, though I believe agricultural associations were the main driving force behind change. Generally it can be said that some types of associations could not be found in the countryside which would be found in the towns, (which is understandable, e.g. museum associations, workers' associations) or were rare (reading associations, political associations).[27]

Even in the last years before the First World War, Wallachia was a strongly religious area, though the ideas of the intelligentsia that religion was a private matter and that the Catholic Church should not have institutional influence on public life started to spread even here, especially from Valašské Meziříčí and Vsetín. The secularization of society (anti-clericalism) was mainly supported by the progressive movement; in contrast, clericalism was formed as a defensive reaction by political circles linked to the Catholic ideology. In 1899 the clerical *Noviny z Pod-Radhoště* started to be published in Valašské

---

24 Ibid.

25 Noviny z Pod-Radhoště, 17. 2. 1905, p. 3.

26 SOkA Vsetín, collection Pozůstalost Matouše Václavka [The Estate of Matouš Václavek], inventory no. 109: Kořaleční mor a židovstvo na Valašsku [The Spirit Plague and Jews in Wallachia].

27 The Palacký Reading Association in Velké Karlovice owed its existence to the presence of a specific group—qualified glassmakers. The protocol for the general meeting of this association from 27 April 1912 states that the glassmakers were going to leave Karlovice, which would cause the association to lose 24 members, 16 of which the association owed its existence and activities to. As a result, the general meeting decided to disband the association. See SOkA Vsetín, OÚ Vsetín, box 92, inventory no. 361.

Meziříčí. The district governor notified his superiors that the official editors were, in his opinion, only puppets, and that it was the parish priest in Valašské Meziříčí who was in charge of the editorial board. The first three issues of the newspaper confined themselves to criticism of political and local events. However, by the fourth issue from 11 November, the governor stated it had crossed the limits by containing agitation and incitement against the government and the Jews, and was therefore confiscated.[28]

With the establishment of the Catholic and Political Union for the political district of Vsetín in 1912, the clerical camp had reached political maturity. The eight-member committee of this political association included the parish priest in Hovězí, the parish priest in Halenkov and the catechist in Vsetín. The full list of members of the Catholic and Political Union comprised 187 members, mainly peasants, workers (i.e. the uneducated dependent strata), parish priests and catechists. It is typical that there were not many clerks and very few artisans or traders in the association, and that the list included only two teachers and no solicitors or doctors. In contrast, the Vsacko Politicial Association in Vsetín, established in late 1911, had far fewer workers and peasants, with more clerks, artisans and traders, while most importantly, the nucleus of the association was formed by teachers, solicitors and doctors.[29]

In their periodicals (*Noviny z Pod-Radhoště* and *Palacký* respectively), the clerical and progressive camps attacked each other vociferously. The atmosphere was especially tense during the general elections of 1907 and 1911 when Tomáš Garrigue Masaryk stood as a candidate for the electoral district of the Wallachian towns, as he was known for his negative stance towards the Catholic Church. The pre-election special edition of *Noviny z Pod-Radhoště* from 21 May 1907 was nothing other than a two-page gutter campaign against Masaryk. It is well known that Masaryk won in both these elections. However, the clerical camp continued to dominate the rural electoral districts in Wallachia.

Even after the election, both Masaryk and the clerical deputies from Wallachia (mainly Kadlčák) remained in close contact with their electoral district, which contributed to rural areas being drawn into political life. The deputies held meetings to inform their voters what they had been doing in Parliament. For example, Kadlčák organized approximately forty meetings in his electoral district in the winter season of 1910–1911 alone.[30]

In the countryside, where there were no solicitors, doctors or other representatives of the intelligentsia, the advocates of progressive ideas were mainly teachers. This can be seen in the activity of teachers in the Sokol movement, which also took root in large Wallachian municipalities. For example, in 1912, three of eleven members of the committee of the Sokol Gymnastic Union in Nový Hrozenkov were teachers, and in 1913, seven of eleven members of the committee of the Sokol Gymnastic Union in Velké Karlovice were teachers.[31] Rural parish priests strived to maintain their influence in the local environment and viewed any "competition" with suspicion. According to Barbora Machová and Eva

28 SOkA Vsetín, OÚ VM, box 13, pres. 1899/497.
29 Noviny z pod Radhoště, 24. 2. 1912, p. 5; Palacký 15. 12. 1911, p. 5.
30 Noviny z pod Radhoště, 4. 3. 1911, p. 2.
31 SOkA Vsetín, OÚ Vsetín, box 92, inventory no. 362.

Šipöczová, in terms of their function, teachers and parish priests both had real power over the community. If there were any disagreements between them, the devout and conservative society traditionally stood by the parish priest because it was a slow and painful process for a "stranger" to introduce new ideas.[32]

One example was from 1901, when three peasants from the municipality of Choryně filed a complaint against the head teacher Pavel Zgabaj over religious matters. The teacher allegedly insisted that the sea had high and low tides and that this phenomenon had helped the Israelites to cross it and kill the pharaoh, which people wrongly considered to be a miracle. During another history lesson the teacher claimed that pagan priests had lured people by offering them gifts, which was what priests continued to do.

When discussing the complaint with the district school board, the mayor of the municipality stated that a number of students had claimed they had been forced to make the statement by their classmate, Grygařík, who was an altar server. The former head teacher had had a good relationship with the parish priest, but when, like his predecessor, the current head teacher had been appointed organist, he had been dissatisfied with the fee set by the parish priest. Subsequently, the parish priest dismissed the teacher from his post as organist.

Zgabaj assessed the situation in such a way that after coming to the school in the early 1890s he managed to change the situation there and promote interest in the school. However, this favourable interest in the school had aroused the animosity of the parish priest, who until then had been used to controlling everything in the municipality. The teacher had not adopted the behaviour of his predecessor or taken a servile, humiliating position towards the parish priest in front of the public. The parish priest had then asked two pupils who were altar servers to become his informers.

It is interesting (and definitely not usual for villages) that at its meeting, the Choryně municipal committee voted to submit an appeal to the authorities to protect the head teacher and school from similar attacks.[33]

A Few Notes Regarding National Agitation in the Countryside

The Czech national ideology was not autochthonous to Wallachia, but had been brought by the nationalist activists who migrated there as solicitors, teachers, clerks, etc. Many of them did not come from Wallachia, though we can also find natives among them who were interested in the national ideology during their studies. For instance, the articled clerk and later independent solicitor, František Barvič from Velké Karlovice, working at the Mikyška Attorney's Office in Valašské Meziříčí, embraced the Sokol ideals during his

32 Barbora Machová—Eva Šipöczová, *Reflexe vztahu venkovského učitele a lokálního společenství na pozadí událostí zaznamenaných ve školních kronikách na Moravě na přelomu 19. a 20. století*, Národopisná revue Strážnice 24, 2014, no. 2, pp. 117–127, here p. 122.

33 SOkA Vsetín, OŠV Valašské Meziříčí, box 100, inventory no. 228

studies in Prague; he exercised at Tyrš's Gymnastic Union of Prague.[34] It was such people who brought a tradition of active national and community life with them to Wallachia and around whom national organizations formed.

The central area from which Czech national life spread was undoubtedly Valašské Meziříčí. The employees of Mikyška's Attorney's Office were crucial for setting things in motion in the town: in addition to Barvič these included J. Sobotka, R. Kašlík, J. Baše and naturally Mikyška himself, albeit he was relatively cautious. For example, in 1869 he was appointed chairman for a mass meeting [*tábor lidu*] which took place near Hranice, but he did not appear because apparently he was worried about the reaction of the Austrian authorities, so he was replaced by the aforementioned articled clerk, Richard Kašlík.[35] The opening of a Czech grammar school in Valašské Meziříčí at the beginning of the 1870s was of great importance, as was the establishment of the Museum Association in Valašské Meziříčí in 1884, in which the grammar school teachers played an important role.

In June 1891 a special train with visitors going to the Provincial Anniversary Exhibition in Prague was dispatched from Valašské Meziříčí. The train to the Provincial Anniversary Exhibition in Prague was dispatched from Valašské Meziříčí on 26 June 1891 and people had to sign up as early as possible. Provincial Deputy Karel Bubela represented the organizational committee. A year later, in 1892, another great success was the Wallachian Ethnographic Exhibition in Vsetín, which was the first of twelve other exhibitions in Moravia. One of the initiators of the Vsetín exhibition was Dušan Jurkovič. The "Wallachian Village" became very popular at the Great Ethnographic Exhibition in Prague in 1895.

Rural teachers were not only highly active in agricultural, savings and credit union associations, but they also took part in the establishment of important national associations and the local branches of national unions and Sokol. Nationalist associations were established relatively late in Wallachia. As late as spring 1911, the progressive newspaper *Palacký* complained that there was not a single local branch of the National Union in the political district of Vsetín except in Velké Karlovice, where it was established in 1910.[36] Not even the towns were in a better situation in this respect; the meeting to establish the local branch of the National Union in Valašské Meziříčí took place as late as April 1911.[37] The local branch of the National Union came into existence in Vsetín in 1912.[38]

Newspapers were very important for spreading nationalist ideas. Wallachia began to have its own local newspaper from 1885 with the establishment of *Valašské hlasy*

---

34 *Úroda čtyřiceti let Sokolské župy valašské Fr. Palackého 1893–1933*, Valašské Meziříčí 1933, p. 23.

35 Jiří Demel (ed.), *Sokol nad Bečvami: historie a současnost tělovýchovné jednoty Sokol ve Valašském Meziříčí 1864–2004*, Valašské Meziříčí 2004, pp. 4–5; Zdeněk Kment, *Kulturní a společenský rozvoj Valašského Meziříčí v letech 1853 až 1948*, Valašské Meziříčí 2008, p. 13; Jaroslav Šťastný, *K dějinám Muzejní společnosti ve Valašském Meziříčí (1883–1900)*, Acta Universitatis Carolinae—Philosophica et Historica, 1974, pp. 87–129, here p. 91.

36 Palacký, 10. 3. 1911, p. 6.

37 Palacký, 14. 4. 11, p. 6.

38 Palacký, 21. 6. 1912, p. 6.

[Wallachian Voices] (publication ceased in 1891). Newspapers which were published later included *Noviny z Pod-Radhoště* (from 1899), *Valašsko* [Wallachia] (1904-06), *Valašské noviny* [The Wallachian Newspaper] (from 1907, renamed *Palacký* in 1908), Boj Valašska [The Wallachian Fight] (from 1908), *Cíl* [Aim] (1911–1913) and *Přehled* [Overview] (1912–1913).

Conclusion

Important economic, social and cultural changes related to modernization processes significantly affected and gradually transformed the way of life even in the countryside. The state's regulating and modernizing activity played a fundamental role in this, as the Habsburg state, through its regulations, decrees and administration offices, reacted to the needs of the period. The most important manifestation of state discipline in the countryside was the new system of schools established at the end of the 1860s.

The changes were further related to two mutually connected, though not identical, types of activities. After breaking free from subservience to the manorial lords and establishing municipal governments, and as a consequence of the development of community life and, in the late 19th century, even political life (the extension of political rights), local self-initiatives and civil society also started to develop. Their strongest manifestation was with associations and the cooperative system. Throughout the second half of the 19th century, increasingly stronger national agitation gradually and with growing intensity manifested itself even in rural areas, dragging the countryside into national life, or, at least, into the national discourse.

Civic/national identity as a concept of self-perception gained significance amongst an increasing number of people from the countryside only after the isolation of the rural communities had been overcome through the organizational and communication channels of civil society. This is why it is important to follow the formation and development of such channels (newspapers, educational and agricultural associations, the education system, and political parties).

The wave of social and economic changes was also felt in poor and peripheral regions such as Wallachia in the eastern part of Moravia. The analysis showed that, as a result of the former period of serfdom, the local people were used to fatalism and paternalism; therefore, they had to learn to take initiatives themselves, just as they had to be persuaded of the importance of education. They were most open to those changes which provided them with tangible, i.e. economic, benefits. Therefore, they were most drawn to the agricultural associations and credit unions, which helped them adopt more efficient methods in agriculture and secure cheap loans.

Bibliography

Josef ADAM et al., *Velké Karlovice 1714–2014*, Velké Karlovice 2014.

Ladislav BALETKA, *Vsetín. Město a čas* [Vsetín. The Town and Time], Vsetín 2008.

Stanislav BALÍK et al., *Český antiklerikalismus. Zdroje, témata a podoba českého antiklerikalismu v letech 1848–1938* [Czech Anti-Clericalism. The Sources, Topics and Form of the Czech Anti-Clericalism in 1848-1938], Praha 2015.

Jan BERNARD, *Přednášky konané v hospodářském spolku na Hovězí, a konečný návrh na zřízení rolnické školy v okresu* [Lectures held by the Agricultural Association in Hovězí, and the final proposal regarding the establishment of a peasant school in the district of Vsetín], Brno 1886.

Jiří DEMEL (ed.), *Sokol nad Bečvami: historie a současnost tělovýchovné jednoty Sokol ve Valašském Meziříčí 1864–2004* [Sokol over the Bečvas: The History and Present of the Sokol Gymnastics Union in Valašské Meziříčí, 1864-2004], Valašské Meziříčí 2004.

Ruth DÖRNER, *Staat und Nation im Dorf*, München 2006.

See Lukáš FASORA—Jiří HANUŠ—Jiří MALÍŘ (eds.), *Sekularizace venkovského prostoru v 19. století* [The Secularization of Countryside in the 19th Century], Brno 2009.

Norbert FRANZ, *Durchstaatlichung und Ausweitung der Kommunalaufgaben im 19. Jahrhundert. Tätigkeitsfeld und Handlungsspielräume ausgewählter französischer und luxemburgischer Landgemeinden im mikrohistorischen Vergleich (1805–1890)*, Trier 2006.

Silvestr KAZMÍŘ, *Nový Hrozenkov. Poohlédnutí za historií rázovité valašské dědiny 1649–2009* [Nový Hrozenkov. Looking Back on the History of a Distinctive Wallachian Village, 1649-2009], Nový Hrozenkov 2009.

Pavel KLADIWA, *The Transformation and Social Activation of Rural Areas. The Bohemian Lands in 1861–1914 (A Preliminary outline of the issue)*, Moderní dějiny/Modern History 26, 2018, no. 1, pp. 1–29.

Zdeněk KMENT, *Kulturní a společenský rozvoj Valašského Meziříčí v letech 1853 až 1948* [The Cultural and Social Development of Valašské Meziříčí from 1853 to 1948], Valašské Meziříčí 2008.

Rudolf KUČERA, *Civil Society. The Concept and Its Historicisation*, Dějiny—Teorie—Kritika 2007, no. 2, pp. 219–231.

Barbora MACHOVÁ—Eva ŠIPÖCZOVÁ, *Reflexe vztahu venkovského učitele a lokálního společenství na pozadí událostí zaznamenaných ve školních kronikách na Moravě na přelomu 19. a 20. století* [A reflection on the relationship between the country teacher and the local community against the background of events recorded in school chronicles in Moravia at the turn of the 20th century], Národopisná revue Strážnice 24, 2014, no. 2, pp. 117–127.

Richard PAVLÍK, *Kronika města Vsetína z let 1850–1960* [The Chronicle of the Town of Vsetín from 1850 to 1960], Vsetín 1960.

Jan PETRUS, *Statistika hejtmanství valašskomeziříčského* [The Statistics of the District Governor's Office in Valašské Meziříčí], Holešov 1896.

Jaroslav Šťastný, *K dějinám Muzejní společnosti ve Valašském Meziříčí* [About the history of the Museum Association in Valašské Meziříčí] *(1883–1900)*, Acta Universitatis Carolinae—Philosophica et Historica, 1974, pp. 87–129.

Úroda čtyřiceti let Sokolské župy valašské Fr. Palackého 1893–1933 [The Harvest of Forty Years of František Palacký's Sokol Regional Organization in Wallachia], Valašské Meziříčí 1933.

Matouš Václavek, *Vlastivěda moravská. 2. Místopis, Vsatský okres* [The National History and Geography of Moravia. Toponymy. The District of Vsacko], Brno 1902.

The Role of Teachers and Parish Priests as Agents of Economic, Social and Cultural Change in Rural Areas 1861–1918*

Andrea Pokludová

Abstract

The aim of this study is to explain the role and function of clergymen and teachers as exponents of progress in the agricultural and social life of the countryside in the second half of the 19th and early 20th century, i.e. after the abolition of the corvée and before the First World War. The selected problem was investigated by the method of micro-history. The micro-historical approach refuted the stereotypical concept in Czech historiography of clergymen as anti-modernization elements in society at the beginning of 20th century. The main focus is that some of them, as with teachers, contributed towards agricultural developments in the countryside by communicating new ideas about agriculture and the credit economy.

In recent years Czech historiography has focused particularly on the modernization of the Czech lands in the second half of the 19th and the early 20th century. The processes of industrialization and the formation of a civil society have already been dealt with to such an extent that we can consider them as a solid basis for comparison within Central Europe, while other key topics such as the modernization of the countryside are currently at the stage of basic research and the first partial outputs.[1] It is true that works on the

* The study was published as part of the grant GAČR 17-02986S: The Transformation and Social Activisation of the Rural Milieu in Moravia and Austrian Silesia in 1861–1914. The study is partly based on the text: Andrea POKLUDOVÁ, *Village teacher at the turn of the 19th and 20th centuries. An important representative in the modernization of rural society*, Časopis Matice moravské 137, 2018, pp. 295–319.

1 Magdalena Beranová, *Dějiny zemědělství v Čechách a na Moravě*, Praha 2010, pp. 248–301. From the latest works this realtes to Jitka Balcarová's studies, which examine the role of German agricultural associations in the region of Austrian Silesia and the credit cooperative system, i.e. topics related to those in the submitted study. Jitka Balcarová, *Počátky německého venkovského úvěrového družstevnictví v rakouském Slezsku v 2. polovině 19. století: organizační základna a aktéři*, Prameny a studie 2, 2016, no. 59, pp. 56–75; Jitka Balcarová, *Německé zemědělské spolky v rakouském Slezsku druhé poloviny 19. století: stavovská svépomoc, solidarita, jednota a uvědomělost*, Historica. Revue pro historii a příbuzné vědy, 2017, no. 2, pp. 31–44.

economic and social development of the Czech lands in the "long" 19th century cover the basic trends in the transformation of the countryside after 1848; however, if we ask ourselves who was the initiator of the numerous changes which subsequently led to the irreversible transformation of rural society, it is insufficient to reply that it was the peasants based on our knowledge of the patterns of behaviour and actions attributable to the peasantry on the threshold of the modernization process.[2]

The abolition of the corvée during the revolutionary turmoil of 1848 was welcomed by the rural population, though they were unable to entirely grasp and adopt as their own the other demands from civil society, i.e. calls for local government and civil rights.[3] The reason for this was that the value system of the rural people was based on traditional piousness and respect for authority. The opinions and attitudes of the peasantry were aptly described by the trainee solicitor Jan Kozánek in the proclamation *Co jest konstituce, Svoboda tisku, Národní garda* [What is the Constitution, Freedom of the Press, the National Guard]. He gave a lecture to the Czech people in Austrian Silesia on the ongoing society-wide changes through the comprehensible form of a dialogue between a parish priest, burgher and farmer. In order to give the reader an idea of the intellectual world of the peasantry, we have included a passage from the lecture where a farmer expresses his doubts about the establishment of the municipal government demanded by the burghers: "What does a commoner know of how to govern people? They had better keep to their work and leave governing to the clerks." The reply of the clergyman, a traditional, incontrovertible authority for rural people, captures the basic idea of the transformation of the countryside: "Neighbours, you are mistaken. Who better understands a peasant's work than the peasants themselves?"[4] Rural chronicles from the late 19th century depict life in the countryside as follows: "The people were so wretched and numbed by the manorial system that they did not even know that they could thrive. This mental numbness had become second nature to them. They merely laughed at any attempts at progress, seeing them as stupid novelties, and they were strengthened in their opinions when these attempts were not successful. 'My father and grandfather did it that way' was the first

2 Zdeněk Jindra—Ivan Jakubec, *Hospodářský vzestup českých zemí od poloviny 18. století do konce monarchie*, Praha 2015, pp. 145–199; Jana Machačová—Jiří Matějček, *Problémy obecné kultury v českých zemích 1781–1989*, Opava 2008, p. 245; Jiří Matějček, *Příspěvek k popisu materiálních pozic chudého venkovského obyvatelstva, řemeslnického a průmyslového dělnictva v českých zemích ve druhé polovině 19. a na začátku 20. století*, in: Zdeněk Kárník (ed.), K novověkým sociálním dějinám českých zemí, vol. 2, Z dob rakouských a předlitavských (1848–1918), Praha 1998, pp. 116–119; Jiří Matějček, *Rok na vsi. Sonda do sociální situace na jihomoravské vesnici v poslední čtvrtině 19. století*, Slezský sborník 96, 1998, pp. 264–284.

3 Josef Vochala, *Rok 1848 ve Slezsku a na severovýchodní Moravě*, Opava 1948; Jiří Radimský—Milada Wurmová (eds.), *Petice moravského lidu k sněmu z roku 1848*, Praha 1955.

4 Zdeněk Fišer, *Zpravodajství Jana Kozánka z Opavy z let 1845–1849*, Přerov 1999, pp. 73–78. Further descriptions of the events in rural society in the revolutionary years 1848/49 were depicted by Josef Vochala in the work *Rok 1848 ve Slezsku a na severovýchodní Moravě.*

and last rule."[5] Teachers, who were generally the authors of chronicles, knew from their own experience that traditions and customs carried more weight in the countryside than "novelties". Any changes were condemned beforehand with reference to the actions of the ancestors, which mainly concerned the running of farms. Despite the Theresian school reforms, the education level of the rural population in the mid-19th century was generally low; illiteracy was more the norm than the exception.

It was only on the eve of the First World War that the sources mentioned the ongoing changes in the daily lives of rural people. With the introduction of new methods, small-scale agricultural production gradually broke free from the vicious circle of low productivity. Changes were noticeable in the rural population's patterns of behaviour and mentality. Some men began to show an interest in public affairs, i.e. in municipal politics, which even in the countryside was transforming from being dominated by notables to a modern "party" structure.[6] In defending its interests, the rural population used the right of petition and other legal instruments such as appeals against official decrees and regulations.[7] Local-government representatives gradually stopped being the servile executors of official authority. We can see the influence of the secularization process within the male section of the rural population. Residues of traditional society survived in pious country women, the upbringing of children, and the rural population's generally low level of education.

The Role of Teachers and Priests in the Rural Society of the Second Half of the 19th Century

From the sources it seems that the initiators of ongoing changes in rural society were representatives of the intelligentsia, i.e. mainly clergymen and teachers.[8] The key role of Catholic clergymen and teachers was based on their education and the fact that their work

5 http://digi.archives.cz/da/permalink?xid=123551CC67134CA48AAEADCFA65E6FF0&scan=73#scan72

6 Pavel Pospěch, *Rolník—Haná—Příklad Josefa Vysloužila*, in: Lukáš Fasora—Jiří Hanuš—Jiří Malíř (eds.), Člověk na Moravě 19. století, Brno 2004, pp. 169–181.

7 Andrea Pokludová, *Sviadnov v letech 1848–1918*, in: Tomáš Adamec et al., Sviadnov, Sviadnov 2017, pp. 31–80.

8 Jana Machačová—Jiří Matějček, *Nástin sociálního vývoje českých zemí 1781–1914*, Opava 2002, chapter „Funkce a funkční skupiny" [„Functions and Function Groups"]; Jiří Pokorný, *Lidová výchova na přelomu 19. a 20. století*, Prague 2003, p. 108; Andrea Pokludová, *Formování inteligence na Moravě a ve Slezsku 1857–1910*, Opava 2008, chapters dealing with the teaching profession pp. 193–216, a list of relevant references and sources dealing with the topic, pp. 312–313 and 319; Tomáš Kasper—Markéta Pánková, *Učitel ve střední a jihovýchodní Evropě: profesionalizace učitelského vzdělávání: historické a systematické aspekty*, Praha 2015; Pavla Vošahlíková, *Rákoska v dílně lidskosti: česká škola v 19. století očima účastníků*, Praha 2016; Jitka Padrnosová, *Učitel. Příklad Jana Jaroslava Jelínka*, in: Lukáš Fasora—Jiří Hanuš—Jiří Malíř (eds.), Člověk na Moravě 19. století, pp. 111–123; A. Pokludová, *Formování inteligence na Moravě a ve Slezsku*, chapters dealing with the teaching profession pp. 193–216, a list of the relevant references and sources dealing with the topic,

was carried out directly in rural areas. In particular, the clergymen in the countryside in the mid-19th century were representatives of the intelligentsia who enjoyed high social prestige.[9] In comparison with the clergy, the social status of rural teachers in the mid-19th century was lower. It derived not only from their dependent position on ecclesiastical administration, but also from the low income connected with the teaching profession. It was only with the Imperial Act on *Volksschulen* (the so-called Hasner's Act of 1869) that teachers' institutes were established and the rules set for the economic and social security of qualified teachers. The pedagogical studies lasting four years for *Volksschulen* teachers at teachers' institutes, with an examination of their teaching competence at the end, replaced the unsatisfactory professional preparation of two years at teachers' preparatory schools. The system of appointing teachers certified the teacher's expertise, qualification and experience. With the ongoing process of the professionalization of employment at the turn of the 20th century, teachers' tariff incomes improved significantly, which ultimately led to an increase in teachers' prestige in rural society. During the second half of the 19th century, the social habitus of rural teachers changed against a background of continuous society-wide changes, some of which will be dealt with later.

The state also played a significant role in the modernization process within the countryside, namely the district governors' offices which monitored the activity of local authorities.[10] They mainly ensured that legislation was observed in education and public healthcare. An important role was played by agricultural unions in the economic development of the countryside, whose establishment on a district level was initiated by *C. k. moravskoslezská společnost pro zvelebení orby, přírodoznalství a vlastivědy* [The Imperial-Royal Moravian-Silesian Association for the Improvement of Ploughing, Natural Science and National History and Geography].[11] Agricultural unions were established to defend the economic interests of the countryside, i.e. the peasantry. Although the peasantry formed the majority of its membership, they were not the most active; these were the members of the intelligentsia, whose intellectual curiosity made them more open to innovation in agricultural production. The above-mentioned thesis can be documented by criticism of the peasantry's indifference given in 1886 at a shareholders' meeting of *Hospodářská jednota pro severovýchodní Moravu* [The Agricultural Union for North-East Moravia] by the doctor and provincial deputy Rudolf Kallus. The most relevant passages are as follows: "As the saying goes: God helps those who help themselves; when, however,

pp. 312–313 and 319; Andrea Pokludová, *Učitel*, in: Milan Myška—Aleš Zářický (eds.), *Člověk v Ostravě v XIX. století*, Ostrava 2007, pp. 31–43.

9 http://lidemesta.cz/archiv/cisla/8-2006-2/vychova-knezi-a-jejich-pusobeni-na-prelomu-18.-a-19.-stoleti.html?language=cs

10 Pavel Kladiwa, *The Transformation and Social Activation of Rural Areas. The Bohemian Lands in 1861–1914 (A Preliminary outline of the issue)*, Moderní dějiny/Modern History 26, 2018, no. 1, pp. 1–29.

11 Kai Struve, *Peasant Emancipation and National Integration. Agrarian Circles, Village Reading Rooms and Cooperatives in Galicia*, in: Torsten Lorenz (ed.), Cooperatives in Ethnic Conflicts. Eastern Europe from the late 19th until the mid 20th Century, Berlin 2006, pp. 229–250, here p. 249.

the peasantry do not mind their own affairs, being utterly indifferent and idle, they cannot and must not ask others to act and think for them. —The Agricultural Union is the only centre where all questions concerning the peasantry can be discussed and negotiated, and yet the participation of peasants in this association is so negligible that without the selfless and tractable work of the other estates it would have most likely ceased to exist long ago.—The glorious clergy, teachers and other intelligentsia take part frequently in the bustle of the association; the peasantry, however, do so only sporadically."[12]

The role and function of clergymen and teachers can be interpreted as agents of economic, social and cultural change in the rural milieu using a microhistorical approach against the background of the activity of *Filiální hospodářský spolek Paskovský* [The Paskov Filial Agricultural Association], later renamed The Agricultural Union for North-East Moravia, i.e. one of the oldest Moravian agricultural unions. Unlike older agricultural associations, the agricultural associations from the second half of the 19th century were not enclosed microcosms of agrarian scholars and theorists, but functional platforms for the activation of the peasantry and the transfer of innovations to agricultural production. In many respects the scope of activity of the Paskov Filial Agricultural Association/The Agricultural Union for North-East Moravia was connected to figures from public life who had spent part of their life in the submontane municipality of Palkovice, which is why the events in this municipality in the second half of the 19th and the early 20th century are related to the issue of teachers and clergymen as innovators in country life. The peasantry from this municipality also participated in the membership of the union more than peasants from other municipalities.[13] They established a local Agricultural Association in 1909.[14]

History of the Agricultural Association in Paskov in the Context of the Membership of Teachers and Priests

The founder of the Paskov Filial Agricultural Association (1862) was Eduard Vrána, a teacher at the *Volksschule* in Paskov, who was the son of Sebestián Vrána (Wrana), a patriot and rector of the school in Palkovice.[15] The peasants, who the association's activities were

12 State District Archive (SOkA) Frýdek-Místek, collection Hospodářská jednota pro severovýchodní Moravu, Kniha zápisů hospodářské jednoty severovýchodní Moravy 1879–1886; record from June 14th 1886.

13 Josef M. Kadlčák, *Jednatelská zpráva*, Opavský Týdenník 9. 3. 1887, příloha, p. 1. The membership of the Agricultural Union included the representatives of 17 municipalities from the district of Místek, incorporating a total of 29 villages.

14 SOkA Frýdek-Místek, collection Okresní národní výbor Frýdek-Místek (1860)1945–1960(1961), Spolkový katastr okresu Místek.

15 The Provincial Archive Opava (ZAO), Římskokatolická fara Kozlovice: P VI 1. Eduard Josef Vrána was born in 1827 in Kozlovice, where his father held the position of assistant teacher; J. Vochala, *Rok 1848 ve Slezsku*, p. 67; Jaromír Šupina, *Šebestián Vrána*, Sborník Státního okresního archivu ve Frýdku-Místku 6, 2005, pp. 67–76.

primarily aimed at, always had their representatives on the association committee, though it was the members of the intelligentsia who organized the activities of the meetings in the early years. They ran the association office including the treasury, held educational lectures and established the association's library. At the end of the first decade of its existence the association almost ceased to exist. The generation of founders from the intelligentsia had either left the region, such as the teacher and secretary of the association, Eduard Vrána, in 1865, or had died.[16] New impetus for the association's activities came from Ludvík Kubala, a young peasant and inventor, later a provincial deputy, who became one of the heads of the association in 1874 at the age of twenty-four. Kubala represented a type of peasant-innovator rarely found in the rural community, who, thanks to his education and unique personality traits, freed himself from the traditional patterns of behaviour.[17] He actively cooperated on the association committee with Josef Mnohoslav Kadlčák, an ambitious young teacher (in 1878–1880 a teacher in Palkovice, later a prominent Moravian politician, deputy and senator), the Palkovice parish priest Ferdinand Baar, and Rudolf Kallus of Frenštát, a doctor and provincial deputy.[18] With the new management, the association's meetings were transferred from Paskov to the administration centre of the district—Místek. With its change of statutes in 1881, the association was renamed The Agricultural Association for North-East Moravia.[19] After twenty-five years in existence (1887), the association numbered 266 members, made up of 149 peasants, 21 clergymen, 20 teachers, 13 clerks and three doctors, solicitors and engineers. Representatives of the intelligentsia made up a quarter of the membership, though in comparison with the majority of the peasantry they still represented the more active, progressive and innovative part of the membership.

The association's goals adapted to the modernizing processes in society. After years of preparation, a one-year agricultural school was opened in Místek in 1880, whose activities had a direct impact on the development of the neighbouring countryside. The association provided expert reports regarding numerous legislative questions—retired farmers, the insurance of the peasantry, the right of domicile [*Heimatrecht*] and usury. The lecturers

16 J. Šupina, *Šebestián Vrána*, p. 71.

17 Jaromír Kublák, *Ludvík Kubala, sedlák, vynálezce a buditel selského stavu na Moravě*, Brno 1941, pp. 581–590; Zdeněk Fišer, *Hospodářská jednota záhlinicko-kvasická (1861–1912)*, Chropyně 1997. In terms of the association's activity, the work of František Skopalík is described in relation to numerous aspects of modernization in the Moravian countryside, i.e. land consolidation, drainage, etc. In a local context, a more modern-minded peasant could be found in almost every village in the last third of the 19th century: P. Pospěch, *Rolník—Haná—Příklad Josefa Vysloužila*, pp. 169–181.

18 Miloslav Oliva—Jiří Figura, *Kadlčákův Frýdlant nad Ostravicí*, Frýdek-Místek 2009.

19 https://archive.org/details/vlastiveda_moravska-jicin-mistek/page/n33. In my opinion the initiative came from a circle of men who maintained close ties to the supraregional centres of events and who came to be at the head of the association in the first years of its existence. I would like to name especially the mining councillor Franz Kleinpeter (a leading expert in mining and metallurgy in the region), a representative of the Moravian Agricultural Association and a recognised expert in forestry, and Valentin Kostelník, a merchant in Frenštát and a deputy to the Moravian Provincial Assembly in Brno.

included František Ladislav Chleborád, national economist and pioneer of the cooperative system; the above-mentioned Ludvík Kubala, a promoter of modern dairy farming; J.M. Kadlčák, a prominent regional expert in beekeeping; and Alois Žert, a teacher at the agricultural school in Místek. From the grant programme of the Moravian Agricultural Society it was possible, within a few years, to establish cattle breeding in the region. In addition, quality seed stock, vegetable seedlings, fruit trees, and natural and (in the early 20th century) artificial fertilisers were provided to the members. Costly agricultural machines, such as honey extractors, which the members could borrow, were acquired using the association's funds.

Even though numerous personal disputes took place over the decades between prominent figures of the union related to priorities in its programme, the list of projects which contributed to a substantial transformation in regional agriculture is extensive: livestock breeding, larger profit from fields, modern fruit farming and beekeeping, land consolidation, the cooperative system and the establishment of modern dairy farming. On the eve of the First World War, questions regarding the transport service and its electrification in the countryside began to be discussed by the union. In addition to lectures, agricultural periodicals designed for rural readers were distributed among the union's members, which helped to maintain the literacy of the rural adult population. It is necessary to mention one more area of the association's activity: the promotion of Czech nationalist ideals in a rural setting which had been indifferent to national matters. With the change of statutes in 1881, the union openly declared itself a Czech association through Section 3, with Czech as the official language of the association in the multi-ethnic borderland. Through its extensive network of members, within half a century the Agricultural Union had contributed to a transformation in the everyday life of rural society, which tends to be ignored by the chronicles. Therefore, in terms of the judicial and political districts, the interaction between the provincial and rural milieu was not restricted to markets, traditional festivities (fairs) or commuting from the village to town for work, as there existed a vibrant network of associations and professional organizations.

In many respects the activities of The Agricultural Union for North-East Moravia had a direct impact on the transformation of everyday life in the submontane municipality of Palkovice, in which the above-mentioned functionaries and active members of the association, i.e. above all Eduard Vrána, P. Ferdinand Baar and J. M. Kadlčák, spent part of their professional careers. Even Ludvík Kubala had close ties to Palkovice. His wife came from the local bailiff's [*Vogt*] house, where they lived for a couple of years, and after he committed suicide in Budapest, he was buried in Palkovice.[20] Peasant innovators, clergymen and teachers interacted with local farmers, allowing for the multi-level transfer of information which ultimately led to the modernization of life in the municipality. Within the developing network of economic and political ties, the representatives of the intelligentsia were an important link in the interaction between the submontane municipality of Palkovice and the outside world.

20 Noviny Těšínské, issue 23, p. 4.

The priest Ferdinand Baar was born on 28 March 1834 in Štramberk into the family of the burgher Jan Baar. Before he was appointed spiritual administrator of the parish office in Palkovice in 1871, he performed four years of spiritual and pastoral service at a women's prison in Valašské Meziříčí. At the parish office in Palkovice he replaced the spiritual administrator, Karel Kaštýl, who was also a progressively minded priest in matters of the national economy. As early as 1869, i.e. just before the development of self-help cooperative finance in the monarchy, he helped to establish the Civic Savings Bank in the municipality. Just like his predecessor, Ferdinand Baar was aware of the importance of self-help credit finance in the countryside and collaborated with the management of the bank for many years. Usury-free credit was much needed in the municipality throughout the entire second half of the 19th and early 20th century. He founded the *Hospodářská besídka* [Agricultural Association] in 1871, which, however, ran up against stiff competition in the form of the reading association established by a local teacher. He was more successful with his project for a hospital, which he established in the old school building in 1872 through the parish office, the management of which was partly financed by leasing grave sites. In the late 19th century, he was active in the municipal council, which named him an honorary citizen in his senior years. In terms of modernizing the municipality, he publicly supported the regulation of the Olešná river flowing through the municipality, which burst its banks almost every year and caused damage to the crops and property of the local peasants. He had a lifelong interest in the affairs of the municipality and felt such a strong bond to it that at the end of his life he asked the consistory in Olomouc if he could remain in Palkovice until the final days of his life. His request was granted and he died in Palkovice on 25 May 1919.[21]

From the census files we can partly reconstruct the economic background of the parish office from 1880 to 1910. In 1880 the clergyman Baar shared the parish office with his widowed mother and married sister, hiring a maid to help out. The files describe the family members in different arrangements for the entire period monitored. The cattle that were bred in the cowshed included a cow, a heifer and a calf. In 1890 the parish farm numbered two cows and two pigs. Ten years later the files enable us to view lively farm activity through the parish office, with the breeding of two cows, two pigs, one goat, forty-eight hens, fourteen ducks, four geese and twenty-three further unspecified items of poultry. A considerable amount of forage crops and fodder was needed to raise so many farm animals, which was undoubtedly supplied from the meadows and fields belonging to the parish office. The census from 1910 described similar management; the number of cows had now increased to three and the situation with the poultry had also changed slightly.[22] From the data on the farm animals we can see that a large farm existed through the parish office, and also that in 1900 the census taker recorded that the clergyman was the owner of an arable farm in the secondary column for professions. The clergyman would not have raised the cattle and poultry himself, but being an experienced farmer, he

21 SOkA Frýdek-Místek, collection Farní úřad Palkovice, box no. 8, documents related to Ferdinand Baar, the parish priest in Palkovice.

22 SOkA Frýdek-Místek, collection Okresní úřad Místek, Palkovice—census sheets 1910.

would have delegated such jobs to farm workers. From the economic aspect of the parish, rural clergymen were supposed to take an interest in the prosperity of the parish farm.

It is not clear from the sources who arranged Baar's membership of the Paskov Filial Agricultural Association. At the time of his arrival in the municipality, the Palkovice residents who were members of the association included four wealthy farmers and the teacher Anton Hoffschneider. One of the clergymen might also have introduced him to the association, for example, the dean of Místek. Within a short time he had established himself in the association as a man with a good knowledge of peasant issues. At the association meetings he led heated debates about the lack of land and other social issues affecting the countryside, such as the causes of economic decline amongst peasant homesteads. At the external meetings of the union he offered practical advice to the peasants, e.g. regarding the protection of cattle from the spread of infection, or the prevention of dodder (*Cuscuta*) weed infestation in fields, which was very common in the region in the early 1880s. He was actively engaged in the establishment of the Winter Agricultural School in Místek. In 1876 he was elected onto the association committee, and in the first half of the 1880s he held the position of chairman. As has been mentioned above, there were conflicting opinions concerning the activities of the Agricultural Union, which contributed to his decision to stand down as chairman in the following years. There was an escalation in his dispute with the secretary of the association, J.M. Kadlčák, in the mid-1880s concerning the financial aspect of building the Agricultural School in Místek. In later years these two activists set aside their differences over these issues. When J.M. Kadlčák became head of the National Catholic Party in Moravia, the ageing clergyman mentioned him in the parish chronicle with considerable respect, which cannot be said about other teachers he came into contact with while working as the spiritual administrator at the parish office in Palkovice.

A parish vicar was appointed for the first time in the history of the Palkovice parish in 1888. Usually it was a new priest who after a few years was entrusted with the position of spiritual administrator in one of the parishes, which is why he never made a special mark in history. A completely different situation arose when Valentin Zavadil was appointed assistant Parish priest in Palkovice in 1903.[23] The so-called *hetzchaplain* came to the Palkovice parish office as a young priest who was enthusiastic about social work and who had gained theoretical knowledge about dealing with social issues in developed industrial countries during his theological studies.[24] He was not the only clergyman who intended to put into practice the theoretical knowledge gained during his studies in the spirit of the *Rerum novarum* encyclical.[25] The young supporter of Christian socialism, eager for change, gained the support of the ageing parish priest for his activities. In 1907 he established a

23 Valentin Zavadil was born on 18 January 1879 to the family of a peasant, František Zavadil, in Čelechovice. He was ordained on 5 July 1903 in Olomouc. Land Archive in Opava, Department Olomouc, Roman Catholic parish office in Kokory.

24 Pavel MAREK, *Čeští křesťanští sociálové: příspěvek k problematice programových a organizačních základů českého politického katolicismu v letech 1894–1938*, Olomouc 2011, pp. 157–158.

25 P. MAREK, *Čeští křesťanští sociálové*, p. 120.

branch of *Všeodborové sdružení křesťanského dělnictva Moravy a Slezska* [The Union of Christian Workers' Association in Moravia and Silesia] in the municipality; the "association's" flag was consecrated in the presence of Josef M. Kadlčák on 5 August 1908. In 1908 he established a consumer cooperative called *Svépomocný potravní spolek* [Self-Help Food Association], which became competition for the five local traders. In 1912 the association numbered 268 members; every tenth inhabitant of the municipality was a member. With the financial participation of *Občanská záložna v Palkovicích* [The Civic Credit Union in Palkovice], the cooperative bought a mill close to the parish office which was falling into disrepair, rebuilt it and ran a grocery store there. It also set up the new headquarters of the Credit Union there. For several years the cooperative attempted to procure an innkeeper's licence, despite the fact that there were already three pubs in the municipality. The municipal council repeatedly refused to grant the licence. Although the cooperative did not acquire an innkeeper's licence, from 1909 it ran a cooperative distillery, which also angered some of its fellow citizens. In a region affected by alcoholism, which the clergy were the first in line to campaign against, one would have expected high-profile public demonstrations against the excessive consumption of alcohol rather than a profitable cooperative distillery. Under Zavadil's leadership, the Christian Social Party was formed in the municipality, which, on the eve of the Great War, ran in the municipal election and contributed to the division of the local political scene. The ambitious young clergyman finally became the scapegoat concerning the local dispute surrounding authority in the school and the polarization of public life, which will be clear from the reconstruction of events in the following text. Each of the participants in the events described both above and below was, to a certain extent, an agent of modernization in rural society.

Throughout his life, the clergyman Ferdinand Baar met several like-minded teachers at the Agricultural Union who wanted to improve life in the countryside. However, he had a more authoritarian attitude towards them concerning the Palkovice school, which eventually became an area of polarization in Palkovice society.[26] When Ferdinand Baar came to Palkovice in 1871, Anton Hofschneider, a native of Suché Lazce in Austrian Silesia, was teaching at the newly built local school. Before his appointment he had taught at a nearby school in Místek. A graduate of the two-year teacher preparatory school in Opava (1852), he also represents a teacher of the older generation; however, thanks to his numerous extra-curricular activities, he became an advocate of modern approaches in beekeeping and orcharding in the municipality. His interest in orcharding was based on the latest trends in this area; for example, he cultivated high-quality varieties of fruit trees. In 1868 he established a grafting nursery in the municipality, thereby going above and beyond the theoretical and practical preparation of pupils in questions of agricultural small-scale production set by the Education Law. In beekeeping, too, he conducted experiments with new types of beehives in order to increase honey production. In addition to arable farming and cattle breeding, the sale of honey and fruit was a significant source of income

26 Lukáš Fasora—Jiří Hanuš—Jiří Malíř (eds.), *Sekularizace venkovského prostoru v 19. století*, Brno 2009; Stanislav Balík et al., *Český antiklerikalismus. Zdroje, témata a podoba českého antiklerikalismu v letech 1848–1938*, Praha 2015.

for the peasants and new practices could help them become competitive in the market. Some clung to the old ways and ignored the activities of teachers in these areas, but the more modern minded in the agricultural associations cooperated with the teachers in practical terms. Hofschneider's great interest in orcharding and beekeeping, which are very closely connected, was not unusual amongst rural teachers, as is known from the life of the Moravian teacher, MP, senator and author of several essays on beekeeping, J.M. Kadlčák.[27] Hofschneider and Kadlčák not only shared similar interests, but they also both taught at the school in Palkovice, where J.M. Kadlčák was appointed as a teacher on 1 November 1878. This period came to an end with A. Hofschneider's premature death in May 1879.[28] It is unknown whether he died of typhoid fever during an epidemic in the municipality or of another illness as the parish register cannot be verified. J.M. Kadlčák came to the municipality as a skilled expert in modern farming practices. He knew the head teacher from the Agricultural Union for North-East Moravia with a branch in Místek, where they were both active members.[29]

Typical Political Disputes between Teachers and Priests in the Countryside

The roots of the animosity between the teachers and clergymen in the municipality can be traced back to Hasner's Education Law, i.e. the beginning of the liberalization process of primary education. One area of conflict was the religious examination, specifically whether the religious examination was superior to that of general knowledge (reading, writing and mathematics). From a wider perspective it was a clash over authority: the social habitus of the head teacher/teacher versus the catechist/parish priest/dean in local society. In a society that was transforming from traditional to modern, authority played an important role, and teachers from the "new" schools were supposed to have authority both in school and outside of it. The issue, therefore, was not the secularization of teaching, but the dilemma facing teachers of whether they would lose esteem in the eyes of the pupils and parents if they chose the religious examination over a specialized one. The fact that such a situation could arise demonstrates the problematic communication between the school and the ecclesiastical administration regarding the coordination of examination dates. In 1874, the teacher Hofschneider did not bring his pupils in time to the religious examination taking place at a church in the presence of the dean of Místek, as at the same time they were sitting examinations at school. In the eyes of the waiting clergymen and the conservative-minded inhabitants of the municipality, the teacher's behaviour had violated good

27 M. Oliva—J. Figura, *Kadlčákův Frýdlant nad Ostravicí.*

28 SOkA Frýdek-Místek, collection Základní devítiletá škola Palkovice, Kronika národní školy v Palkovicích [Chronicle of the National School in Palkovice], founded by Antonín Hofschneider in 1870. Book 1, unpaginated.

29 SOkA Frýdek-Místek, collection Okresní úřad Místek (1742) 1850–1945 (1950), Hospodářská jednota severovýchodní Moravy v Místku [The Agricultural Union of North-East Moravia in Místek Association].

manners, as the clergy held the most respected and influential position in the hierarchy of local society. However, the teacher also had sympathisers among the locals, who, while not approving of his actions publicly, at least did not pillory him. The polarization of the inhabitants of the municipality into one camp sympathizing with the school, and one camp sympathizing with the parish office, can be found in sources concerning the oldest associations in the municipality even before this dispute about symbolic power over the school and pupils. This could be seen when the parish priest, F. Baar, established an agricultural association, and the teacher Hofschneider immediately set up a "rival" reading association *Lidumil* [Philanthropist], which flourished, unlike the "parish" agricultural association.[30]

Another area of contention in the peaceful cohabitation between the teacher and the inhabitants of the municipality was the school, not only as an institution but also as a building. After the issuing of the Municipal Law and the Provincial Implementation Acts, the establishment, maintenance and running of schools fell under the remit of the independent activity of the local municipalities. The law did not distinguish between towns and municipalities. The plans for the construction of a school were submitted by the local school board to the district school board, which had them assessed by a medical officer, technician and expert on education. The committee meeting of the advisory body either authorised construction or recommended some essential alterations to the project so that it would be in compliance with building regulations. The construction proceedings were to ensure that the school buildings were not damp and dark and thus did not endanger the health of children and young adults. School gardens, exercise areas and bathrooms were to be provided by the school. Only project documentation which met the building and hygiene standards was returned to the local school board, which presented it to the local municipality.[31] The initiative to erect a new school building usually came from the local school board; however, the district school board often exerted pressure on the local school board to take steps in the matter of a new school building. The members of the local school board found themselves under pressure both from the district school board and their fellow citizens/voters. In compliance with the legislation, some members of the local school board were local representatives who had a knowledge of municipal finance as well as their fellow citizens' attitudes towards investing municipal funds in municipal education. Therefore, building a new school became a political issue in many municipalities, which divided opinion among the inhabitants. Some inhabitants took the anti-modernization stance that not only were the old school buildings with up to 300 pupils per one or two teachers in compliance with the regulations, but also that providing accommodation for the teacher near the school, as required by the state, was a luxury.

30 The Moravian Provincial Archive Brno, collection B 40/I land registry 437 h Spolkový katastr okresu Místek [The Associational Register of the District of Místek]. The federal statutes were approved by the governor's office on 27 December 1870 under reference number 22,471. The activity of the association was suspended only with the outbreak of the First World War and was not renewed afterwards. It was deleted from the federal register in 1921.

31 *Nařízení o zdravotnictví na školách obecných v království Českém*, Praha 1891, pp. 2–12.

Furthermore, they considered school attendance for older children and young adults as unnecessary, and showed absolutely no understanding of new subjects that developed precise motor skills or physical fitness in pupils. In Palkovice, they rejected the teaching of art, natural history and physical education. Hofschneider wrote in the school chronicle that the parents considered these subjects to be literally nonsense, as they were of the conservative opinion that it was sufficient for their children to learn the basics of general knowledge and the catechism. However, according to the teacher, these local farmers' knowledge of the laws of nature was only superficial, or, in his words, "ignorance about nature and its effects is enormous among the citizens". This ignorance could have had a direct impact on the productivity of the local peasants and Passekers (owners of land that had to be cleared before use). A minority of the town's modern-minded inhabitants saw the school as an important institution, not only for educating children and young adults, but also for the life of the town; they did not consider the old school building worthy of being called a school. The mayor of the municipality also numbered among them, but in order to push through the construction of a new school building it was necessary to gain the votes of the majority of the local municipality. In these local disputes over the new school the political state authority played an important role, which monitored the independent activities of the municipalities. As is clear not only in Palkovice, the disputes among the locals over whether to build a new school, which could drag on indefinitely, would come to an end when the municipality received a firm reminder of its obligations. A new school building was thus constructed in Palkovice in 1872, and a second teaching position for a temporary teacher was created, which was held by J.M. Kadlčák for five years.[32]

The teaching profession was connected with numerous open interviews. At that time it was not common to automatically fill a position vacated by a deceased head teacher with another teacher working at the same school; instead, there were interviews for the position. Three experienced teachers applied for the post, whose qualifications corresponded to their age, ranging from thirty to forty. All of the applicants emphasised their ability to play the organ in their CVs. One had a certificate to teach at German schools, but this was unnecessary in a purely Czech municipality such as Palkovice.[33] Why the local school board chose Adolf Winkler cannot be deduced from the sources. For a quarter of a century this teacher was at loggerheads with a number of Palkovice's representatives and the public regarding the school building. After teaching there for several years, the number of children per class exceeded the norms set by the education laws and regulations. The head teacher's difficult position within the local community is documented in the school chronicle. The head teacher's successor wrote that 20 of the 26 years working at the school represented a "series of injustices" for the head teacher Winkler. The years of fruitless negotiations with the municipal council and the local and district school boards

32 SOkA Frýdek-Místek, collection Archiv obce Palkovice, box no. 1, inv. no. 42; SOkA Frýdek-Místek, collection Základní devítiletá škola Palkovice, Kronika národní školy v Palkovicích, founded by Antonín Hofschneider in 1870. He remained a teacher until 8 October 1883.

33 SOkA Frýdek-Místek, collection Okresní školní rada Místek, inv. no. 132, box no. 62.

were finally brought to an end by a regulation from the provincial school board in Brno (1902) concerning the construction of the school building by the district council, with all the expenses connected with the construction to be paid by the municipality. The municipality immediately began its construction and it was completed within several months; however, it is likely that the cheapest building option was chosen.[34]

Adolf Winkler followed in the footsteps of his predecessor and for many years defended the important role of education for rural children, even though his opponents remained strong, despite the modernization trends in society. The arguments of his opponents were similar to those many years before. Beyond a basic knowledge of reading, writing and mathematics, they considered education to be useless. Craft work was slowly asserting itself as a necessary skill for girls. There was considerable resistance among the locals to physical education. In addition, local representatives had refused to provide funds to build a school playground. Some even spread false news among the locals about the harmful effect of physical education on children's health; allegedly, exercise led to children developing a goitre. The decision of the municipal council not to provide funds to build a playground was immediately revoked by the imperial-royal district council; the municipality had to build the exercise area as requested by the school authorities. The opponents of the enlargement of the school building argued that such an operation would be expensive. No sooner had the municipality paid off the loan it had taken out to build the school (1872) than it wanted to expand it with new classrooms. The key question, therefore, was where to find the necessary funds from the municipal budget. The protests grew from the biggest taxpayers in the municipality against the usual surtaxes which normally covered budget deficits. We must also consider the issue from their perspective. The state monitored the running of the local municipalities through the district councils, but did not finance them. The state authorities monitored the activities of the municipalities in their independent activities, but they were not interested in how the municipalities were to obtain the additional finance for growing expenses and investments. It was possible to gain subsidies that would partly cover the expenses, but it was still necessary for municipalities to have their own sources of financing. Furthermore, it was not only schools that the municipalities had to finance from their budgets. The system in itself, therefore, contributed to a division of opinion among the inhabitants of the municipalities.

During his career, the head teacher Winkler was re-elected to the position of expert on the district school board in 1894 and 1900. In 1874 and 1877 he held the position of deputy chairman at the *Místecko-novojičínská učitelská jednota Komenský* [The Komenský Teachers' Union of the Regions of Místek and Nový Jičín].[35] He was appointed as a delegate to the provincial education conference four times. Therefore, being a teacher in a village did not necessarily mean career stagnation if the person was willing to work and to self-educate. A village teacher in the late-19th and early-20th century no longer lived in poverty along with the local poor. It is true that they were not among the highest

34 SOkA Frýdek-Místek, collection Archiv obce Palkovice, box no. 1, inv. no. 42.

35 Edvard DORAZIL, *Zpráva jednatelská o dvaceti pětileté činnosti Místecko-novojičínské učitelské jednoty "Komenský" za dobu od 1870 až do 1895*, Příbor 1896, p. 20.

earners in rural society, but their income and social status were comparable to that of a clergyman in local society. Like the parish priests they were educated and had a secure income, pension and the right to vote in the municipal election in the first electoral body of the so-called notables.[36]

As was common with rural teachers, Winkler and his wife ran a small farm on the estate and land provided by the municipality together with the school accommodation. He probably enjoyed beekeeping and orcharding and like his predecessors, he was involved in Místek's agricultural union. Not only was he interested in improving agriculture but also his fellow citizens, and under his leadership the Lidumil reading association flourished. Being an excellent organ player, he devoted himself to playing with a group of singers. He prepared liturgical music performances with them, but after years of disputes with the parish priest he gave up leading the choir and playing the organ. The animosity between the school and the parish office grew ever deeper and escalated under the last pre-war head teacher.

When he retired in 1905 after 42 years of teaching, he left his successor a modern five-grade school with the professional positions of a head teacher, two teachers and two assistant teachers. Craft work was taught by a female industrial teacher and religion by a catechist. On 28 November 1905 an experienced teacher, Metoděj Bartoník, born on 25 September 1863 in the Municipality of Kokory, was appointed to the vacated position. It is possible that he was directed, or at least inspired, towards becoming a teacher by the Kokory head teacher, musician and patriot, Antonín Geisler, who could have been a model worth following for the village boy.[37] Before he was accepted at the teachers' institute in Příbor, he completed three years of studies at the *Realgymnasium* in Přerov. He passed his school-leaving examination in 1884. He was appointed as a temporary teacher at the school in Čeladná; after two years of teaching he passed an aptitude test.

His career advancement was in line with his teaching abilities. In August 1889 he was appointed temporary head teacher at the school in Trojanovice, which became a permanent appointment from 15 December 1890. After nine years he moved position and was appointed head teacher at the school in Kunčičky near Baška. The sources suggest he must have been a very energetic man. As soon as he discovered that the school building in his new area needed repairs, he negotiated with the municipality to have them done. Like the teacher Adolf Winkler in Palkovice, he negotiated for several years with representatives from the local municipality and the appropriate authorities to have a new school built. He believed that a hygienic and modern-equipped school was required to give children and young adults a proper education. He was uncompromising when it came to poor school attendance. During his first year of teaching in the municipality he had already

36 SOkA Frýdek-Místek, collection Archiv obce Palkovice, box no. 1, inv. no. 36. A list of eligible voters for the 1891 municipal election.

37 Opavský týdenník, 16 January 1891, no. 3, pp. 1–2. The father of the Olomouc canon and prelate Jindřich Geisler, founder of the music association Žerotín, was also a civically engaged man. In Kokory he established a music and singing association and a municipal library, and he introduced numerous innovations in agriculture.

filed a criminal complaint against parents who did not send their children to school. He continued to educate himself even while carrying out the demanding duties of a teacher. He attended agricultural courses organized by the agricultural school in Místek. He was a teacher who was fully aware of his society-wide role and function, promoting the interests of the school in accordance with the legislation. From among the locals this led to people either sympathising with him and his colleagues or opposing them.

At the peak of his career aged 42 he was appointed head teacher at the five-grade school in the neighbouring village of Palkovice. The teaching staff of the school comprised seven teachers and a catechist. There had already been nine teachers and a catechist working at the school from the 1908/1909 school year. As far as modernization processes were concerned, even at this village school we can see the beginnings of the feminization of education. When a female teacher was first appointed at the school under the then head teacher Adolf Winkler, he had asked the authorities to fill the position with a man as there was an aversion to women being appointed teachers in the municipality. The authorities pandered for a short time to the persisting traditionalism of the local men, but within ten years women had become a common feature among the teaching staff. With its 396 children in the school year 1908/1909 and its modern teaching aids, the school was more like an urban school than a traditional rural one. The annual salary of the teacher Bartoník was 3,000 crowns plus 60 crowns remuneration. The basic pay of permanently appointed teachers ranged from between 1,200 to 2,000 crowns a year.[38] The lowest wage of 900 crowns was paid to the craft-work teacher (industrial). The teaching staff did not include the catechist, Valentin Zavadil, who taught religion in all classes.[39]

The head teacher, Metoděj Bartoník, became the personification of the progressive democratic camp; he came to the municipality two years after the assistant and catechist Valentin Zavadil. As was mentioned above, he had been appointed head teacher in Palkovice for his teaching and leadership skills, which were necessary for managing a five-grade school. Like every civic-minded man of his time, he was involved in the local cultural life and politics. His political views eventually led him to the so-called progressive democratic camp of the local representatives and sympathisers. After only a few months of being active in the municipality he had become one of the leading participants in the ongoing polarization of the local political scene.

38 In order to compare the income level of teachers we have included the salaries of university educated doctors employed at the City Hospital in Moravian Ostrava in 1908: Senior consultant and hospital director F. Neugebauer had a basic annual salary of 3,000 crowns, plus extra pay of 1,180 crowns and the option to use a hospital flat. Senior consultant Sederl had a salary of 3,000 crowns, plus extra pay of 840 crowns, plus annual housing benefit of 1,000 crowns. Secondary doctors were entitled to a basic annual salary of 2,160 crowns, an extra pay of 840 crowns and housing benefit amounting to 800 crowns. Other doctors' salaries were 1,440 crowns, plus extra pay amounting to 840 crowns and housing benefit of 500 crowns.

39 SOkA Frýdek-Místek, collection Základní devítiletá škola Palkovice, Book 2. 1899–1925, unpaged.

The division of opinion in the local political scene was a long-term process.[40] At the centre of the dispute was the management of municipal funds, specifically the sources of funding for the development of the municipality. In an already divided society, any dispute contributed to the tense atmosphere and the spread of uncivilized behaviour such as libel, denunciations to the authorities and petty vandalism of political rivals' property. This had made the municipality notorious on a district level, which was how the situation was perceived by the imperial-royal district governor, who took an apolitical stance in the dispute outlined below. Therefore, it cannot be said that if the position of head teacher had been filled by an ardent Catholic and member of the Christian Social Party, like the abovementioned teacher and politician, J.M. Kadlčák, that there would have been consensus in the municipality and the municipal council. Perhaps the reputation of the school and its teaching staff would not have suffered due to the dispute. At this point we also have to mention the text of §54 of the Amendment Act of the Education Law.

In the ideological conflict over authority between the clergy and the teachers, the head teacher Bartoník did not believe that the authority of the clergymen was greater than that of the teachers at school. This was based on the basic principles of the Education Law of 14 May 1869 and §36 of the Amendment Act of the Education Law of 1883.[41]Although this act did not mention authority, it did deal with the equal rights and responsibilities of permanently appointed teachers of religion and of head teachers.[42] The conservative-minded ecclesiastical administrator of the parish, Ferdinand Baar, who was not in favour of interconfessional education, clung to the symbolically higher esteem of the clergy, despite society-wide developments. The young assistant, Valentin Zavadil, took a similar stance, sending a complaint to the provincial school board in Brno on 10 December 1909 about the offensive and illegal behaviour of the head teacher Metoděj Bartoník towards him; specifically, that he had reduced the authority of the religion teacher in the eyes of the pupils. The subject of the dispute was a sermon in which Zavadil stated that reading the inappropriate literature which could be found in the school library [author's note: Machar's poems and Zola's *La Conquête de Plassans*] could pose a potential threat to the moral and religious education of children and young adults. The following day in response to the Sunday sermon the head teacher conducted an investigation in the school into whether the school library had lent the incriminating books to any of the pupils. He defended his actions before the district school board by arguing that his intention was to protect the good name of the school in the eyes of the public. Furthermore, he also mentioned that some time before he had forbidden the catechist to use inappropriate physical punishment on the pupils, highlighting the religion teacher's violation of the school rules. The main investigation was conducted by the district school board, but in addition to the school authorities it was also closely watched by the archbishop's consistory in Olomouc, where the catechist had also complained about the head teacher.

40 SOkA Frýdek-Místek, collection Archiv obce Palkovice, inv. no. 5. Kniha protokolů 1889–1907 and Kniha protokolů 1908–1923.

41 Reichsgesetzblatt für die im Reichsrate vertretenen Königreiche und Lände, Wien 1869, p. 277.

42 Reichsgesetzblatt für die im Reichsrate vertretenen Königreiche und Länder, Wien 1883, p. 203.

During the investigation into the administrative nature of the complaint, the district school board came to the conclusion that by investigating without the board's consent the head teacher Bartoník had indeed violated the school's regulations and that his actions could have led to reducing the authority of the catechist in the eyes of the pupils. In the presence of the vicegerent secretary, the board decided that his punishment would be an admonition by the district school inspector. In the report to the provincial school board the writer stressed that in the decision-making process they had taken into account the "well-known and unpleasant situation in Palkovice" and the hitherto exemplary running of the school by the head teacher.[43]

The abovementioned affair formed a prologue to the events of 1911, when conflict flared up again and gained in intensity.[44] This time the parish office in Palkovice complained to the provincial school board in Brno and to the archbishop's consistory in Olomouc about insufficient teacher supervision during religious exercises and the Feast of Corpus Christi. During the investigation, head teacher Bartoník mentioned the fact that supervision had been approved at an education conference in compliance with the school regulations of 24 September 1905. The teaching staff appealed to the Ministry of Culture and Education against the decree by the provincial school board, which increased teacher supervision during religious exercises. After the ministry rejected the complaint, increased teacher supervision was accepted by the school. In this symbolic dispute over authority it was the clergy who "won". In addition to this administrative matter, the provincial school authorities had received several complaints regarding the poor situation concerning the school and the teaching staff, but also petitions claiming the exact opposite. From the correspondence it is evident that this was just another aspect of the political struggle in the municipality, with the writers from both parties describing the main conflicts in the municipal council.[45] However, we cannot omit §54 of the Education Law relating to the behaviour of teachers outside of school. As a result, school authorities may have come to the conclusion that the political involvement of the head teacher reduced his esteem in the eyes of the public.

To what extent the friction was reduced after the assistant and catechist, Valentin Zavadil, was transferred to the parish in Nová Ves in 1912 cannot be verified from the sources. The imperial-royal district governor believed that the division of opinion in the municipality was such that whether the assistant remained or left would have changed nothing. The deanery was inclined towards the position of the ageing parish priest, Baar, who claimed that Zavadil's transfer would weaken the position of the Christian Social Movement in the municipality. From the correspondence of the consistory it is evident that it did not approve of all the young clergyman's actions, such as his position as

43 SOkA, collection Okresní školní rada Místek, inv. no. 132, box no. 62.

44 Ostravský kraj, no. 49, vol. 5. 18 June 1910. Palkovice § 57. Head teacher Bartoník and the canonical visit to the school.

45 Ostravský kraj, no. 61. 3 August 1910, p. 3. Z Palkovic, no. 64. Palkovice. The report reads: Somebody has smeared the windows of the Self-Help Association, chaplain and assistant with tar. Defamatory messages are being written on the walls and fences.

secretary of the consumer cooperative. Finally, it decided to transfer the "controversial" clergyman. On the eve of the First World War, rural society was divided in a similar political way to that of the towns, while the process of secularization was also in evidence.[46]

In the early 1870s—the period of the priest Baar's arrival—the municipality of Palkovice was a typical, underdeveloped submontane village, where the majority of residents earned their living by farming. In this respect, the economic structure of the population of the municipality was preserved until the beginning of the First World War; only migration to the neighbouring industrial cities for work increased. The local agricultural small-scale production was modernized over the course of half a century. According to the municipal chronicle, the fields were not being ploughed properly as late as the mid-19th century. The farming tools were generally wooden, while the land was not drained of water and was fertilized irregularly every six years. The harvests were generally small, which led to a lack of straw, and thus leaves and moss were used as litter for livestock in winter. The peasants gradually implemented changes in the last third of the 19th century. Farmers started to drain the land of water and to fertilize it; they also used limestone. By 1900 the peasants had acquired threshing machines with whims; there was also, apparently, one sowing machine in the municipality. Orcharding was developing as well.[47] The activity of The Agricultural Union of North-East Moravia had a considerable share in this; it procured stud bulls, high-quality grain and fertilizer for the municipality and organized external shareholders' meetings in the municipality connected with educational lectures related to current topics. On 27 August 1882 an agricultural congress for the peasantry was held in the municipality, organized by P. Ferdinand Baar, the chairman of The Agricultural Union of North-East Moravia, where the prominent national economist, F. L. Chleborád appeared and gave a presentation entitled *What Is the Situation Today?* Perhaps surprisingly for some of the attendees he did not speak about the poor material state of the peasantry; instead, in the spirit of strengthening national awareness, he warned against German cultural nationalism.[48] However, he spoke out most vociferously against the widespread alcoholism in the countryside. The lecturer revealed that the Catholic clergy would be at the forefront of the enlightened fight against the "plague of the spirit", as it was called then.[49] The content of the prominent national economist's presentation highlights another role and function of the clergy in the countryside, which was the fight against the social decline of peasant families caused by alcoholism, which had various roots in the village community and was an integral part of the vicious circle of poverty. It, therefore, made an absurdity of the Christian Social Association's decision to open a distillery in the municipality; the opposition's criticism in this respect was more than justified. With their involvement in the activities of the agricultural unions, the Catholic clergy passed on information regarding the self-help credit system, consumer cooperatives and modern agricultural methods. The unions distributed agricultural journals and

46 SOkA Frýdek-Místek, collection Farní úřad Palkovice 1760–1954, inv. no. 101, box no. 13.

47 SOkA Frýdek-Místek, collection Archiv obce Palkovice, Kronika Palkovice, vol 1.

48 Našinec, 30. 8. 1882, issue 102, p. 3.

49 Našinec, 1. 9. 1882, issue 103, pp. 2–4.

newspapers. As has already been outlined, the clergy engaged mainly in beekeeping and orcharding. The parish gardens were exemplary in the municipality. The parish priests were in contact with the local peasantry not only through the Christian ministry and education, but also through their activity in local government.

The two above-mentioned Catholic clergymen, who worked together at the Palkovice parish office for a short period of time, are not an exception in the history of the Czech clergy. The role of clergymen in the Czech national movement is generally known for the earlier half of the 19th century, but this was also a feature in the countryside and small towns during the entire second half of the 19th century. The stereotypical image of the Catholic clergyman as being against modernization starts to become less convincing when rural society is studied at a micro-historical level. In the case of clergymen, clinging to traditional values and old systems can be seen in the Christian ministry and school education. As far as the older generation is concerned, remnants of the clergy's traditional charitable activities were apparent in social issues. The generation of clergymen influenced by the *Rerum novarum* encyclical also implemented a modern Christian-social programme in villages. The *hetzchaplains* in particular took part in many aspects of everyday rural life. They often knew about the problems the rural people had from their own experiences as youths. The data concerning the make-up of the intelligentsia shows that a considerable number of people who joined the seminaries were intelligent young men from the countryside. As in any other socio-professional group, it is necessary to consider the personality traits of each individual, i.e. the fact that there also existed clergymen who did not take part in any of the above-mentioned activities, but were merely involved in spiritual and pastoral service.

In the epilogue to his work on the clergy in Bohemia from 1848 to 1914, Tomáš W. Pavlíček stated that "over time it was teachers instead of priests who were at the forefront of progress".[50] In the above-mentioned text, the areas in rural life where teachers were at the forefront of progress are outlined over time. Personality traits played the same role in their behaviour and actions as was the case for clergymen. Even if some of them limited themselves to the modernization obligations set for the teaching profession by laws and school regulations, they would still have had a considerable share in the modernization of the countryside. They provided children and young adults with a standardized public education. It was only in the early 20th century that requests from the more modern-minded peasants were heard in rural schools; in addition to theoretical knowledge, they also wanted to communicate practical information about orcharding and gardening to older pupils. The obligation to establish school gardens was mentioned above and school chronicles show that teachers taught grafting, orcharding, market gardening, flower growing, as well as the study of medicinal herbs.[51] There was a vast amount of information passed on to pupils through the subject which would be called horticulture in

50 Tomáš Pavlíček, *Výchova kněží v Čechách a jejich role v náboženské kultuře (1848–1914)*, Praha 2017, p. 462.

51 SOkA Frýdek-Místek, collection Základní devítiletá škola Palkovice, Kronika školy obecné v Palkovicích 1899–1925.

today's school curriculum. Teachers also taught older pupils the basics of the national economy, in particular the meaning of saving and self-help credit cooperatives.[52] In addition to educational activity, teachers also influenced their pupils in social hygiene. They taught children basic hygiene habits, but if this had no effect, they could address the situation using other means. Although physical punishment was prohibited, teachers were allowed to wash a child who came to school dirty. Discipline did not only apply to personal hygiene, which constituted a serious health risk both for the class and the municipality as a whole, but also to other basic rules of behaviour, e.g. compulsory school attendance. Here the teacher had to exert influence on the pupils as well as their parents, who tended to disagree with the idea that education led to an improvement in the child's social status. The words recorded in the school chronicle by the head teacher concerning the peasants' attitude to school attendance were not only related to pre-war Palkovice: "Parents cannot wait until the moment their children finish school and start working in a factory to help bring in money to the family. All the arguments that they are ruining their health and shortening their lives if they work in a factory from such a young age are futile."[53] The state monitored the fulfilment of rural teachers' obligations through regular school inspections and could sanction a teacher for failing to follow them.

The professionalization of teaching was closely related to teachers' charity. With the introduction of tariff salary grades and better financial reward for teachers in the last quarter of the 19th century, the permanently appointed teacher was no longer a man supporting his family on the verge of a subsistence wage, and instead became part of the middle-income stratum. With this change in social status, those teachers who used to receive local charity now became the organisers of many charity events. Being aware of the appalling social conditions experienced by the rural lower classes and the poor, they initiated Christmas clothes collections and the organization of Christmas parties, where small presents were given to the children. They were also behind the village soup kitchens, which provided the poorest pupils with hot soup during the winter months; for many children this was their only substantial hot meal of the day.[54] Some parents may have been motivated to send their children to school as a result of these charitable activities.

In a reactionary move, the state used an amendment to the Education Law of 1883 to monitor teachers' free-time activities, even though in social practice this would have been entirely against society-wide developments. It depended on the level of the local civil society whether a teacher's after-school activities, such as orcharding, beekeeping, music, ethnography or history ultimately became public activity, with the teacher communicating new ideas. If a network of civil engagement was being formed in the municipality through the societies which teachers joined, as was implied above, then they had the possibility to pass on their knowledge and experience. We traditionally view associations as one of the lynchpins in the formation of civil society. The thesis concerning the

52 Ibid. The Raiffeisenka was established in Palkovice by local teachers on 14 March 1909 and pupils were given piggy banks.

53 Ibid.

54 Ibid.

interconnectedness of associations' activities with municipal politics at the turn of the 20th century also proved to be valid in a rural context. Permanently appointed teachers who had the right to vote in municipalities and who participated in the activities of associations in the municipality also usually took part in local political affairs. As with every other participant in public life, they eventually became embroiled in the disputes connected with holding public office and the polarization of opinion in local politics. There was far less controversy in teachers' cultural activities; for example, the establishment of singing, reading, charity and sports associations, though, as has been mentioned above, in a divided rural society, even cultural events could lead to conflict. The least controversial areas, therefore, would have been gardening, orcharding, beekeeping and other agricultural activities, which might have be an inspiration for some peasants. There were several factors which determined whether teachers and clergymen became respected figures and exponents of progress in the locality, in particular the level of the civil society and the personality traits of the peasants as well as the clergy and teachers.

Conclusion

The aim of this study was to explain the role and function of clergymen and teachers as exponents of progress in the agricultural and social life of the countryside in the second half of the 19th and early 20th century, i.e. after the abolition of the corvée and before the First World War. Instead of looking at the issue globally, a micro-historical approach was chosen, which allowed us to interpret our findings within the wider context of the modernization process. To a certain extent, the micro-historical approach refuted the stereotypical concept of clergymen as anti-modernization elements in society. During the period examined, clergymen still played an important role in spreading ideas concerning the national community in rural society. Some of them contributed towards agricultural developments in the countryside by communicating new ideas about agriculture and the credit economy. In the late 19th century, we can encounter the progressive activity of the *hetzchaplains*, who also spread the ideas of the Christian Social Movement to the countryside.

In the countryside, teachers made up the second group from the intelligentsia who the rural population came into everyday contact with. In comparison with the clergy, the teaching profession underwent a process of professionalization during this period and as a result of their education, the teachers were the nearest in social status to the parish priest. Like clergymen, with their knowledge, experience and lifelong learning, teachers became advisors to rural inhabitants in many areas of everyday life. If the suitable conditions for civil engagement existed in the municipality, teachers would establish associations and take part in local political affairs.

The network of associations in the region formed a platform to introduce numerous innovations to rural societies. These associations distributed newspapers to the countryside, redistributed donations and organized educational lectures. The peasantry became active and politicized as a result of the associations' activities. In this research, the aim was not to focus on the history of specific associations in municipalities, but to describe activity which had a regional impact and was linked to the political scene. Only in this context is it possible to highlight the importance of rural clergymen and teachers as exponents of modernization.

Bibliography

Jitka BALCAROVÁ, *Německé zemědělské spolky v rakouském Slezsku druhé poloviny 19. století: stavovská svépomoc, solidarita, jednota a uvědomělost* [German agricultural associations in Austrian Silesia in the second half of the 19th century: professional self-help, solidarity, unity and awareness], Historica. Revue pro historii a příbuzné vědy, 2017, no. 2, pp. 31–44.

Jitka BALCAROVÁ, *Počátky německého venkovského úvěrového družstevnictví v rakouském Slezsku v 2. polovině 19. století: organizační základna a aktéři* [The beginnings of the German rural credit cooperative in Austrian Silesia in the second half of the 19th century: organizational base and actors], Prameny a studie 2, 2016, no. 59, pp. 56–75.

Stanislav BALÍK et al., *Český antiklerikalismus. Zdroje, témata a podoba českého antiklerikalismu v letech 1848–1938* [Czech anti-clericalism. Sources, themes and the form of Czech anti-clericalism in the years 1848–1938], Praha 2015.

Magdalena BERANOVÁ, *Dějiny zemědělství v Čechách a na Moravě* [History of agriculture in Bohemia and Moravia], Praha 2010.

Edvard DORAZIL, *Zpráva jednatelská o dvaceti pětileté činnosti Místecko-novojičínské učitelské jednoty "Komenský" za dobu od 1870 až do 1895* [The General report on 25 years of activities of the Teachers's association "Komenský" in Místek and Nový Jičín], Příbor 1896.

Lukáš FASORA—Jiří HANUŠ—Jiří MALÍŘ (eds.), *Sekularizace venkovského prostoru v 19. století* [Secularization of rural space in the 19th century], Brno 2009.

Zdeněk FIŠER, *Hospodářská jednota záhlinicko-kvasická (1861–1912)* [Economic association Záhlinice-Kvasice], Chropyně 1997.

Zdeněk FIŠER, *Zpravodajství Jana Kozánka z Opavy z let 1845–1849* [Reporting by Jan Kozánek from Opava from 1845–1849], Přerov 1999.

Zdeněk JINDRA—Ivan JAKUBEC, *Hospodářský vzestup českých zemí od poloviny 18. století do konce monarchie* [The economic rise of the Bohemian lands from the middle of the 18th century to the end of the monarchy], Praha 2015.

Tomáš KASPER—Markéta PÁNKOVÁ, *Učitel ve střední a jihovýchodní Evropě: profesionalizace učitelského vzdělávání: historické a systematické aspekty* [Teacher in Central and South-Eastern Europe: professionalization of teacher education: historical and systematic aspects], Praha 2015.

Pavel KLADIWA, *The Transformation and Social Activation of Rural Areas. The Bohemian Lands in 1861–1914 (A Preliminary outline of the issue)*, Moderní dějiny/Modern History 26, 2018, no. 1, pp. 1–29.

Jaromír KUBLÁK, *Ludvík Kubala, sedlák, vynálezce a buditel selského stavu na Moravě* [Ludvík Kubala, a farmer, inventor and awakener of the peasant state in Moravia], Brno 1941.

Jana MACHAČOVÁ—Jiří MATĚJČEK, *Nástin sociálního vývoje českých zemí 1781–1914* [Outline of the social development of the Bohemian lands 1781–1914], Opava 2002.

Jana MACHAČOVÁ—Jiří MATĚJČEK, *Problémy obecné kultury v českých zemích 1781–1989* [Problems of general culture in the Bohemian lands 1781–1989], Opava 2008.

Pavel MAREK, *Čeští křesťanští sociálové: příspěvek k problematice programových a organizačních základů českého politického katolicismu v letech 1894–1938* [Czech Christian Socials: A Contribution to the Problems of the Programmatic and Organizational Foundations of Czech Political Catholicism in the Years 1894–1938], Olomouc 2011.

Jiří MATĚJČEK, *Příspěvek k popisu materiálních pozic chudého venkovského obyvatelstva, řemeslnického a průmyslového dělnictva v českých zemích ve druhé polovině 19. a na začátku 20. století* [Contribution to the description of the material positions of the poor rural population, craft and industrial workers in the Czech lands in the second half of the 19th and at the beginning of the 20th century], in: Zdeněk Kárník (ed.), K novověkým sociálním dějinám českých zemí [On the Modern Social History of the Bohemian Lands], vol. 2, Z dob rakouských a předlitavských (1848–1918) [english], Praha 1998, pp. 116–119.

Jiří MATĚJČEK, *Rok na vsi. Sonda do sociální situace na jihomoravské vesnici v poslední čtvrtině 19. století* [From the Austrian and pre-Lithuanian times], Slezský sborník 96, 1998, pp. 264–284.

Nařízení o zdravotnictví na školách obecných v království Českém [A year in the village. A probe into the social situation in a South Moravian village in the last quarter of the 19th century], Praha 1891.

Miloslav OLIVA—Jiří FIGURA, *Kadlčákův Frýdlant nad Ostravicí* [Kadlčák's Frýdlant], Frýdek-Místek 2009.

Jitka PADRNOSOVÁ, *Učitel. Příklad Jana Jaroslava Jelínka* [Teacher. The example of Jan Jaroslav Jelínek], in: Lukáš Fasora—Jiří Hanuš—Jiří Malíř (eds.), Člověk na Moravě 19. století [A Man in 19th-century Moravia], Brno 2004, pp. 111–123.

Tomáš PAVLÍČEK, *Výchova kněží v Čechách a jejich role v náboženské kultuře (1848–1914)* [Education of priests in Bohemia and their role in religious culture], Praha 2017.

Andrea POKLUDOVÁ, *Formování inteligence na Moravě a ve Slezsku 1857–1910* [Formation of intelligence in Moravia and Silesia], Opava 2008.

Andrea POKLUDOVÁ, *Sviadnov v letech 1848–1918* [Sviadnov in the years 1848–1918], in: Tomáš Adamec et al., Sviadnov, Sviadnov 2017, pp. 31–80.

Andrea POKLUDOVÁ, *Učitel* [Teacher], in: Milan Myška—Aleš Zářický (eds.), *Člověk v Ostravě v XIX. století* [A Man in 19th-century Ostrava], Ostrava 2007, pp. 31–43.

Jiří POKORNÝ, *Lidová výchova na přelomu 19. a 20. století* [Folk education at the turn of the 19th and 20th centuries], Prague 2003.

Pavel POSPĚCH, *Rolník—Haná—Příklad Josefa Vysloužila* [Paesant - Haná - The Example of Josef Vysloužil], in: Lukáš Fasora—Jiří Hanuš—Jiří Malíř (eds.), Člověk na Moravě 19. století, Brno 2004, pp. 169–181.

Jiří RADIMSKÝ—Milada WURMOVÁ (eds.), *Petice moravského lidu k sněmu z roku 1848* [Petition of the Moravian people to the parliament from 1848], Praha 1955.

Kai STRUVE, *Peasant Emancipation and National Integration. Agrarian Circles, Village Reading Rooms and Cooperatives in Galicia*, in: Torsten Lorenz (ed.), Cooperatives in Ethnic Conflicts. Eastern Europe from the late 19th until the mid 20th Century, Berlin 2006, pp. 229–250.

Jaromír ŠUPINA, *Šebestián Vrána*, Sborník Státního okresního archivu ve Frýdku-Místku 6, 2005, pp. 67–76.

Josef VOCHALA, *Rok 1848 ve Slezsku a na severovýchodní Moravě* [Year 1848 in Silesia and northeastern Moravia], Opava 1948.

Pavla VOŠAHLÍKOVÁ, *Rákoska v dílně lidskosti: česká škola v 19. století očima účastníků* [Reed in the workshop of humanity: a Czech school in the 19th century through the eyes of participants], Praha 2016.

An Era of Ethnic Protection: "Defending" the Rural German Speakers in Hungary during the Late 19th and Early 20th Centuries

John C. Swanson

Abstract

In this paper John C. Swanson examines the work of organizations and individuals in the German Empire and in Cisleithanian Austria to "defend" the rural German speakers in inner Hungary during the late nineteenth and early twentieth centuries. "Germans" in Germany and Austria felt a duty to guide and protect their ethnic brethren and to prevent them from being magyarized. Swanson argues that what took place at that time was a series of negotiations between new notions of Germanness brought to the rural communities and local concepts of Germanness based on an understanding of tangible belonging. He describes the work of various organizations, and he focuses on the attempt by the circulation of the German-Hungarian catechism to challenge the rural German speakers to think in a new way about what their Germanness meant.

What took place during the late nineteenth and early twentieth centuries in Hungary could be explained as a transformation of "peasants into Germans" (and for some of them: "peasants into Hungarians") or "German-speaking Hungarians into Volksdeutsche", yet I do not see a simple shift from a premodern identity to a modern one or from an ethnic identity to a civic one or even vice versa. A process definitely took place in rural Hungary, but it could not be described as such a linear process. What I saw in the documents, in my discussions, and in the communities was an on-going struggle between different forms of thinking and different ways of understanding oneself, one's neighbours, as well as the immediate and wider world.

I discovered at the rural level—in the villages where German speakers lived—a kind of tangible belonging: by the late nineteenth century people understood themselves as Germans, but that sense of being German was local. Their identity was from the "centre looking out", instead of from "borders looking in".[1] Because we know that things changed and that some German speakers clearly developed a sense of belonging to the wider German Volk, I then tried to discover what kind of ideas, concepts, new ways of thinking arrived in the villages and encouraged rural dwellers to think differently. I found new, more abstract ideas about Germanness coming to the rural communities from a new Hungarian-German leadership (often people who came from these villages but lived in Budapest), from the Hungarian state, and from Germany. (Borrowing terminology from Rogers Brubaker's triadic nexus we could see two of these as "the nationalizing state" and "homeland nationalism".)[2] In this paper I will discuss only the new notions of Germanness brought to the rural communities in Hungary from the German Reich and to a smaller extent from Cisleithanian Austria.

In early 2002 I travelled to the small community of Nagynyárád in southern Hungary, where I met Antal Weisz, more commonly known as *Tóni bácsi* [uncle Tóni]. I was there to talk to him about German life in the village: before, during, and after the Second World War. Tóni bácsi talked for hours. He told me about his family's loyalty to Hungary, about the hardships they had to endure as Germans, and about a better time before the war.

The story about his grandfather's education was among the most intriguing that I heard. Born in 1868 into a Swabian, Catholic peasant family speaking German at home, Tóni's grandfather was sent to Nagyharsány as a young boy to learn Magyar. This practice was traditional: children—mainly boys, though not just boys—were placed in neighboring villages to learn a different language. The affair was often reciprocal, with Hungarian children in turn coming to German communities. *Tóni bácsi* could not tell me very much about the tradition. He guessed that it had faded out in his home village by the early twentieth century, when Magyar became the language of instruction in the village elementary school.

It was exactly this type of activity that worried and even terrified German speakers throughout Central and Eastern Europe. The thought of Antal Weisz's grandfather learning Magyar in Nagyharsány would have angered a great number of people in the late nineteenth century, specifically Reich Germans and German Austrians. Many of these overly conscious Germans worried about losing their ethnic kin to the Magyar cause. Sending children to learn Magyar and letting them live outside the German world would have been seen as capitulation in the battle against magyarization. Germandom needed to be protected. The vanguard of the Volk in Germany and Cisleithania began to organize and propose programs to prevent assimilation, to reach out to their brethren abroad, and to awaken them. They formed so-called protection organizations (*Schutzvereine*), and although much of their activity in the late nineteenth and early twentieth centuries

1 For a longer explanation of "tangible belonging", see John C. Swanson, *Tangible Belonging: Negotiating Germanness in Twentieth-Century Hungary*, Pittsburgh 2017.

2 Rogers Brubaker, *Nationalism Reframed: Nationhood and the National Question in the New Europe*, Cambridge 1996.

focused on developing and fostering German education, they financially supported other projects as well.[3]

Interest in "Germans in an alien world" [*Deutsche in der Fremde*] dates back to before the formation of the German Empire in 1871. In the 1840s writers, including Wilhelm Stricker in *Die Verbreitung des deutschen Volkes über die Erde*, were writing about Germans abroad [*Auslandsdeutsche*].[4] Yet, most "pan-German" activity took root in the late nineteenth century, as Germans in the new Germany and in Cisleithanian Austria saw German communities abroad as "outposts in a hostile environment".[5] During the 1880s in the western half of the Habsburg Monarchy, especially in its capital city of Vienna, various associations materialized, such as the All German Movement [*Alldeutsche Bewegung*] of Georg Ritter von Schönerer, which devoted attention to Germans across Cisleithania.[6] As many German speakers throughout the Habsburg lands grew disillusioned in the late nineteenth century because of the empire's concessions to non-German nationalities, they often oriented themselves toward the new German Reich.[7] Germany began to take on a more seminal role after 1871, as "Germans" sought to redefine Germandom and to distinguish those who belonged from those who did not.

One of the leading protection organizations in the late nineteenth and early twentieth centuries was the German School Association [*Deutscher Schulverein*], which aimed at establishing and supporting German schools abroad in order to preserve Germandom outside the German Reich.[8] It dispersed funds to assist schools and libraries, as well as to provide scholarships.[9] In actuality, there were two German School Associations. The first one was founded on 13 May 1880 in the Austrian half of the Habsburg Monarchy and focused on the German school question in Cisleithania, initially in South Tyrol. Its founding members believed that education in the mother tongue should not be left to the state but needed to be supported by independent organizations such as the German School Association.[10] One of the new organization's many chapters, the Universal German

3 The Bauernbund, for example, received at least moral assistance from both Germany and Austria. Paul GINDER, *Ein verhinderter Demokratisierungsversuch im Vorkriegsungarn: Aus der Geschichte des deutschungarischen Bauernbundes von Bonnhard/Bonyhád 1908–1921*, Suevia Pannonica 7, 1989, No. 17, p. 121.

4 Ernst RITTER, *Das Deutsche Ausland-Institut in Stuttgart 1917–1945: Ein Beispiel deutscher Volkstumsarbeit zwischen den Weltkriegen*, Wiesbaden 1976, pp. 6–7.

5 See Max Hildebert BOEHM, *Das Volkstum des Grenz- und Auslanddeutschtums*, in: Ingeborg Weber-Kellermann (ed.), Zur Interethnik: Donauschwaben, Siebenbürger Sachsen und Ihre Nachbarn, Frankfurt a. M. 1978, pp. 93ff.

6 The tensions in Cisleithania increased after Austro-German protests broke out in 1897 over a new ordinance establishing Czech, alongside German, as an official administrative language in Bohemia and Moravia. A. J. P. TAYLOR, *The Habsburg Monarchy 1809–1918*, New York 1948, pp. 181ff.

7 R. BRUBAKER, *Nationalism Reframed*, 115. See also Rudolf JAWORSKI, *Vorposten oder Minderheit? Der sudetendeutsche Volkstumskampf in den Beziehungen zwischen der Weimarer Republik und der ČSR*, Stuttgart 1977, pp. 34–35.

8 Otto DANN, *Nation und Nationalismus in Deutschland 1770–1990*, Munich 1993, p. 191.

9 E. RITTER, *Das Deutsche Ausland-Institut*, p. 19.

10 Norbert PROHASKA, *Der Deutsche Schulverein: Beiträge zum 120. Gründungstag*, Vienna 2000, pp. 4–5.

School Association [*Allgemeiner Deutscher Schulverein*], established in Berlin in 1881, was particularly interested in the school question in Hungary. (Its founding members had already carried out an investigative journey to Transylvania in 1875.[11])

The Berlin association aspired to extend the work of the organization to Germans beyond Austria—beyond Cisleithania—to Germans throughout the world.[12] The Kingdom of Hungary, with more than 2.5 million German speakers, figured prominently in this context. As German speakers began to organize in Hungary, especially in Transylvania but also in regions around Budapest and in the south, they provided more reasons for Reich Germans to lend support. The Hungarian-German People's Party [*Ungarländische Deutsche Volkspartei*], for instance, received funding from the Berlin-based organization.[13] Reich Germans strove to assist Germans abroad (whom they saw as their brothers and sisters) in strengthening their Germanness and awakening their "unconscious" neighbors. In November 1881 the Universal German School Association formulated its perspective in an open letter:

> Above all, it is the Germans in Hungary and Transylvania who need our help. Despite legal guarantees for the equality of languages, the dominant Magyar minority has for the last few years worked diligently to destroy German education in the lands of the Hungarian crown. (...) Therefore the Magyar should thank the Germans not only that they brought about freedom from the Turkish domination but also that the light of European culture has reached the Hungarian lands. (...) The organization of the Allgemeiner Deutscher Schulverein would like to be in the position to construct a shield that could be activated wherever modern barbarism threatens the areas of German culture (*Bildung*).[14]

The goals and activity of the Universal German School Association, however, were not always compatible with the desires of those affected. Hungarian publications heavily criticized the organization for dictating to Germans outside of Germany. Ambros Neményi in 1882 pointed out that there were no Hungarian Germans and no Saxons in the organization in Berlin. It was composed only of Reich Germans, whose goal it was to save the

11 Jonathan Kwan mentions both Wilhelm Wattenbach and Wilhelm Groos as founding members. Jonathan KWAN, *Transylvanian Saxon Politics, Hungarian State Building and German Public Opinion: The Case of the Allgemeine Deutscher Schulverein Scandal (1882)*, unpublished paper, p. 16.

12 Erwin BARTA—Karl BELL, *Geschichte der Schutzarbeit am Deutschen Volkstum*, Dresden 1930, p. 117.

13 Günter SCHÖDL, *Alldeutscher Verband und deutsche Minderheitenpolitik in Ungarn, 1890–1914: Zur Geschichte des deutschen "Extremen Nationalismus"*, Frankfurt a. M. 1978, p. 9.

14 Quoted in Gerhard WEIDENFELLER, *VDA, Verein für das Deutschtum im Ausland, Allgemeiner Deutscher Schulverein (1881–1918): Ein Beitrag zur Geschichte des deutschen Nationalismus und Imperialismus im Kaiserreich*, Frankfurt a. M. 1976, p. 172.

Germans abroad, ignoring the fact that they had never asked for assistance.[15] There is also absolutely no evidence that the efforts of the organization reached the rural German-speaking population of inner Hungary.

Other political organizations, such as the Pan-German League [*Alldeutscher Verband*], also took an interest in Central Europe.[16] The league initially concerned itself with colonial questions, but after 1900 its attention turned to Germans in Austria-Hungary as it strove to move toward an "all German unity" [*alldeutsche Einheit*] in cultural, economic, and political affairs.[17] The Pan-German League's declared mission was "the care and support of German national efforts in all countries where members of our Volk struggle for their uniqueness, and the aggregation of all Germans in the world for this goal".[18] But like the Universal German School Association, the Pan-German League did not seem to reach the German-speaking villagers of Hungary either, especially those in inner Hungary.

Yet another organization that strove to improve the conditions for German life in Hungary, the Association for the Preservation of Germandom in Hungary [*Verein zur Erhaltung des Deutschtums in Ungarn*], was founded in 1907 in Vienna. It was one of the few Austro-German organizations that focused on Hungarian Germans. (Much of its attention fell on the Germans in western Hungary, but it did reach out to all Germans in the country.) The first issue of its quarterly journal *Deutsch-Ungarn* listed its ten goals.[19] The first goal was "the encouragement of German education as the most important educational tool of the Volk", while its practical objectives included helping Hungarian-German peasants get a fair price for their goods, providing housing for German apprentices, artisans, and merchants, and trying to halt the emigration of Germans from Hungary or at least steer migration toward German states. The last goal—"an important duty"—was to distribute "true reports" concerning the almost "daily violence" against the Germans in Hungary.[20]

Like the members and leadership of the Universal German School Association and the Pan-German League, those who supported and belonged to the Association for the Preservation of Germandom in Hungary were (I would argue) more concerned about their own Germanness than about Germans in Hungary. They strove to enlarge their own world through their preoccupation with faraway brethren: their primary motive was

15 Ambros NEMÉNYI, *Hungaricae Res: Ein Commentar zu dem Aufruf des "Allgemeinen deutschen Schulvereins" in Angelegenheit der Unterdrückung der Deutschen in Ungarn und Siebenbürgen*, Budapest 1882.

16 Before 1894 the organization was known as the Allgemeiner Deutscher Verband. Ritter has described its work as more political compared to that of the Allgemeiner Deutscher Schulverein. E. RITTER, *Das Deutsche Ausland-Institut*, pp. 18–19.

17 G. SCHÖDL, *Alldeutscher Verband*, p. 13.

18 Quoted in Friedrich GOTTAS, *Die Deutschen in Ungarn*, in: Adam Wandruszka—Peter Urbanitsch (eds.), Die Habsburgermonarchie, 1848–1918, vol. 3, *Die Völker des Reiches*, Wien 1980, p. 404.

19 According to the card catalog in the Austrian National Library in Vienna, the German-language *Deutsch-Ungarn* was published between 1912 and 1919, but the library had volumes from only 1912 and 1913. I have been unable to find other volumes in Budapest or in Germany.

20 *Deutsch-Ungarn*, no. 1, 1912.

to enrich the meaning of their own Germandom as they played the benefactor in others' lives. They blamed themselves for allowing conditions to deteriorate to the extent that had occurred in Hungary (as a result of the magyarization efforts) and for the lack of a unified Germandom in the country. An article in the first issue of *Deutsch-Ungarn* argued that the real objective was to "build a unified [German] consciousness (...). Every member of the Volk who has been lucky enough to feel what it means to be German will care, according to his own ability, to help awaken and strengthen Germandom in Hungary."[21] The association established local chapters in Vienna and throughout Austria. There was even a chapter in Chicago, where its members proclaimed: "We are and will remain German!"[22] The chapters raised money for their projects. A two-heller stamp was circulated in Austria after 1908 with the name of the organization at the top, an image of a young man in the middle, and the statement "Here the German will not die—trust therein!" at the bottom.

Scholarly publications and more literary ones also appeared in the late nineteenth and early twentieth centuries, with the purpose of informing the German and Austro-German public of the oppressive conditions that their "unconscious" fellow Germans faced in places such as Hungary. Booklets, like those published in 1874 by Guido von Baußern and Franz Löhrer, were neither very popular nor very influential.[23] That situation had changed by the early twentieth century, when works about fellow Germans found a wider audience. One of the most significant authors was Adam Müller-Guttenbrunn (1854–1923)—a Danube Swabian from the Banat who spent much of his adult life in Vienna. Müller-Guttenbrunn used his talents to educate Germans in Germany and Austria, as well as to awaken the "unconscious" Germans in Hungary. One of his most powerful novels was *Götzendämmerung* [Twilight of the idols], the title being identical to that of a work by Nietzsche, which in turn alludes to Wagner's opera *Götterdämmerung* [Twilight of the gods]. The book was based on the political conditions of 1905–1906 in Hungary, specifically the franchise, and it suggests that no resolution to the social question would be possible without a solution to the nationality question. It is a literary work that plays on the emotions of the reader, which is somewhat disturbing for the twenty-first-century mind. Quite by accident but exactly a hundred years after its publication I read *Götzendämmerung* in the Austrian National Library in Vienna. Much more than I expected, I was drawn to the characters, to the feeling of loss and oppression that the protagonists faced, even though some of the language was somewhat farcical. On almost every page was an instance of the Germans of Hungary being mocked and humiliated for being German. If I, in 2007, was inadvertently moved by the pompous style of Müller-Guttenbrunn, I can only imagine what readers in the early twentieth century must have experienced.

Rural Swabian readers of Müller-Guttenbrunn's works, however, must have been few and far between, due to the protection organizations' lack of direct contact with inner

21 *Deutsch-Ungarn*, no. 1, 1912.

22 *Deutsch-Ungarn*, no. 3, 1912.

23 Baußern wrote a pamphlet titled *Das Erwürgen der deutschen Nationalität in Ungarn*, and Franz Löhrer's book carried the title *Die Magyaren und andere Ungarn*. F. Gottas, *Die Deutschen in Ungarn*, p. 393.

Hungary. More than likely most of this type of literature, including *Götzendämmerung*, never reached them. We do know that publications, including school material, sent to rural communities were often confiscated by the Hungarian authorities, since Hungarian civil servants monitored all mail and packages. Anything that could be seen as pan-German agitation faced fierce opposition and rarely reached the general public.[24] Receiving publications considered to be pan-German was treason. And locals were fearful. For example, when a fifty-kilogram box containing approximately sixty German-language books and journals arrived on the doorstep of the innkeeper in the village of Tevel in 1912, he became nervous. The return address read "Vienna Women's and Girls' Chapter of the Association for the Preservation of Germandom in Hungary". The innkeeper immediately sought out the school director of the village, Stefan Kirez, who also served as president of the local reading association. The problem was obvious. Receiving books from such an organization would be seen as a betrayal of the fatherland. To make matters worse, some of the publications were anti-Hungarian, and one of them stated that to be a member of the Association for the Preservation of Germandom in Hungary one must be an "Aryan" (meaning German). The school director wrote to the unknown sender that such anti-Hungarian books were not welcome in Tevel. In reply, Elle Triebnigg, herself a Tevel native living in Vienna, offered an apology for having sent the anti-Hungarian material.[25]

The exact details of the reception that projects of the Universal German School Association, the Pan-German League, or the Association for the Preservation of Germandom in Hungary found in the rural Swabian villages will probably never be entirely clear. Whether a rejection of anti-Hungarian sentiments was solely due to fear of retaliation or to some extent reflected true sentiments is very much open to interpretation. But whatever information reached these German speakers from and about the protection organizations, it must have gradually established a foundation for the subsequent espousal of an alternative worldview. We must assume that the shift away from a local, tangible identity and toward a larger and more abstract one was preceded by a period when information about a united German group was trickling into the villages and slowly taking effect until at some point it became self-evident. That process must have intensified somewhat around this time, when the protection organizations countered magyarization efforts with attempts to germanize German-speaking peasants. As the Swabians were being courted by powerful contenders in the relentless game called nationalism, the idea must have begun to crystallize in their minds that there were now alternatives to choose from and that it was time to start weighing the advantages of each.

One of the pieces of literature (or propaganda, depending on the point of view) that we know to have reached the villages and to have had an influence on rural German speakers was the *Deutschungarischer Katechismus* [German-Hungarian catechism], written by

24 F. Gottas, *Die Deutschen in Ungarn*, p. 394.

25 Johann Eppel (ed.), *Tevel: Zweieinhalb Jahrhunderte schwäbische Ortsgeschichte in Ungarn, 1701–1948*, Budapest 1988, pp. 366.

Otto Hermann Krause in 1906 and circulated in the villages of southern Hungary in late 1907.[26] These instructions on how to be German took the form of a religious document—the question-and-answer format of the catechism—which was meant to appeal to the mindset of pious peasants and artisans in inner Hungary.[27] The language of the catechism was accessible to rural dwellers: it was straightforward and repetitive. The text was written with "peasant shrewdness", in their own "rough peasant tongue", according to Paul Ginder.[28] German-speaking villagers read it, memorized it, and passed it on.[29]

The first question inquired, "What is a German-Hungarian [*Deutschungar*]?" The answer: "Every German who is born in Hungary is a Deutschungar."[30] The catechism evidently dismissed the complexity of this question and implied that Germans were Germans and Hungarians were Hungarians. They were two separate groups based on actual differences. One's sense of self was to be defined by being German, not by living in Hungary. And being German meant not only being distinct but also being superior to others. Hungarians may have created the Kingdom of Hungary, but the catechism instructed its reader that the culture in Hungary was purely German, since the country had no culture before the arrival of the Germans.

The language of the catechism may have been simple and repetitive, yet it was anything but precise. The booklet employed expressions such as nation, race, and Volk to mean similar things that were differentiated from each other in a randomly artificial way. Nation, for example, usually referred to groups in Hungary that were not Hungarian, which most literature in the early twentieth century would have called nationalities. Germans were a nation, just like Serbs, Croats, Slovenes, Italians, Romanians, Ruthenians, Slovaks, Bulgarians, Armenians, Gypsies, and Jews. (It should be pointed out that the catechism separated Gypsies and Jews as distinct nations, although Hungarian and German propaganda did not always do so.) Magyars were sometimes a nation, but most often a race or a Volk—two concepts that were frequently used as synonyms but never clarified. Hungary, according to the language of the catechism, was simply the country and Magyar, the race (or *Volk*). To a certain extent, this treatment foreshadows the later practice many scholars used to distinguish Hungarians from Magyars, and the catechism went so far as to contend that Hungary should be called *Ungarország* (land of the Hungarians—a combination of the German word for "Hungarian" and the Hungarian word for "country"), not *Magyarország* (land of the Magyars).

---

26 Initially the catechism's author was unknown, but later it was found to have been Krausz, who lived in Pomáz, near Budapest. P. GINDER, *Ein verhinderter Demokratisierungsversuch*, p. 121.

27 The majority of the villagers were familiar with similar religious documents. Péter GUNST, *Die bäuerliche Gesellschaft Ungarns in der Zeit zwischen den beiden Weltkriegen*, Budapest 1991, pp. 218–219.

28 P. GINDER, *Ein verhinderter Demokratisierungsversuch*, p. 121. See also F. GOTTAS, *Die Deutschen in Ungarn*, p. 400.

29 Harold STEINACKER, *Aus den Anfängen der deutschen Bewegung im Vorkriegsungarn: Der Deutschungarische Katechismus von 1907*, Südostdeutsches Archiv 2, 1959, p. 53.

30 For a discussion of the difference between German Hungarian [*Deutsch-Ungar*] and Hungarian German [*Ungarndeutsch*] see J. SWANSON, *Tangible Belonging*.

The catechism confused its readers by contradicting itself in many ways, always with the intention of separating German speakers from Magyar ones. If Hungary was the land of the Hungarians, not of the ethnic Magyars, and Germans were a nation in Hungary, then Germans should logically have been Hungarians, but at times the catechism argued against this view. If Germans voiced the intention to become Hungarian [*Ungar*], which from certain sections of the catechism we may conclude to be acceptable, they were all of a sudden declared to be "dumb, narrow-minded, and foolish". If a Hungarian defiled a German by calling him a stupid Swabian, a Swabian pig, or a Swabian dog [*buta sváb, disznó sváb*, or *kutya sváb*], then, according to the catechism, the German was to "give the person a good Swabian slap in the face". At the same time, if someone told him that he was not a German but rather a Swabian, he was to answer that he had "never heard such a stupid thing. The Swabian is German."[31]

Literature such as the German-Hungarian catechism encouraged people to think in rigid categories, but without supplying an adequate explanation of what those represented. If I abandon my search for linguistic rationale, however, I can find a certain logical pattern in the general format—the religious model. Emulating the laws given to Moses by God, the catechism proclaimed the ten commandments of the German Hungarian:

1. Speak, where you can, only German.
2. Marry only a German girl.
3. Speak only German with your children. Teach them to pray only in German, and strive to send them to German schools, and when there is no such school in your community, send them to schools where German is also taught.
4. Uphold your religion and respect the religion of others. But attend only German mass and German sermons.
5. Be upstanding and honest, so that everyone, even those speaking other languages, respects you as a German.
6. Respect the language of others who also respect your language.
7. In the local community house you should speak only German, and you should tolerate only a notary who can also understand German.
8. Speak only German with your servants, since those who eat of my bread should speak with me only in my language.
9. Obtain a respectable German newspaper.
10. Do not get corrupted during the representative elections. Give your vote only to someone who publicly states that he will fight for the rights of the Germans.

In a religious mode, the catechism presents language and blood as the icons of salvation. Mother tongue and blood [*Muttersprache* and *Mutterblut*] were sacrosanct: "holier than religion". To be Catholic was a choice, to be German was ordained by God. God provided one with language and blood, and a violation of either was a sin in the eyes of

31 This and all subsequent direct references to the catechism come from H. Steinacker, *Aus den Anfängen der deutschen Bewegung*, pp. 61ff.

the Almighty: "One can change his beliefs, but not his language or blood." This type of rhetoric resonated with the pious rural German speakers, as they began to contemplate their loyalties to the German Volk.

We know that the German-Hungarian catechism was delivered to parts of Hungary in late 1907 and early 1908, often in packages with the return address of Vienna, Müller & Hagemann.[32] Frequently, the local notaries and gendarmes monitored these packages and confiscated them, as well as threatened the recipients.[33] Some feared repercussions and either avoided reading the catechism (for this we have no evidence) or returned it, as did the innkeeper in Tevel, while others read it with great interest. According to Paul Ginder, the catechism was "studied" [*einstudiert*] and passed on.[34] There are letters in support of the catechism—sent from various Hungarian Germans to the publisher of the booklet—which Harold Steinacker cites in his 1959 article about the origins of the German movement in Hungary. The letters came from all over, a few from inner Hungary. Wilhelm Plesz, a twenty-three-year-old living in Bikal, in Baranya county, wrote that he had been moved by the publication and that he would try to pass it and its message on to others. He considered it a "guide for his adult life". He also requested additional material. Another letter sent by a group of men in Szentendre, near Budapest, thanked the sender for the booklet but bemoaned that it had arrived too late: Germans in Hungary had already become slaves to the Magyars; no one cared that they were Germans. Others, such as the letter writer in Mágocs (Baranya county), also complained that too many Germans in his village and the neighboring ones just wanted to become Hungarians.[35]

The effectiveness of German propaganda was undoubtedly limited at first, but the terms of the later full-blown struggle over the interpretation of Germanness were being established during this period, as Reich German and Austrian protection organizations took an interest in the German-speaking peasants of Hungary. The opportunity arose now for rural Swabians to be members of a community of Germans that was larger than that of Hungarian Germandom, a community based solely on ancestry rather than citizenship. This idea sparked the imagination of some Swabians, as they read with enthusiasm pieces of literature and propaganda such as the German-Hungarian catechism.

32 F. Gottas, *Die Deutschen in Ungarn*, p. 400; H. Steinacker, *Aus den Anfängen der deutschen Bewegung*, p. 53.

33 H. Steinacker, *Aus den Anfängen der deutschen Bewegung*, p. 53.

34 P. Ginder, *Ein verhinderter Demokratisierungsversuch*, p. 121.

35 H. Steinacker, *Aus den Anfängen der deutschen Bewegung*, pp. 79ff.

Bibliography

Erwin BARTA—Karl BELL, *Geschichte der Schutzarbeit am Deutschen Volkstum*, Dresden 1930.

Max Hildebert BOEHM, *Das Volkstum des Grenz- und Auslanddeutschtums*, in: Ingeborg Weber-Kellermann (ed.), Zur Interethnik: Donauschwaben, Siebenbürger Sachsen und Ihre Nachbarn, Frankfurt a. M. 1978, pp. 78–94.

Rogers BRUBAKER, *Nationalism Reframed: Nationhood and the National Question in the New Europe*, Cambridge 1996.

Otto DANN, *Nation und Nationalismus in Deutschland 1770–1990*, Munich 1993.

Johann EPPEL (ed.), *Tevel: Zweieinhalb Jahrhunderte schwäbische Ortsgeschichte in Ungarn, 1701–1948*, Budapest 1988.

Paul GINDER, *Ein verhinderter Demokratisierungsversuch im Vorkriegsungarn: Aus der Geschichte des deutschungarischen Bauernbundes von Bonnhard/Bonyhád 1908–1921*, Suevia Pannonica 7, 1989, No. 17, pp. 120–138.

Friedrich GOTTAS, *Die Deutschen in Ungarn*, in: Adam Wandruszka—Peter Urbanitsch (eds.), Die Habsburgermonarchie, 1848–1918, vol. 3, *Die Völker des Reiches*, Wien 1980.

Péter GUNST, *Die bäuerliche Gesellschaft Ungarns in der Zeit zwischen den beiden Weltkriegen*, Budapest 1991.

Rudolf JAWORSKI, *Vorposten oder Minderheit? Der sudetendeutsche Volkstumskampf in den Beziehungen zwischen der Weimarer Republik und der ČSR*, Stuttgart 1977.

Jonathan KWAN, *Transylvanian Saxon Politics, Hungarian State Building and German Public Opinion: The Case of the Allgemeine Deutscher Schulverein Scandal (1882)*, unpublished paper.

Ambros NEMÉNYI, *Hungaricae Res: Ein Commentar zu dem Aufruf des "Allgemeinen deutschen Schulvereins" in Angelegenheit der Unterdrückung der Deutschen in Ungarn und Siebenbürgen*, Budapest 1882.

Norbert PROHASKA, *Der Deutsche Schulverein: Beiträge zum 120. Gründungstag*, Vienna 2000.

Ernst RITTER, *Das Deutsche Ausland-Institut in Stuttgart 1917–1945: Ein Beispiel deutscher Volkstumsarbeit zwischen den Weltkriegen*, Wiesbaden 1976.

Günter SCHÖDL, *Alldeutscher Verband und deutsche Minderheitenpolitik in Ungarn, 1890–1914: Zur Geschichte des deutschen "Extremen Nationalismus"*, Frankfurt a. M. 1978.

Harold STEINACKER, *Aus den Anfängen der deutschen Bewegung im Vorkriegsungarn: Der Deutschungarische Katechismus von 1907*, Südostdeutsches Archiv 2, 1959, pp. 48–49.

John C. SWANSON, *Tangible Belonging: Negotiating Germanness in Twentieth-Century Hungary*, Pittsburgh 2017.

A. J. P. TAYLOR, *The Habsburg Monarchy 1809–1918*, New York 1948.

Gerhard WEIDENFELLER, *VDA, Verein für das Deutschtum im Ausland, Allgemeiner Deutscher Schulverein (1881–1918): Ein Beitrag zur Geschichte des deutschen Nationalismus und Imperialismus im Kaiserreich*, Frankfurt a. M. 1976.

Subjects or Citizens?
Party Politics and the Peasants' Right to Vote in Romania (1866–1918)

Sorin Radu

Abstract

In Romania, the construction of democracy went hand in hand with the foundation of the modern state (1859), with the Occident serving as the main model for political elites. The 1866 Constitution instituted a modern political system based on the separation of state powers and censitary suffrage, which was essentially a reflection of the division of Romanian society: on the one hand, a small rich and educated elite, and on the other hand, a poor rural class with very limited education, but with an overwhelming demographic significance. An interesting ideological debate took place at the end of the 19th century in Romania on the theme of electoral reform, concerning the limitation of the number of electoral colleges, moving away from censitary suffrage, and even than the enactment of universal suffrage. Our study focused on the debate between the political parties on electoral reform and analyses the projects of social and political emancipation of the peasants until the Great War.

In the second half of the 19th century, Romania began to rapidly catch up with European civilization in terms of economic, social and political life. A strategy of modernization was developed and implemented by the Liberals and Conservatives. Although the two parties differed in terms of methods and pace of modernization, they complemented each other in the administration of the country, which benefited modernization.[1] It was against this background that an intense debate took place regarding how modern Romania should move forward. Parties, political groups and leading personalities of the time were involved in this argument. The problems they debated and tried to solve were diverse: agrarian relations, industrialization, cultural development, political system, and status of the peasants.

---

1 Gheorghe Iacob—Luminiţa Iacob, *Modernizare—europenism. România de la Cuza Vodă la Carol al II-lea*, vol. 1, *Ritmul şi strategia modernizării*, Iaşi, 1995, pp. 135, 136.

In this context, the democratization of electoral legislation in terms of extending the franchise was of key importance. As the voting qualification requirements established by electoral law were very high, over 90% of the population could not participate in public affairs. Corruption in the electoral colleges was notoriously widespread and many people believed that this problem had to be dealt with in order to get Romania out of its crisis and speed up modernization. Limiting the number of electoral colleges and lowering the requirements for voting—extending even as far as universal suffrage—were identified as the only ways to bring democracy to political life. Electoral reform could provide the stimulus to improve social, economic and political conditions in Romania. The parties which were in favour of such change (the Liberal Party and the Social Democratic Party) had different views on the franchise extension and they also faced a strong opponent in the Conservative Party. They were opposed to the extension of the electorate, believing that the peasants were not ready and that universal suffrage would bring anarchy to the country.

The debate on the extension of electoral rights became even more interesting when it was discovered that no common view prevailed among those who favoured the democratization of the franchise. There were differences of opinions between the National Liberal Party and the Social Democratic Workers' Party in Romania concerning the extension of electoral reform and the tactics to be pursued to achieve it.

Changing the electoral system in order for the peasants to gain the right to vote—which was also common in other European countries—became one of Romania's major problems in the 20th century, which needed a rapid solution. The debate around the reform and the modernization of the electoral system, allowing the peasants to become voters, took place in the press, in Parliament, and through the publication of pamphlets, organizing conferences and public meetings, and involved the political and cultural elite of the time.

Regulating the Right to Vote in Romanian Principalities

At the beginning of the 19th century in the Romanian principalities (Moldova and Wallachia), the concepts of democracy, elections, voters, and representation were still imprecise and not understood by most of the political elite. *The Organic Regulations* of 1831 (drawn up under the guidance of Russia which had occupied the principalities) regulated for the first time the conditions for organizing a legislative body by establishing an elected assembly [*Obşteasca Adunare*]. The conditions for voters and candidates were established, providing at the same time sanctions against those who perpetrated fraud or violated electoral rules. Naturally, this legislative assembly represented the interests of the high nobility and high clergy, while the criteria for voting were wealth and rank. The programme of the revolutionaries of 1848 included the introduction of modern principles of representative governance based on the separation of state powers and a substantial extension of the franchise. The *Wishes of the National Party* as well as the *Constitutional Project for Moldova,* drawn up by Mihail Kogălniceanu, called for a general assembly made up of representatives from all the social classes based on the principle of the civil and political equality of citizens. Among its 22 points, the Proclamation of Islaz also demanded equality of political rights; a general assembly made up of representatives from all the classes, and universal suffrage. The defeat of the revolutions in Moldova and Wallachia postponed this programme of reform. The Treaty of Paris of 1856 concluded between France, England, Austria, Prussia, Sardinia and Turkey on one side, and Russia on the other, established the political and electoral regime for the Romanian principalities. The treaty imposed the convocation of an *ad hoc* assembly in each principality, which would decide the definitive organization of the two countries. The electoral colleges were convened in January 1857 in order to establish the *ad hoc* divans. Despite the limitations, the election of representatives from various social classes was an important benchmark in the history of the representative regime. In spite of the fact that the divans were consultative rather than legislative assemblies, and that their existence was the result of the will of foreign powers, the fact that representatives from all of the classes of the nation were reunited in the same assembly was something new and had positive consequences for the period which followed immediately after.[2]

The Paris Convention of August 1858, which was to debate the will of the Romanian population as expressed through the *ad hoc* divans, introduced modern principles for the separation of state powers and representative governance. In each principality, public power was entrusted to the prince and an elected assembly. Legislative power was granted to the elected assembly, which was chosen for a seven-year term. The convention had several annexes, some of them representing electoral law for an elected assembly in each principality composed of members chosen for each district and town by citizens who were divided into primary or direct electors. The former had an income of 100 ducats; those in the second category either had an income of 1,000 ducats or—in the towns—financial, industrial and commercial capital worth 6,000 ducats. To be eligible to vote, you had to be over 25, hold Moldavan-Wallachian citizenship and be of the Christian faith. The elected assemblies performed the function of the Parliament—voting on and adopting laws which were later sanctioned by the prince. These electoral provisions allowed access for only a very small elite into the electoral body.[3] Despite this, the Paris Convention was of great signif-

---

2 Alexandru Dimitrie XENOPOL, *Primul proiect de Constituţie a Moldovei din 1822. Originile Partidului Conservator şi ale celui Liberal*, Bucureşti 1898, pp. 23–28; Alexandru Dimitrie XENOPOL, *Istoria partidelor politice în România. De al origini pînă la 1848*, vol. 1, part 1, Bucureşti 1910, pp. 230–233; D. V. BARNOVSCHI, *Originile democraţiei române. "Cărvunarii". Constituţia Moldovei de la 1822*, Iaşi 1922, pp. 110–257; Eugen LOVINESCU, *Istoria civilizaţiei române moderne*, Bucureşti 1997, pp. 36, 50–51, 71, 106–109, 134–136; Jean C. FILITTI, *Des origines du régime représentatif en Roumanie*, Bucureşti 1931, pp. 3–11; Ilie GĂNESCU—Constantin Gr. ZOTTA—Alexandru KOSTACHI, *Dreptul electoral român*, Bucureşti 1937, pp. 10–12; Dan BERINDEI (ed.), *Istoria românilor*, vol. 7, part 1, *Constituirea României moderne (1821–1878)*, Bucureşti 2003, pp. 67–69; 83–88.

3 Eleodor FOCŞENEANU, *Istoria constituţională a României 1859–1991*, Bucureşti 1992, pp. 19, 20; Apostol STAN, *Putere politică şi democraţie în România 1859–1918*, Bucureşti 1995, pp. 9–12; Georges M. LAHOVARY, *Histoire d'une fiction. Gouvernement des Partis*, Bucarest 1887, pp. 175, 176; Gheorghe TĂTĂRESCU, *Regimul electoral şi parlamentar în România*, Bucureşti 2004, pp. 24–26.

icance as it created the foundations of the nation state in 1859 as well as the constitutional framework for its development.

When Romania became a nation state following the unification of Moldova and Wallachia in 1859, the mechanisms for organizing and modernizing the country became a controversial political issue between the conservative groups, which the electoral system favoured, and the liberals, who advocated the democratization of the political regime. The prince's desire to modernize the country was opposed by the elected assembly, which mainly represented the interests of the aristocracy.[4] As a result, he launched an initiative to implement structural reforms in the Romanian society which included electoral reform. In May 1864, Prince Alexandru Ioan Cuza had the *Expanding Statute of the Convention of Paris, 19th of August 1858,* and the reform of the electoral law validated by a plebiscite. The statute, which had the force of a basic law, and the electoral institution remained in place until the Constituent Assembly voted for a new electoral law in 1866. Cuza's statute introduced a bicameral legislature made up of the Moderating Body and the Chamber of Deputies. The electoral body was divided into two colleges, each one with two categories of voters based on income and wealth. The colleges sent two categories of deputies to the chamber: from the towns and the counties. Each of these two colleges was made up of primary and direct voters. In order to be a primary voter, a tax of 80 lei had to be paid in towns of up to 15,000 inhabitants, and a tax of 110 lei in the larger towns. The peasants had to pay a tax of 48 lei. Their vote was indirect; one hundred voters appointed a delegate who voted for a deputy. Direct voters were men who paid a contribution of at least four golden coins (1,200 francs) in the municipality where they lived, knew how to read and write and were over 25 years of age, as well as intellectuals and pensioners with a minimum pension of 2,000 lei per year. Those eligible had to have an income of at least 2,400 francs and there was a secret ballot for direct voters, but not for the primary ones. The Moderating Body consisted of members by right and 64 members appointed by the prince.[5]

The franchise law designed by Cuza obviously led to a slight increase in the number of those who could vote, but due to the absence of data we cannot give a precise percentage by which this number grew.[6] Cuza's reforms opened the way for modernization in all fields of public life and created the foundation for the development of new political life. Nonetheless, the democratization of the political regime was still at an early stage. The restrictive electoral provisions imposed by the Paris Convention were replaced in 1864 by a more lenient franchise law—but which allowed the executive power to interfere in the development of democratic political activity. This limited the proper functioning of

4 A. Stan, *Putere politică şi democraţie în România*, pp. 13–15.

5 Mattei Dogan, *Analiza statistică a "democraţiei parlamentare" din România*, Bucureşti 1946, p. 7; E. Focşeneanu, *Istoria constituţională a României*, pp. 21–22; A. Stan, *Putere politică şi democraţie în România*, pp. 30–33; Dan Berindei (ed.), *Istoria românilor,* vol. 7, part 1, pp. 523–525; G. Lahovary, *Histoire d'une fiction*, pp. 177–180; G. Tătărescu, *Regimul electoral şi parlamentar în România*, pp. 26–30.

6 Leonida Colescu, *Statistica electorală. Alegerile generale pentru Corpurile Legiuitoare din 1901 şi 1905*, Bucureşti 1905, p. 6.

an appropriate political framework for the complex process of transformation which the state and society underwent.[7] The abdication of Prince Alexandru Ioan Cuza and the ascendency to the throne of a foreign prince, Carol of Hohenzollern, marked a new phase in the evolution of the political regime in Romania.

Regulating the Right to Vote in the Constitution of 1866

The political regime established in 1866 was essentially liberal, built according to the West European model. Although it was a compromise between liberalism and conservatism, the new political regime did not mean a pact for the division of power between the bourgeoisie and the large landowners, but the establishment of rules for governing in the spirit of political democracy and the affirmation of opinions without administrative restrictions, the implementation of a government through chosen representatives. Individual and collective liberties, which ensured the existence of an autonomous press and the preservation of parties and various professional and political associations, were under threat due to the electoral limitations which made the Chamber and the Senate the privilege of a relatively educated and prosperous minority. The ability of citizens to exercise power was thus regulated by economic conditions as well as cultural and intellectual levels.[8]

The Constitution adopted in June 1866 and the accompanying electoral law introduced essential changes to the franchise system.[9] According to the provisions of articles 58–63 of the Constitution for the election of deputies, the electoral body was divided in each county and into four colleges, while article 68 and pursuant established two colleges for the election of senators based on wealth and social origin. These provisions were adopted after intense debates between the liberal and conservative groups. Where some of the liberals supported universal suffrage, stating that citizens' and political rights were absolute and predetermined, the conservatives believed that political rights had to be earned based on ability or work.[10]

---

7 Dan BERINDEI, *Societatea românească în vremea lui Carol I (1866–1876)*, Bucureşti 2002, p. 111.

8 Apostol STAN—Mircea IOSA, *Liberalismul politic în România. De la origini pînă la 1918*, Bucureşti 1996, p. 100; Apostol STAN, *Grupări şi curente politice în România între Unire şi Independenţă*, Bucureşti 1979, pp. 187, 209.

9 Alexandru PENCOVICI, *Desbaterile Adunării Constituante din anul 1866 asupra Constituţiunei şi a legei electorale din România*, Bucureşti 1883; Paraschiva CÂNCEA—Mircea IOSA—Apostol STAN (eds.), *Istoria Parlamentului şi a vieţii parlamentare din România*, Bucureşti 1983, pp. 151–171; Tudor DRĂGAN, *Începutul şi dezvoltarea regimului parlamentar în România pînă în anul 1916*, Cluj-Napoca 1991, pp. 184–259; E. FOCŞENEANU, *Istoria constituţională a României*, pp. 25–33; Anastasie IORDACHE, *Instituirea monarhiei constituţionale şi a regimului parlamentar în România 1866–1871*, Bucureşti 1997, pp. 56–93; D. BERINDEI (ed.), *Istoria românilor*, vol. 7, part 1, pp. 560–564.

10 A. STAN, *Putere politică şi democraţie în România 1859–1918*, pp. 57–62.

The constitutional provisions regarding the electoral system were developed by the electoral law promulgated by King Carol on the 28th of July 1866.[11] For the Chamber of Deputies the electoral body was divided into each county and four colleges. College I was for those with a yearly income of at least 300 golden coins (3,000 lei); college II was for those with an income of between 100 and 300 golden coins; college III was for the towns, comprising of tradesmen and industrialists who paid an annual tax of 80 lei. All those with liberal professions, retired officers and state pensioners were exempted from the voting restrictions in this college. These three colleges chose the deputies by direct election.[12] The peasants were in college IV—the college for all those who paid tax to the state, no matter how small, and those who did not belong to any of the categories above. Their vote was indirect; 50 registered voters appointed a delegate who in turn voted for the deputy.[13] For the Senate, the electoral body was divided into each county into two colleges. The first one comprised of all landowners who had an income of at least 300 golden coins (3,000 lei). The second one comprised of all property owners in the towns who had an income of between 100 and 300 golden coins. The universities of Iaşi and Bucharest each had the right to vote for a senator from among their professors. Eligible senators included the heir to the throne (over 18), and metropolitan and eparchial bishops.[14] The electoral eligibility of every citizen depended on fulfilling the following requirements: Romanian citizenship, aged 21 and over, and compliance with the provisions of the articles regarding voting requirements.[15]

Although the electoral body and participation in the voting process were still far from representative of the whole nation, it is obvious that political life had become more mature in the years following the adoption of the Constitution in comparison with the period under Cuza, as more citizens were now involved. The peasants were viewed as subjects of the state rather than citizens, while their contribution towards the state's economic development was not in proportion to their political representation. The pace of elections was particularly intense, the appointment of a new government usually meant the dissolution of legislative bodies and new elections. The governments always managed to ensure a parliamentary majority for themselves.[16]

The small number of voters led to electoral manipulation, while the law allowed for a wide range of electoral abuses and fraud. Furthermore, pressure from the government on voters, theft at the ballot box, vote riggings, forcing citizens to vote using an open ballot paper, placing ghost voters on electoral lists—all of these abuses were the results of the

11 George D. Nicolescu, *Parlamentul român 1866–1901*, Bucureşti 1903, pp. 10–11.
12 A. Pencovici, *Desbaterile Adunării Constituante*, p. 344.
13 A. Pencovici, *Desbaterile Adunării Constituante*, pp. 344–345.
14 A. Pencovici, *Desbaterile Adunării Constituante*, p. 345.
15 A. Pencovici, *Desbaterile Adunării Constituante*, pp. 345–346.
16 D. Berindei, *Societatea românească în vremea lui Carol I*, pp. 163–164.

implementation of the franchise statute of 1866.[17] In 1883, C. G. Dissescu—an eminent legal expert—stated that the voting requirements in Romania were higher than in England. The voters who voted in England in college I could not have voted anywhere else in Romania than in college IV.[18] Three decades later, the famous legal expert concluded that the electoral law of 1866 had produced some "rotten apples", including its aristocratic character, the restricted electoral colleges, electoral corruption, the stifling of a civic spirit, and overly powerful political parties.[19]

According to data published by Leonida Colescu, 6,879 direct voters participated in the electoral process in colleges I and II of the Senate in 1883. The situation in the Chamber was the following: 3,388 people participated in the voting process in college I; 4,814 people in college II, (2,355 in the first college and 4,524 in the second); 15,382 in college III; and 626,906 indirect voters in college IV.[20] Of the 157 deputies to the Chamber, the first three colleges elected 124 deputies, more than three-quarters of the total, while college IV only elected 33 deputies.[21] In a population which numbered 4,774,969 inhabitants in 1883, 657,369 direct and indirect voters participated in the voting process.

To a certain degree, the law established in 1866 did not correspond to the liberal principles contained in the Constitution. The voting requirements for citizens, which were more restrictive than those in Cuza's statute, coupled with the division of the voters in the colleges ensured the predominance of the wealthy in Parliament and the marginalization of the peasants. This was despite the fact that the principle of equal rights of Romanian citizens had been established in the Constitution. Furthermore, the relatively small number of voters and the lack of appropriate measures against interference from central and local authorities in the voting process encouraged fraud.[22] College IV, where the peasants indirectly expressed their vote, was often called the "dowry" of the government. The provisions of the electoral law of 1866 favoured the conservatives, who succeeded in controlling their position by including special electoral provisions in the fundamental law of the state so that they could not be changed by ordinary laws, but only by a constituent assembly which could only be convened under certain circumstances.[23] On the other hand, as the political scientist Daniel Barbu discovered, if the dilemma of liberals in 19th-century Europe was how to set a political agenda encompassing both aristocratic privileges and democratic expectations, then the Romanian liberals were more preoccupied with limiting the people's democratic aspirations which Cuza had encouraged, than with the conservatism of the great landowners. Therefore, the main aim of the Constitution

17 Crisan T. Axente, *Essai sur le régime représentatif en Roumanie*, Paris 1937, p. 351; M. Dogan, *Analiza statistică a „democraţiei parlamentare" din România*, pp. 8–9; G. Nicolescu, *Parlamentul român 1866–1901*, p. 13.

18 Constantin G. Dissescu, *Chestiunea revizuirii legii electorale*, Bucureşti 1883, p. 12.

19 Constantin G. Dissescu, *Dreptul constituţonal*, Bucureşti 1915, p. 873.

20 See L. Colescu, *Statistica electorală*, table A, p. 10.

21 P. Câncea—M. Iosa—A. Stan (eds.), *Istoria Parlamentului*, p. 165.

22 Keith Hitchins, *România 1866–1947*, Bucureşti 1996, p. 37.

23 P. Câncea—M. Iosa—A. Stan (eds.), *Istoria Parlamentului*, p. 155.

of 1866 was to reject the political consequences of the Paris Convention (1858) and of the statute imposed by Cuza in 1864. The Constitution of 1866 was meant to obliterate the memory of the peasant electoral colleges which had voted in the ad-hoc assemblies of 1857 and had tried to bring the rural question onto the public agenda. Liberals believed strongly that the peasants did not have the necessary political education to have representatives among them. By removing the peasants from the public sphere in 1866, the political elite re-established the relationships and the social hierarchies established in 1831 through the Organic Regulation.[24] Nonetheless, there were radical groups within the Liberal Party which were in favour of the democratization of the electoral system.

The Electoral Reform of 1884

The Romanian citizens' right to vote was slightly extended by changes to the Constitution[25] and the electoral law[26]in 1884. Basically, the electoral colleges from the Chamber of Deputies were reduced from four to three, and the requirements to enter one of the colleges were lowered. There was no longer any distinction between primary and direct voters, and the category of those exempt from fulfilling the voting requirements was extended. The electoral law divided the electoral body for the Chamber into three colleges. In addition to the other general conditions for electoral eligibility which existed in the previous law, Romanian citizens had to have a rural or urban income of at least 1,200 lei per year and belong to college I (which comprised of colleges I and II). No exemption from the voting requirements was allowed in this college, which voted for 75 deputies or 40% of the total number of members of the Chamber (183 deputies). College II was for all urban citizens who paid a direct annual tax of any nature of at least 20 lei to the state. Those who practised liberal professions, retired officers and those who had at least a primary education were exempt from the voting requirements. This was the largest college in terms of the number of direct voters but only elected 70 deputies or 38% of the members of the Chamber. College III was made up of direct and indirect voters. In general, anyone who was a Romanian citizen, over 21 years old and paid any amount of tax to the state belonged to this college if they were not registered in the other two. However, direct voters were only those who had a rural income of at least 300 lei and were educated. Exemption from the voting requirements was only granted to teachers, priests, and those who paid an annual royalty of at least 1,000 lei. The remaining voters from this college voted indirectly (50 voters/one delegate). College III had 38 deputies. In the Senate the electoral body was made up of two colleges. In the first college were those who had a rural

24 Daniel Barbu, *The Nation Against Democracy. State Formation, Liberalism, and Political Participation in Romania*, Studia Politica. Romanian Political Science Review 5, 2005, no. 3, pp. 550–554; Daniel Barbu, *Hainele cele noi ale statului. Liberalismul românesc între două revoluţii 1848–1917*, Henopoliana 13, 2005, no. 1–4, p. 53.

25 Monitorul Oficial [MO], no. 51, 8./20. 6. 1884.

26 MO, no. 52, 9./21. 6. 1884.

or urban income of 2,000 lei per year. According to the electoral law this college voted for 60 senators or 50% of the total number of members of the Senate. College II of the Senate was made up of all the direct voters in the towns and villages who had a rural or urban income of between 800 and 2,000 lei, as well as tradesmen and industrialists who paid a specific tax called a class I or II patent. Fifty senators were elected by this college or 42% of the total number of members of the Senate. The remaining 8% was made up of senators by right: the crown prince, metropolitans and bishops, and two senators chosen from among the professors from the universities of Yassi and Bucharest.[27]

Electoral eligibility was determined by being a Romanian citizen over the age of 21 and belonging to the Christian faith. Those who could not vote included beggars, prisoners, people who were bankrupt, paid servants, those who had been condemned for crimes or misdemeanours under the Penal Code, and those who owned brothels or organized gambling. The criteria for eligibility remained identical to those contained in the electoral law of 1866.[28]

An increase of more than double the number of voters registered in the electoral lists was recorded for the first Senate and Chamber elections based on the new electoral system in October 1888. Therefore, the number of those who voted directly in the Chamber election in the three colleges was 62,948 in 1888 compared to 23,584 in 1883, and in the Senate election the number of direct voters from the two colleges increased from 6,879 in 1883 to 15,467 in 1888.[29]

However, the new electoral law did little for the majority of the population, leaving the peasants without proper representation in Parliament. The peasants voted indirectly and the electoral changes of 1884 only gave them the right to elect eight more representatives, while those subject to voting requirements had the right to elect a further 27. Despite the acrimonious debates between conservatives and liberals, the review of the Constitution and the electoral law did not result in any fundamental changes to the electoral rules. The electoral system adapted slowly and with difficulty to the country's need to modernize. The five categories of voters were recruited almost exclusively from the ranks of landowners and urban property owners, one category consisted of city dwellers and only one was representative of the rural population. In other words, of the 295 parliamentarians, 257 were chosen by a few thousand large landowners and city inhabitants, and only 38 by almost 5 million peasants.[30]

The analysts of the time believed the Parliament was a "fiction" because the "elections from which it resulted are, in their turn, fictions and do not count. Thus the Parliament should represent the citizens' volition, so that the government could be the expression of the Parliament."[31] Despite the intense debate surrounding the modernization of the

27 G. Nicolescu, *Parlamentul român 1866–1901*, pp. 9, 16–19.

28 G. Nicolescu, *Parlamentul român 1866–1901*, pp. 20–21.

29 L. Colescu, *Statistica electorală*, table no. 1, pp. 14–1.

30 Gheorghe Tătărescu, *op. cit.*, pp. 36, 37.

31 Ibid., p. 150.

electoral system, which involved the political and intellectual elite of Romania, no fundamental changes were made to the electoral legislation after 1884.

In terms of electoral statistics, in the legislative elections of March 1907, 114,721 voters were registered on the electoral lists for the Senate and Chamber of Deputies, of whom 74,332 voted.[32] In the year 1911, the adult population (over 21) of Romania was 3,024,928 inhabitants, of whom 1,644,302 were men. Of those with direct voting rights for the Chamber of Deputies, there were 15,301 voters in college I, 33,270 voters in college II, and 101,339 direct and delegate voters in college III, totalling 49,910 voters. In the Senate the situation was the following: college I had 11,164 voters and college II had 12,757, totalling 24,921 voters. In conclusion, only 6.1% of adult men had a direct vote for the Chamber and 1.5% had a direct vote for the Senate. Of these, only 74.2% of those registered on the electoral lists for the Chamber of Deputies and 72.2% of those registered on the lists for the Senate participated in the elections of 1911.[33] This means that approximately 75,194 Chamber voters and 17,993 Senate voters elected a Parliament which was supposed to be representative of a population of over 7 million inhabitants. This was why the issue of broadening the electoral system became one of Romania's main problems at the turn of the 20th century.

Political Parties and the Peasants' Right to Vote

The Liberals and the Peasants' Right to Vote

Between 1866 and 1914 the National Liberal Party was the main political force which governed Romania, as well as being the principal modernizing agent of the state. The Liberals were not a unified political organization as they were constantly divided by political interests and views which differed in their radicalism.[34] Depite their differences, they continued to support electoral reform either by extending the franchise, by lowering the voting requirements, or by proposing radical reforms such as universal suffrage. In a simplified interpretation, the Romanian literature presents the existence within the National Liberal Party of two large ideological groups: the "old" Liberals who supported a moderate programme of political modernization and electoral reform in gradual stages by lowering the voting requirements, the social and educational improvement of the peasants, ending electoral corruption; and the "young" Liberals who advocated radical reforms, as well as universal suffrage for men and agrarian reform, in the belief that granting the peasantry the right to vote would raise their political consciousness and transform them into citizens, rather than waiting for them to be educated.

---

32 George D. NICOLESCU, *op. cit.*, p. 33.

33 Leonida COLESCU, *Statistica electorală. Alegerile generale pentru corpurile legiuitoare din 1907 și 1911*, București 1913, table no. 1, p. 7; M. DOGAN, *Analiza statistică a „democrației parlamentare" din România*, pp. 10–11.

34 Cristian PREDA, *Modernitatea politică și românismul*, București 1998, p. 158.

When modern Romania was founded, most Liberals, like the Conservatives, believed that the principle of universal suffrage was "not required due to the cultural level at which our society stands".[35] One promoter of electoral reform was C.A. Rosetti, a famous revolutionary from 1848 who had been educated in the West and who in the pages of his newspaper *Românul* promoted the idea that the democratization of the state could only occur by giving the peasants the right to vote.[36] Initially, C.A. Rosetti supported the merger of colleges I, II and IV into one college where the peasants would vote indirectly through delegates (100 peasants electing one delegate), while college III, which represented the urban population, would have remained separate. Regarding the Senate—with the significant comment that "it could be abolished"—he proposed merging the two colleges, lowering the voting requirements and abolishing the privilege whereby some people were senators by right.[37] The dispute concerning the granting of political rights to peasants was one of several which would lead to political ruptures within the Liberal Party. For example, a group of independent Liberals led by Dimitrie Brătianu left the party, followed later by a group of radical liberals led by C.A. Rosetti.[38]

When the Liberal Party initiated a review of the Constitution with the support of King Carol in 1884, it was stated in the preamble to the review drawn up by Vasile Boerescu that universal suffrage was the ideal, but the nation could not benefit from it if it was still immature politically. The hasty adoption of universal suffrage would have meant its transformation from a useful political tool into a "double-edged sword". By taking the path of moderate and gradual progress, future generations would inevitably bring about the complete democratization of Romanian political life.[39]

The radical liberals led by C.A. Rosetti, unsatisfied with a governmental project they saw as "crooked and unfair", supported the introduction of a single college and drew up a draft for the appropriate electoral law.[40] It stated that the electoral body was to consist of a single college in every county, where the educated citizens and those who paid a direct tax of 25 lei per year to the state would vote directly, while the others were to vote through delegates. The number of deputies was determined proportionally according to the population of each county.[41] The Liberal Party as a whole, but also the opposition Conservative Party, were lukewarm in the extreme towards Rosetti's proposal. The leader of the Liberal Party, Ion C. Brătianu, rejected the idea of a single college, while the "old" Liberal, A. Stolojan, believed that "universal suffrage is dangerous because I cannot give

35 Alexandru Dimitrie Xenopol, *Istoria partidelor politice în România. De la origini pînă la 1866*, vol. 1, part 2, Bucureşti 1910, p. 535.

36 Especially no. 23, 27, 28 April 1881.

37 Românul, 29. 8. 1882.

38 Paraschiva Câncea, *Formarea opoziţiei unite şi acţiunile sale în februarie–martie 1888*, Studii şi Materiale de Istorie Modernă 3, 1963, p. 316.

39 Apostol Stan, *Vasile Boerescu (1830–1883)*, Bucureşti 1974, p. 108; Vasile Boerescu, *Discursuri politice*, vol. 2 (1874–1883), Bucureşti 1910, pp. 1463–1515.

40 Românul, 2. 9. 1883; Dezbaterile Corpurilor Legiuitoare [DCL], The Extraordinary Session 1883–1884, no. 61, 21. 12. 1883, p. 768.

41 Românul, 31. 12. 1883.

political power to those whose social ideas are wrong and who see anyone who is not one of them as the enemy".[42]

C.A. Rosetti's radical supporters were extremely dissatisfied with the watering down of the changes to the electoral law and began an intense propaganda campaign in favour of a single college, which was viewed as an intermediary stage before the arrival of universal suffrage. Their propaganda consisted mainly of articles in the *Românul* newspaper, which was also open to the presentation and promotion of socialist ideas and the combative methods recommended by the socialists, including the right to strike, as a way to change the electoral institutions.[43]

The electoral reform of 1884 failed to satisfy all of the parties and political groups. The Conservatives, for example, disagreed with the extent of the changes, but accepted them anyway, hoping that nothing would change in the electoral area. The socialists opposed the reform and pressed for greater participation by the peasants and workers in elections. In light of these attitudes, the Liberal Party tried to compromise and play the role of middleman. Neither were the Liberals content with the three colleges—despite having secured power through them, this was not enough for them to impose their modernization programme on the country. However, unlike the socialists and George Panu's radical democrats, they did not support such radical reform as universal suffrage as they feared that if it became law, it would lead to anarchy as the masses were not yet ready to become involved in political life. The Liberal Party could not openly oppose such democratic reforms as it had always considered itself to be a progressive force. Moreover, there was also a sizeable number of people within the Liberal Party who were in favour of introducing universal suffrage, but towards the end of the 19th century this left-wing faction held little influence.

The Liberal Party often brought up the issue of electoral reform when it was in opposition and could safely promise more, but once in power it found reasons not to keep its promises.[44] This happened, for example, in November 1892, when after a fairly long period in opposition the Liberals promised new electoral reform in the form of the "Iaşi Programme".[45] The initiative for drawing up this document came from Dimitrie A. Sturdza, the newly elected leader of the Liberal Party. While conceding it was necessary to introduce "universal suffrage with proportional representation", the new party policy still considered that this reform was merely an "ideal" to be attained by the party "through gradual reforms". The Liberal Party pushed for reform through evolutionary rather than revolutionary methods and decided to achieve what was possible within the

42 DCL, The Extraordinary Session 1883–1884, no. 68, meeting of 14. 1. 1884, pp. 832–834; George Meitani, *O pagină din istoria parlamentară a României*, Bucureşti 1914, p. 23.

43 Dimitrie Rosetti-Teţcanu, *Colegiul unic cu reprezentarea minorităţilor*, Bucureşti 1884; Vasile Netea, *C. A. Rosetti*, Bucureşti 1970, p. 377.

44 Sorin Radu, *Liberalii şi problema reformei electorale în România (1866–1914)*, part 1, Annales Universitatis Apulensis 4–5, 2000–2001, p. 138.

45 *Programul Partidului Naţional Liberal din 1892 şi Discursurile Preşedintelui Consiliului de Miniştri D. A. Sturdza*, Bucureşti 1897.

conditions of the period, that it "would fight with all the necessary powers which respect the rule of law", with an "honest and conscious application of electoral law".[46] Their position was not significantly different from that of the Conservatives, who rejected this reform *ab initio*, while the Liberals accepted it hypothetically for some time in the future. Once in power in 1895, the Liberal Party ignored this promise, while their programme from December 1906 failed to mention universal suffrage even as a distant ideal, and only pointed to the "rule of law".

A group of "young" Liberals led by I.C. Brătianu emerged within the Liberal Party in the late 19th century. They declared themselves to be supporters of modernization reforms, including universal suffrage.[47] This group of "young" reformers became stronger when Constanin Stere and the "generous" socialists entered the Liberal Party in 1899. The latter had been leaders of the Social Democratic Workers' Party, who had left the party for pragmatic reasons and joined the Liberals with the aim of helping to introduce universal suffrage. Stere believed that if the peasants were not given the vote "Romania will remain moribund in the context of nations, liable to perish as a state and nation".[48] After 1900, an increasing number of Liberals declared themselves to be supporters of the progress, believing that the modernization of Romania could not be achieved without the political and social emancipation of the peasants. As a result, debates on such matters were a constant feature in Parliament.[49]

What was to distinguish not only the Liberal Party's stance regarding the emancipation of the peasants, but also the whole of Romanian society prior to the First World War, was the programme of cultural and social emancipation implemented by Spiru Haret, the Minister of Education in several Liberal governments. In 1905, he published the brochure *The Peasant Question*, in which he argued for the introduction of agrarian radical reform and a wide representation of the peasants in electoral process.[50] The work alarmed more conservative-minded politicians, especially because the author was a high-profile politician. The need for "the introduction of peasants as an active and intelligent factor in our state life"—a phrase which pointed to universal suffrage—risked radicalizing Romanian political life, which suited neither King Carol nor the two largest parties—the Liberals and Conservatives.[51]

Haret's programme made him popular with a large group of supporters, especially former socialists who advocated the political emancipation of the peasants: Vasile G. Morţun, Ioan Nădejde, George Diamandy, Ioan Cantacuzino, Constantin Stere, and

---

46 *Programul Partidului Naţional Liberal din 1892*, p. 19.

47 Mariu Teodorian-Carada, *Efemeridele. Însemnări şi amintiri*, vol. 1, Bucureşti 1930, p. 141.

48 Ştefania Mihăilescu, *Poporanismul şi mişcarea socialistă din România*, Bucureşti 1988, p. 27; Zigu Ornea, *Viaţa lui C. Stere*, vol. 1, Bucureşti 1989, p. 245.

49 Dezbaterile Adunării Deputaţilor [DAD], The Extraordinary Session 1901–1902, no. 9, 6. 12. 1901, meeting of 27. 11. 1901, p. 42.

50 Spiru Haret, *Chestia ţărănească*, Bucureşti 1905, p. 3.

51 Mariu Teodorian-Carada, *Vasile Lascăr*, Bucureşti 1914, p. 112.

others.[52] In the struggle to create a favourable political tide of opinion for electoral reform, an important role was played by the magazine *Viața românească*, which appeared in Iași in 1906 under the management of Stere (he was an important Liberal at the time) and Garabet Ibrăileanu.[53] *Viața românească* rapidly came to prominence, becoming the best and most widely read magazine of the time. It popularized "Poporanist" ideas, which promoted social emancipation for the peasantry through agrarian reform and the political emancipation of the peasantry either through universal suffrage or at least through a single college for the educated. The Poporanists believed that universal suffrage and land distribution to the peasants were interdependent.[54]

The hopes of those who supported the political emancipation of the peasantry were raised when Ionel I.C. Brătianu was elected leader of the Liberal Party in 1909. However, he had to tread cautiously as the party was still dominated by the "old guard" who were closer to the Conservatives. Ionel Brătianu, therefore, declared that in terms of electoral reform it would be better to first introduce a single college for the educated in the county elections, which was "a proper civic education".[55] Brătianu kept his moderate position on gradual electoral reform, which would be augmented by social and cultural reforms to raise the level of the peasantry.[56] With these reticent declarations the leader of the Liberals tried to accommodate the young Liberals as well as the right wing, which still dominated the leadership of the party.[57] The compromise which was finally reached was the gradual political emancipation of the peasantry by establishing a single college for the educated as a first step on the way to universal suffrage.[58] The single college seemed a reasonable compromise between the Liberal groups because at that time it was a progressive reform which could contribute positively to the democratization of Romanian society. The slogan of a single college was promoted across the entire country, with the Liberal Party organizing a series of meetings and public gatherings in the main cities, which continued almost until 1914.[59]

52 Șerban Orăscu, *Spiru Haret*, București 1976, p. 152.

53 Z. Ornea, *Viaţa lui C. Stere*, p. 365.

54 *Către cititori*, Viaţa Românească 1, 1906, no. 1; Constantin Stere, *Momentul ("Cronica internă")*, Viaţa Românească 2, 1907, no. 5, p. 326; Constantin Stere, *Întregirile necesare reformei electorale*, Viaţa Românească 6, 1911, no. 12, p. 474.

55 *Discursurile lui Ion I. C. Brătianu*, vol. 3, p. 42 and 43.

56 *Discursurile lui Ion I. C. Brătianu*, vol. 3, p. 318.

57 Mircea Iosa, *Ion I.C. Brătianu și reformele social-economice liberale (1909–1914)*, Revista de Istorie, serie nouă, vol. 2, no. 9–10, 1991, pp. 545–546.

58 Viitorul 4, no. 1107, 27. 1. 1911; Voinţa Naţională 28, no. 7648, 26. 1. 1911; *Manifestul—program al partidului*, Bucureşti 1911, p. 17.

59 Viitorul 4, no. 1342, 1. 11. 1911; no. 1370, 29. 11. 1911; no. 1385, 14. 12. 1911; Mişcarea 3, no. 249, 14. 11. 1911; no. 250, 15. 11. 1911.

The Conservatives and the Political Eemancipation of the Peasantry

The Romanian Conservatives, as well as their European counterparts, tried to reconcile political moderation with the acceptance of the principle of institutional modernization by adopting the methods of gradualism and prudence. This is why they also favoured a bicameral political system as well as attempts to limit the civil rights and liberties established in the Constitution.[60] The Conservatives were the main group, if not the only one, which consistently opposed reform of the electoral system through the extension of the franchise to less wealthy social categories. They initiated draft laws on several occasions to limit the electoral body, but without success. On the other hand, it is true that there were isolated voices among them who agreed that the peasants should be integrated into political life.

After the arrival of a foreign prince, King Carol of Hohenzollern, and the adoption of the Constitution in 1866, the Conservatives believed Romania had entered a new phase where political conflict was senseless as all the necessary reforms had been implemented. The representatives of the large landowners claimed that until 1866 the political fights and the existence of groups representing different interests had been justified by the need to organize the national state. In 1866 the issue of the organization of modern Romania was considered closed. Starting from such a premise, the Conservatives tried to demonstrate how meaningless it was to have several political groups as nothing else needed building, and all that was left was to organize and administer.[61] Therefore, after 1866 the Conservatives put forward the theory that the electoral system would not require modernization for the foreseeable future. The division into four electoral colleges was, as one deputy declared, "the final expression of democracy, the most perfect form which universal suffrage can provide us with".[62] The electoral law was fair as it regulated the franchise according to "intelligence and wealth". The elites of the state would not be overwhelmed by the poor, uncultivated masses. Political rights could be granted to the peasants when they acquired a political conscience and advanced socially and culturally.[63]

The Conservative view of the modernization of the state's political institutions, specifically the electoral system, was interestingly described by Nicolae Blaremberg in a work published in 1866 entitled *Egalitate, suveranitate şi sufragiu* [Equality, Sovereignty and Suffrage].[64] The Conservative leader based his ideas on the natural rights of man (property and security), which transcended institutions and which could not be limited by the

60 Ioan Stanomir—Laurenţiu Vlad (eds.), *A fi conservator. Antologie, comentarii şi bibliografie*, Bucureşti 2002, pp. 14–15.

61 Vasile Russu, *Cauzele luptelor politice dintre grupările liberale şi conservatoare în anii instabilităţii guvernamentale şi parlamentare (1866–1871)*, Cercetări Istorice, vol. 9–10, 1978–1979, p. 420.

62 A. D. Xenopol, *Istoria partidelor politice în România*, vol. 1, part 2, p. 536.

63 A. Pencovici, *Desbaterile Adunării Constituante*, p. 220.

64 Nicolae Blaremberg, *Egalitate, suveranitate şi sufragiu*, Bucureşti 1866, 76 pp.

law.[65] In his opinion, the criterion for electoral eligibility was the voting requirements. Wealth presumed material independence and strength of character, allowing for the enlightenment of the spirit.[66] Blaremberg could not accept universal suffrage, arguing that "since the mob was most often ignored and always poor, their first concern would always be to satisfy their material and immediate interests".[67] This reform had to be preceded by improving education among the peasants and developing a free press to contribute to the creation of a political conscience.[68] Using this elitist line of thinking, Gr.G. Peucescu claimed in 1878 that political rights had to be earned by every peasant and every citizen through their own efforts, through work and education, and not through gifts from demagogues who were inclined to promise the ends of the earth in order to achieve power.[69] Romanian society would not progress unless it was based "only on its most able citizens", while political rights could only be obtained through "personal merit and reason".[70]

The Conservatives' increasingly sharply focused thinking was based on the idea that state progress had to occur organically by holding on to traditional institutions and not replacing them with foreign imports.[71] The members of "Junimea"—a cultural and political society established by the Conservative youth—believed that the democratization of Romanian society had to come from the "bottom up and not the top down", when the "fund" or level of civilization rose to a level of understanding of modern forms borrowed by the Liberals from Western models by improving educational and economic conditions.[72]

The year 1880 saw the "de jure" establishment of the Conservative Party and the drawing up of its programme and statutes. The party's first political programme did not contain any changes to the electoral legislation or mention of the political emancipation of the peasants. It only expressed trust in the principle of the constitutional monarchy and representation within the legislative bodies.[73]

The Conservatives considered the Liberals' proposals for electoral reform as an "attempt to disturb the legal order" and "a danger which threatens the country". The idea of the peasants being granted the universal vote seemed to be a republican idea, "an attack directed against the stability of the throne as well as the security of people's wealth and honour".[74] Such reform was only necessary in the future when education had spread

65 Nicolae Blaremberg, *Egalitate, suveranitate şi sufragiu*, pp. 16, 17.
66 Nicolae Blaremberg, *Egalitate, suveranitate şi sufragiu*, p. 25.
67 Nicolae Blaremberg, *Egalitate, suveranitate şi sufragiu*, p. 40.
68 Nicolae Blaremberg, *Egalitate, suveranitate şi sufragiu*, p. 71.
69 Grigore G. Peucescu, *Despre partidele politice*, Iaşi 1878, p. 61.
70 G. G. Peucescu, *Despre partidele politice*, p. 94.
71 Timpul 4, 23. 6. 1879, no. 138; Constantin Rădulescu-Motru, *Cultura română şi politicianismul*, Bucureşti 1904.
72 E. Lovinescu, *Istoria civilizaţiei române moderne*, p. 182.
73 *Statutele Clubului Conservator şi programul partidului*, Bucureşti 1880, pp. 8–10.
74 Biblioteca Naţională a României, Colecţii speciale, fond Saint Georges, P.LXVII, D.2, Imprimate politice 1883–1934, f. 13.

and the peasants' level of morality had risen.[75] They did not appear to be frightened by democracy *per se*, but by its "excesses". They did not believe it was the appropriate time for constitutional reform and they employed numerous "arguments" to defend this position. According to them, it was not political rights that the Romanians lacked, but material prosperity and moral fortitude, which combined with education would prevent their "brutalization".[76] Political rights could not precede economic progress—in fact the opposite was true—any reform was meaningless as long as people could not read or write and were unable to judge what was in the public interest.[77] In 1883, Titu Maiorescu, a member of Junimea, admitted that the current electoral law had resulted in electoral corruption. However, this was due to the fact that the majority of the population was illiterate and uneducated, thus lacking the necessary civic education to challenge corruption and abuse in the elections. Therefore, he proposed changes that were indirectly related to the Constitution—compulsory education, permanent judges, administrative decentralization, etc., which would be followed by reform if required.[78] Several leading figures within Romanian culture doubted the political readiness of the peasants, including the poet Mihai Eminescu, who in the 1880s was an editor of *Timpul*, the official Conservative newspaper. Eminescu did not believe that social and political mores could be improved by electoral laws if moral principles were abandoned. Social free-riding, careerism and improvisation would have generated a state of general corruption. Under these circumstances, extending the right to vote would merely have deepened the wounds. Without detailing the mechanisms which made political modernization necessary, the great poet believed that only "the people of the past"—the landed gentry—could maintain an atmosphere of moral rectitude. As a consequence, granting political rights to peasants was seen as an unacceptable "Liberal fantasy".[79]

The Conservative leaders believed that Romania was not ready to undergo new reforms as it was still coming to terms with the present representative regime. Maiorescu argued that the Constitution of 1866 had not been implemented "in all of its essential elements".[80] He directed his critique against those who imported constitutional models from other countries.[81]

At the end of the 19th century, the Conservatives' political discourse focused on a critique of all electoral reform, especially the discrepancies between universal suffrage and the rural population's cultural, social and economic development. For Alexandru Lahovary, an important leader of the Conservative Party, universal suffrage was "a

75 DAD, The Extraordinary Session 1882–1883, no. 47, 30. 12. 1882, meeting of 22. 12. 1882, p. 606.
76 Timpul, no. 194, 4. 9. 1882; no. 202, 16. 9. 1882; no. 203, 17. 9. 1882.
77 Timpul, no. 12, 18. 1. 1883; DAD, The Extraordinary Session 1882–1883, no. 53, 16. 1. 1883, p. 730.
78 DAD, The Extraordinary Session 1882–1883, no. 55, 22. 1. 1883, pp. 765–771; Eugen Lovinescu, *Titu Maiorescu*, Bucureşti 1940, pp. 163–164.
79 Marin Bucur, *C.A. Rosetti—mesianism şi donquijotism revoluţionar*, Bucureşti 1970, p. 426.
80 Titu Maiorescu, *Discursuri parlamentare*, vol. 3, Bucureşti 1899, p. 51.
81 T. Maiorescu, *Discursuri parlamentare*, vol. 3; DAD, The Extraordinary Session 1882–1883, no. 55, 22. 1. 1883, p. 771.

dangerous experiment" because the country was not yet ready and could not risk political innovation which had not yet been tested in the "civilized" West.[82] P.P. Carp was of the opinion that the Liberals and radicals overrated the importance of universal suffrage, especially the benefits of this reform for the peasants.[83] Carp and other Conservative leaders, including Nicolae Filipescu, insisted that Romanian society had to undergo "intellectual and moral reform" and "the regeneration of the public spirit" before the peasantry was granted political rights.[84]

The electoral reform which the Conservative Party was prepared to accept at this stage was the introduction of proportional representation in the distribution of the parliamentary mandates.[85] This principle was accepted by the Conservatives because it did not result in any major changes to the colleges with voting requirements. The Conservatives were forced to come up with some new political ideas in order to be in line—or so they believed—with the modernization trends of the time. This was the large landowners' response to their political opponents' reformist tendencies. It is worth mentioning that this slight shift in the attitude of the Conservatives towards the electoral body occurred when the party was in opposition. For the Conservatives it was more important to halt the disintegration of Romanian society. The "political orgy which separates Romania from the Western world" was to be stopped through a series of economic, social and cultural reforms, and only then could they discuss widening the franchise.[86] On a discourse level, the Conservatives showed themselves to be preoccupied with developing and educating public opinion. No new reforms could be introduced when "there is confusion and improvidence in the mind of every citizen". As a consequence, "our public has to be educated, which means we have to make them clearly understand the present through a thorough knowledge of the past". "This work," wrote C. Rădulescu-Motru in 1900, "of educating the public conscience in our country is the work of salvation and we believe it is the mission of the Conservative Party to do so".[87] With a natural disinclination to speculate on socio-political matters and a scepticism of any changes that might bring about

82 Alexandru LAHOVARY, *Discursuri parlamentare (1888–1891)*, Bucureşti 1915, p. 204; DAD, The Extraordinary Session 1890–1891, no. 20, şedinţa din 5. 12. 1890, p. 155; no. 24, meeting of 11. 12. 1890, p. 204.

83 DAD, The Extraordinary Session 1889–1890, no. 25, meeting of 12. 12. 1889, p. 194.

84 Constantin GANE, *P.P. Carp şi locul său în istoria politică a ţării*, vol. 2, Bucureşti 1936, p. 31, 45; Nicolae FILIPESCU, *Albii şi roşii*, Bucureşti 1894, p. 20; Nicolae FILIPESCU, *Discursuri politice*, vol. 1 (1888–1901), Bucureşti 1912, pp. 29–30.

85 Nicolae FILIPESCU, *Către un nou ideal*, Bucureşti 1898, p. 139; Dimitrie S. NENIŢESCU, *Reprezentarea proporţională a minorităţilor. Studiu asupra sistemelor electorale*, 1895, passim.

86 N. FILIPESCU, *Discursuri politice*, vol. 2, pp. 28–29.

87 Constantin RĂDULESCU-MOTRU, *Cronica politică. Menirea Partidului Conservator. Educaţiunea opiniunei publice*, Noua Revistă Română pentru Politică, Literatură. Ştiinţă şi Artă 1, 15. 4. 1900, no. 8, pp. 338–339.

"an ideal society", the Conservatives at the turn of the century showed no interest in any constitutional reforms.[88]

At the beginning of the 20th century, Conservative thinking made some progress in terms of electoral reform. The Conservatives continued to express their mistrust of peasants' political capabilities, while the concept of political equality seemed unsuited to a backward agrarian society like Romania. Therefore, as before, extending the franchise to the peasant class was contingent upon the expansion of education and the economic development of the peasants.[89] Through the newspapers *Epoca*, *Conservatorul*, *La Politique*, *Seara*, and *Minerva*, and the journals *Săptămîna politică și literară* and *Noua Revistă Română*, the Conservatives further opposed the reform ideas proposed by the Liberals and socialists. The extension of the franchise requested by the other parties, which according to the Conservatives was not supported by anyone in the country, was opposed by the party under P.P. Carp with the slogan: "First culture and economic prosperity in the country, and only after we have an educated rural population who are content with their wealth will we safely extend the franchise."[90]

The opposition of the Conservatives to electoral reform cannot merely be explained by their fear that extending the franchise would result in the loss of their privileged status or because they opposed the modernization of the country. Instead, their opposition resulted from the deep conviction that in a backward country such as Romania with widespread illiteracy and corruption, such a rapid programme of reform would be impossible. The Conservatives claimed that such change would do more harm than good in Romanian society. Without overtly opposing the idea of progress, they tried to slow the tempo of reform, continuously referring to the fact that universal suffrage did not even exist in the advanced countries of Western Europe.

The Social Democrats and Universal Suffrage

The first socialist political groups appeared in Romania at the end of the 19th century and the first Social Democratic Party was established in 1893. In their very first political manifesto, the socialists were in favour of political emancipation for the peasants through universal suffrage. The first cogently argued academic study of electoral reform was by an important theorist, Constantin Dobrogeanu-Gherea, in a work published in 1886 entitled *What Romanian Socialists Want. A Presentation of Scientific Socialism and the Socialist Programme.* Gherea engaged in a debate with the opponents of socialist ideas who argued

88 *Cronica politică și economică. Triumful politicei junimiste*, Noua Revistă Română pentru Politică, Literatură. Știință și Artă 1, 1. 3. 1900, no. 5, pp. 194–195.

89 Nicolae FILIPESCU, *Despre democrație*, București 1908, passim; Emil N. LAHOVARY, *Votul universal*, București 1909, passim; Mariu TEODORIAN-CARADA, *Revizuirea Constituției*, București 1911, passim.

90 *Nimeni nu cere votul obștesc*, Conservatorul 10, no. 203, 17. 9. 1910; *Despre reforma electorală*, Conservatorul 10, no. 271–275, 10. 12. 1910.

that such concepts were incompatible with the reality of an economically backward Romania, particularly in terms of industry and the working class, and with the fact that there was no objective justification for the existence of a socialist movement, let alone a social democratic party. Dobrogeanu-Gherea was in favour of direct universal suffrage for citizens aged over 20 and for the political equality of women.[91] At that time, Dobrogeanu-Gherea's revolutionary ideas triggered a broad debate involving many politicians, while it also marked the start of a long campaign to explain the necessity of universal suffrage to the public.[92]

The correlation between the struggle for universal suffrage and the need to establish a working-class political party was at the centre of the Social Democrats' political activities and propaganda at the end of the 19th century.[93] The introduction of universal suffrage was demanded by the Social Democrats in their election manifestos for the parliamentary elections of 1891 and 1892.[94] An important stage in the socialists' struggle for a democratic electoral system was the establishment of the Social Democratic Workers' Party of Romania (PSDMR), following the Congress of Bucharest from 31 March—3 April 1893. Part of the programme was adopted from Gherea's study *What do Romanian socialists want?*, which was combined with elements from the German Social Democrats' Erfurt Programme.[95] The programme contained only "those reforms which are achievable in society today, the implementation of which would be a huge step towards our ideal (...) the establishment of a socialist society".[96] The first demand was for "equal and direct universal suffrage for all subjects of Romania who have reached the age of 20, irrespective of sex, religion, and race".[97] They also demanded the introduction of proportional representation, equality for women in the law and politics,[98] and the abolition of the Senate.[99] Immediately after the end of the congress, the campaign for the introduction of universal suffrage was stepped up. Here the most important role was played by the press, especially the *Munca* newspaper. The socialist Constantin Mille published an article here in which he hyperbolically claimed that the question of universal suffrage was "a matter of life and death for the socialist party".[100]

The Social Democrats' struggle for universal suffrage involved media campaigns, public lectures and conferences, as well as debates in the Chamber of Deputies, where

91 *Documente din istoria mişcării muncitoreşti din România (1879–1892)*, Bucureşti 1976, pp. 115–116.

92 Constantin Dobrogeanu-Gherea, *Opere completei*, vol. 2, Bucureşti 1976, pp. 306–330.

93 Florea Nedelcu, *Programele mişcării socialiste din România şi lupta pentru cucerirea votului universal (1880–1914)*, Revista de Istorie 23, 1970, no. 2, p. 274.

94 Munca 3, no. 3, 10. 3. 1891; no. 49, 26. 1. 1892; Biblioteca Naţională a României, Colecţii Speciale, fond Saint Georges, Imprimate politice 1883–1934, P. LXVII, D. 2, f. 19.

95 Nicolae Jurca, *Istoria social-democraţiei din România*, Bucureşti 1994, p. 24.

96 *Programul Partidului social-democrat al muncitorilor din România*, Galaţi 1893, p. 18.

97 *Programul Partidului social-democrat al muncitorilor din România*, p. 19.

98 *Programul Partidului social-democrat al muncitorilor din România*, p. 20.

99 *Programul Partidului social-democrat al muncitorilor din România*, p. 22.

100 C. Mille, *Sufragiul universal*, Munca 4, no. 30, 19. 9. 1893; *Documente din istoria mişcării muncitoreşti din România (1893–1900)*, p. 454.

they had a few representatives. For example, in the parliamentary sessions between 1895 and 1898, V. G. Morţun proposed several amendments, demanding the introduction of these reforms together with proportional representation.[101]

During the 4th Congress of PSDMR, which took place in April 1897, major differences appeared between the leaders of the party for the first time, but which were not made public. V.G. Morţun explained his belief to the congress that the socialist movement would not progress until universal suffrage had been introduced. In opposition to the leader of the party, Ioan Nădejde, he considered moving to the Liberals in the belief that universal suffrage could be achieved in five years by acting within that party. Morţun, however, was persuaded to remain in the party.[102] The differences within the PSDMR, especially regarding tactical issues, erupted at the 5th Congress, which took place in April 1898.[103] The congress clearly exposed the existence of two opposing camps within the party. The larger camp was reformist and supported the party's participation in the parliamentary struggle and collaboration with the bourgeois parties (mainly with the National Liberal Party). The second camp was true to the principles of the class struggle and would only participate in elections if they were certain of the result. Until these conditions were fulfilled this group envisaged using other means such as worker strikes and propaganda in the villages and towns.

Because of the predominance of strong reformist personalities within the party, including Ioan Nădejde, V.G. Morţun, I.C. Atanasiu and C. Radovici, the demand for universal suffrage came to the fore towards the end of the 19th century. Although achieving this reform was very important for Romanian society, the strict separation of this demand from other political problems and the exploitation of universal suffrage as a panacea for all the ills of bourgeois society which would usher in socialism, was profoundly mistaken. Universal suffrage changed from being an instrument in the political struggle to an absolute priority, pushing aside other objectives, especially economic ones, which were now the proviso of the workers (through strikes) and the peasants (through social movements and public unrest). Another position was held by the revolutionary group led by I.C. Frimu, Al. Ionescu and Al. Constantinescu, who saw the socialists' collaboration with the bourgeois parties to accelerate the implementation of universal suffrage as "opportunistic hyperbole".[104]

The contradiction between these two tendencies would evolve rapidly and lead to the breakup of the PSDMR following the departure of the reformist intellectuals, also called

---

101 *Deputaţii socialişti în Parlamentul român. Discursuri (1888–1899; 1919–1921)*, Bucureşti 1983, pp. 91, 118–122.

102 N. Jurca, *Istoria social-democraţiei din România*, p. 30.

103 N. Jurca, *Istoria social-democraţiei din România*, pp. 31–32; Constantin Titel Petrescu, *Socialismul în România 1835—6 septembrie 1940*, Bucureşti 2003, p. 143.

104 F. Nedelcu, *Programele mişcării socialiste*, p. 278; Vasile Niculae, *O istorie a social democraţiei române*, Bucureşti 1993, pp. 154–155; *Mişcarea muncitorească din România 1893–1900*, Bucureşti 1965, p. 212; Mircea Iosa, *Încercări de modificare a legii electorale în ultimul deceniu al sec. al XIX-lea*, Revista Istorică 30, 1977, no. 8, p. 1421.

the "generous", to the Liberals after the party congress in April 1899.[105] The actions of the "generous" (V.G. Morţun, I.C. Atanasiu, Al. Radovici and others) had several underlying causes, which we will not elaborate on here. It is sufficient to highlight the fact that after many years of political life, the socialist intellectual elite came to the conclusion that an independent working-class political movement was not possible and that only together with the Liberals they could quickly achieve universal suffrage and implement other reforms.[106] This group formed the left-wing of the Liberal Party and helped accelerate the reform programme. The integration of socialist elements into political parties was not an isolated phenomenon. The same thing happened in France with the socialist M. Millerand, who in 1899 became part of the radical government with Waldeck-Rousseau as its president. His example was followed by Aristide Briand, Réne Viviani and others, who when confronted with revolutionary elements tried to steer the Social Democrats in the direction of reform.[107]

The entry of the "generous" into the National Liberal Party at the end of the century spelled the end of the old social democratic, legalistic and slightly romantic movement, and signalled the beginning of a new stage—that of a radical socialist movement which was strongly working class in character.[108] Despite the fact that after almost a quarter of a century the foundations of the Social Democratic movement had been destroyed, its socialist ideals survived in smaller circles, albeit without political or social resonance within the broad sweep of history.[109]

The "Peasants' Party" and the Political Emancipation of the Peasants

The political representation of the peasants generated interest among intellectuals who attempted to establish an agrarian political body to fight for the political rights of the rural class. In 1880 the teacher Constantin Dobrescu-Argeş established a peasants' committee which demanded the direct right to vote for all educated people, and the indirect vote for illiterate citizens. In October 1895 the "Peasants' Party" appeared on Romania's political stage, whose programme included keeping the three colleges to elect the legislative bodies, but lowering the voting requirements and introducing another division of electoral territories: in college I, rural owners with an income of up to 1,200 lei per year had the vote; in college II, small rural landowners with an income less than 1,200 lei per year had a direct vote if they knew how to write and read, even if they did not have property, and there were delegates for those who were illiterate; in college III the inhabitants of the towns had the vote. The programme also supported the introduction of uninominal voting, the right of

105 N. Jurca, *Istoria social-democraţiei din România*, p. 42–45.
106 Nicolae Jurca, *Istoria social-democraţiei din România*; Z. Ornea, *Viaţa lui C. Stere*, vol. 1, pp. 250–251; Ş. Mihăilescu, *Poporanismul şi mişcarea socialistă*, p. 27.
107 A. Stan—M. Iosa, *Liberalismul politic în România*, p. 332.
108 N. Jurca, *Istoria social-democraţiei din România*, p. 47.
109 N. Jurca, *Istoria social-democraţiei din România*, p. 54.

suffrage and the guarantee of a free secret ballot.[110] Although he believed in the necessity of electoral reform and the broad representation of the peasants in Parliament, Dobrescu-Argeş did not agree with the Social Democrats on the establishment of a "League for the Universal Vote".[111] Dobrescu-Argeş was more in favour of improving the peasantry's political representation in the existing electoral system than revolutionary transformation towards universal suffrage. After four years of limited activity, the "Peasants' Party" disappeared from Romania's political stage.

Another initiative in political agrarianism came from Vasile M. Kogălniceanu, who attempted to establish a new peasants' party in 1906 as a result of his dedication to the cultural, economic and political improvement of the peasantry. Vasile M. Kogălniceanu was the first editor of the *Românul* newspaper and he used it to promote the idea of the apportionment of property and universal suffrage through government reforms. He also supported the Social Democrats' initiatives to legislate for universal suffrage.[112] V.M. Kogălniceanu's ideas regarding the peasant franchise were presented in the pamphlet *The Peasant Question* published in 1906. By emulating the model of the Liberal Spiru Haret, who campaigned for the cultural and economic improvement of the peasantry through the active involvement of teachers, Kogălniceanu supported the political equality of all social classes and universal suffrage. Cultural and economic backwardness could not be allowed to impede these reforms.[113] The manifesto *To the Peasants*, which was launched by the Peasants' Party in 1906, urged peasants to fight for the apportionment of property and the right to vote and not to expect something "for nothing", remaining idle in the hope that someone would give them these rights.[114]

Vasile M. Kogălniceanu believed that universal, direct, equal and secret suffrage had to be the way "to free the peasant class from the political and social slavery which it is in". He was sceptical about the parties' intentions to legislate for this reform, while the political situation showed "we are not only far from universal suffrage, but from the most modest of electoral reforms". Kogălniceanu believed that "universal suffrage is not a panacea for all of the ills this country is suffering from, but it is a powerful way to heal our political life so that millions of peasants can become (...) an electoral body in the true meaning of the word, real citizens". Any electoral reform which did not lead to political equality in the countryside could not be called reform.[115] However, Vasile M. Kogălniceanu's initiative to establish a new peasant political organization never came to fruition.[116]

---

110 *Programul Partidei Ţărăneşti din România*, Bucureşti 1895, p. 5–9; Vasile NICULAE—Ion ILINCIOIU—Stelian NEAGOE (eds.), *Doctrina ţărănistă în România. Antologie de texte*, Bucureşti, 1994, pp. 52–53.

111 Vasile NICULAE, *Liga votului universal*, Magazin Istoric 7, 1973, no. 8, p. 72.

112 V. NICULAE, *Liga votului universal*, p. 72.

113 Vasile M. KOGĂLNICEANU, *Chestiunea ţărănească*, Bucureşti 1906, pp. 87–93.

114 V. NICULAE—I. ILINCIOIU—S. NEAGOE (eds.), *Doctrina ţărănistă în România*, pp. 68–69.

115 *Pentru votul universal. Răspunsul d-lui Vasile M. Kogălniceanu,* Viaţa socială 1, 1910 (August—September), no. 7–8, pp. 17–22.

116 Ion ILINCIOIU, *Vasile M. Kogălniceanu (1863–1942)*, Anale de Istorie 1967, no. 1, p. 132.

After the peasants' revolt of 1907 there were repeated attempts to create a peasants' political organization in various parts of the country. Among the most remarkable was an initiative by the teacher Ion Mihalache, who in the autumn of 1913 proposed the establishment of a "Peasants' League" which aimed to promote agrarian and electoral reform. This was not a political party but a coordinating body which was to speak for all supporters of reform.[117] Mihalache demanded the introduction of universal suffrage because "all the country's children who participate equally in the war, in taxation and all essential matters are equally entitled to rights and leadership". Influenced by the ideas of Nicolae Iorga on the "cultural improvement of the villages", Mihalache understood universal suffrage as "only suffrage for the Romanians and not for the Jews". Such a claim was based on the self-preservation instinct of the nation, at least until the Romanian people became enlightened.[118] Mihalache did not believe that universal suffrage could be introduced at that time because all the governing parties were against it. But in the meantime, he continued, the solution of the single college proposed by the Liberals was preferable for the peasants, teachers and priests.[119] The war would change Ion Mihalache's ideas about the democratization of the country and he would eventually support universal suffrage across the board.

Conclusions

The birth of Romania as a nation state inspired the political classes to implement comprehensive structural reforms in all areas. In 1866, Romanian ideas concerning the constitution fluctuated between copying the West and defining its own identity.[120] The Constitution of 1866 was based on the Belgian model and introduced modern representative governing principles into Romania. From the very outset the Constitution was understood as "too large a coat" for the Romanians. Consequently, although the ruling elite accepted in principle Western European democracy and political modernity, they controlled power through an electoral system based on wealth and education from which the peasants were excluded. The minority political class claimed such a mechanism was theoretically open to all citizens who could gradually gain the right to vote through economic improvement and educational development.

The electoral system adopted in 1866 not only reflected the special interests of the bourgeoisie and the large landowners, but also the immature level of Romanian society which was in a transitional stage towards a democratic regime where the citizens could participate in political life with equal rights. The political and intellectual elites were aware of the shortcomings of the electoral system which resulted in calls for its modernization. Therefore, there

117 Apostol Stan, *Ion Mihalache. Destinul unei vieţi*, Bucureşti 1999, p. 45.

118 V. Niculae—I. Ilincioiu—S. Neagoe (eds.), *Doctrina ţărănistă în România*, p. 73 (Ion Mihalache, „Constituanta").

119 V. Niculae—I. Ilincioiu—S. Neagoe (eds.), *Doctrina ţărănistă în România*, p. 74.

120 C. Preda, *Modernitatea politică şi românismul*, p. 172.

was an interesting ideological debate on this topic in Romania at the end of the 20th century. A limit to the number of electoral colleges, the lowering of the voting requirements, and universal suffrage were all identified as the only ways to create the appropriate conditions for Romania's socio-economic and political development, and to speed up the modernization process.

The opposition of the Conservatives to electoral reform and especially to the universal vote cannot merely be explained by their fear that extending the right to vote would result in the loss of their privileged social status or by their opposition to the modernization process of the country. Instead, their opposition resulted from the deep conviction that such a rapid programme of reforms would be impossible in an underdeveloped country such as Romania with its widespread illiteracy and corruption. The Conservatives claimed that such change would do more harm than good to Romanian society. Without overtly opposing the idea of progress, they only tried to slow the tempo of reform. However, what the Conservatives and Liberals can be accused of was a failure to pay attention to the cultural and economic development of rural areas, with the result that the electoral issue became a vicious circle.

In Romania, political modernization meant the introduction of democratic institutions and representative governing principles. An analysis of the political mechanisms which functioned in Romania in the second half of the 19th century emphasises the discrepancies which appeared in their understanding and application. In other words, these institutions failed to function properly, leading to the emergence of a gap between two worlds: one characterized by authentic progress enjoyed mainly by a small elite; the other by stagnation, poverty, sickness, and illiteracy. It was precisely the disregard of this world which was one of the main causes of Romania's backwardness. Modernization could never be completed as long as it was interpreted as a phenomenon which was only comprehensible to the world of the elites, marginalizing the peasants and the workers. Only sweeping electoral reform could create the conditions to allow modernization to become a general phenomenon. This was the "key" to progress.

Until the majority of the population had greater political access, the wealthy and the educated could not expect democratic political attitudes and behaviour from the population, which would contribute to the formation of a real civil society through the development of the peasants' political conscience. On the contrary, electoral debates emphasized moral behaviour for which there was apparently no cure, such as corruption, 'terror' in elections, demagogy, the creation of a real class of political parasites etc. Nevertheless, the government made insufficient effort towards the development of the educational and economic systems that could improve the peasants' status. Consequently, the educated class did little to prepare the peasantry for public life over four decades, and could even be accused of ignoring it. In terms of the extension of the franchise, there were arguments that it was inappropriate for the peasants because they had not demanded such reforms. Those who proposed electoral reform as a way to politically modernize the state pointed to the shortcomings of the existing elitist political life with the terse phrase "it couldn't be worse if the peasants had the vote". Other arguments were given, such as the peasants' contribution to the economy, their defence of the country, the avoidance of profound social upheaval, and the idea that exercising the right to vote would finally create a political consciousness and democratic electoral behaviour.

An analysis of the political discourse regarding the modernization of the electoral system until the Great War shows that the debate which took place over a period of five decades was part of a larger debate regarding Romania's modernization process. The debate was mainly about whether it was more important to widen the electoral body through radical reform, or whether the priority was to improve the peasants' education and economic situation. The arguments for and against this were serious and well based, though naturally there was a tendency to exaggerate on both sides. The reformists often overstated the importance of universal suffrage and the 'curative' effect it would have on Romanian society. Meanwhile, the opposition overdramatized the disastrous effects which universal suffrage would have on the young state in the early stages of modernity.

Until the First World War, the concept of electoral reform went hand in hand with agrarian reform as part of the debate about modernization. During the war years, circumstances would dictate that a different perspective would be taken, which would usher in a new mood and a different approach from politicians. Romania entered the war on the side of the Entente Powers with the declared aim of annexing Austro-Hungarian territories which had a majority of Romanians (Banat, Transylvania, Bucovina). The peasants were forced to bear the burden of the war, which proved to be a disaster for the poorly trained and poorly equipped Romanian army. After losing the capital Bucharest in December 1916, the institutions of the Romanian state retreated to Moldova. The outbreak of the Russian revolution of 1917 and the danger of Bolshevism in 1917 confused the situation even further in Romania. Against this complicated background, the Romanian political elite decided to accommodate the peasants by giving them universal suffrage as well as radical agrarian reform. For the first time in Romanian history, the social and political integration of the peasant population had become a political reality.[121] The introduction of universal suffrage in Romania was not due to a political growth process of the rural population, rather it was the will of the political class and King Ferdinand. In other words, this was a reform begun from the "top down", which emerged from the debates and controversies surrounding the franchise that had raged from 1866 until 1914. Electoral reform began with a change to the Constitution in the summer of 1917 and the adoption of electoral decrees/laws which introduced universal suffrage for men in 1918-1919, thereby integrating the peasants into the new liberal state order.

121 Sorin Radu, *Electoratul din România în anii democrației parlamentare (1919–1937)*, Iași 2004, pp. 52–73.

Bibliography

Crisan T. AXENTE, *Essai sur le régime représentatif en Roumanie*, Paris 1937.

Daniel BARBU, *Hainele cele noi ale statului. Liberalismul românesc între două revoluții 1848–1917* [The New Face of the State. Romanian Liberalism between Two Revolutions 1848–1917], Henopoliana 13, 2005, no. 1–4, pp. 52–66.

Daniel BARBU, *The Nation Against Democracy. State Formation, Liberalism, and Political Participation in Romania*, Studia Politica. Romanian Political Science Review 5, 2005, no. 3, pp. 549–560.

D. V. BARNOVSCHI, *Originile democrației române. „Cărvunarii". Constituția Moldovei de la 1822* [Origins of Romanian Democracy. "Cărvunarii". The Constitution of Moldavia from 1822], Iaşi 1922.

Dan BERINDEI (ed.), *Istoria românilor* [The History of Romanians], vol. 7, part 1, *Constituirea României moderne* [The Formation of Modern Romania] *(1821–1878)*, Bucureşti 2003.

Dan BERINDEI, *Societatea românească în vremea lui Carol I (1866–1876)* [Romanian Society in Carol I Times (1866–1876)], Bucureşti 2002.

Vasile BOERESCU, *Discursuri politice* [Political Spechees], vol. 2 (1874–1883), Bucureşti 1910.

Nicolae BLAREMBERG, *Egalitate, suveranitate şi sufragiu* [Equality, Sovereignty and Suffrage], Bucureşti 1866

Marin BUCUR, *C.A. Rosetti—mesianism şi donquijotism revoluționar* [C.A. Rosetti—Revolutionary Messianism and Donquijotism], Bucureşti 1970.

Paraschiva CÂNCEA, *Formarea opoziției unite şi acțiunile sale în februarie-martie 1888* [The Development of United Opposition and its Actions in February—March 1888], Studii şi Materiale de Istorie Modernă 3, 1963, pp. 315–350.

Paraschiva CÂNCEA—Mircea IOSA—Apostol STAN (eds.), *Istoria Parlamentului şi a vieții parlamentare din România* [History of Parliament and Romanian Parliamentary Life], Bucureşti 1983.

Către cititori [To the Readers], Viața Românească 1, 1906, no. 1.

Leonida COLESCU, *Statistica electorală. Alegerile generale pentru Corpurile Legiuitoare din 1901 şi 1905* [Electoral Statistics. The General Elections for Legislative Assembly from 1901 and 1905], Bucureşti 1905.

Leonida COLESCU, *Statistica electorală. Alegerile generale pentru corpurile legiuitoare din 1907 şi 1911* [Electoral Statistics. The General Elections for Legislative Assembly from 1907 and 1911], Bucureşti 1913.

Deputații socialişti în Parlamentul român. Discursuri (1888–1899; 1919–1921) [Socialist Deputies in the Romanian Parliament. Speeches], Bucureşti 1983.

Constantin G. DISSESCU, *Chestiunea revizuirii legii electorale* [The Issue of Revising the Electoral Law], Bucureşti 1883.

Constantin G. DISSESCU, *Dreptul constituțonal* [Constitutional Law], Bucureşti 1915.

Constantin DOBROGEANU-GHEREA, *Opere complete* [Complete Works], vol. 2, Bucureşti 1976.

Documente din istoria mişcării muncitoreşti din România (1879–1892) [Documents from the History of Romanian Labour Movement (1879-1892)], Bucureşti 1976.

Mattei DOGAN, *Analiza statistică a "democraţiei parlamentare" din România* [Statistical Analysis of "Parliamentary Democracy" from Romania], Bucureşti 1946.

Tudor DRĂGAN, *Începutul şi dezvoltarea regimului parlamentar în România pînă în anul 1916* [The Begining and the Development of Parliamentary Regime in Romania until 1916], Cluj-Napoca 1991.

Nicolae FILIPESCU, *Albii şi roşii* [Whites and the Reds], Bucureşti 1894.

Nicolae FILIPESCU, *Către un nou ideal* [Towards a New Ideal], Bucureşti 1898.

Nicolae FILIPESCU, *Despre democraţie* [About Democracy], Bucureşti 1908.

Nicolae FILIPESCU, *Discursuri politice* [Political Speeches], vol. 1 (1888–1901), Bucureşti 1912.

Jean C. FILITTI, *Des origines du régime représentatif en Roumanie*, Bucureşti 1931.

Eleodor FOCŞENEANU, *Istoria constituţională a României 1859–1991* [Constitutional History of Romania], Bucureşti 1992.

Constantin GANE, *P.P. Carp şi locul său în istoria politică a ţării* [P.P. Carp and his Position in the Country's Political History], vol. 2, Bucureşti 1936.

Ilie GĂNESCU—Constantin Gr. ZOTTA—Alexandru KOSTACHI, *Dreptul electoral român* [The Romanian Electoral Law], Bucureşti 1937.

Spiru HARET, *Chestia ţărănească* [The Peasant Question], Bucureşti 1905.

Keith HITCHINS, *România 1866–1947*, Bucureşti 1996.

Gheorghe IACOB—Luminiţa IACOB, *Modernizare—europenism. România de la Cuza Vodă la Carol al II-lea* [Modernisation and Europeanism. Romania from Cuza Vodă to Carol th 2nd], vol. 1, *Ritmul şi strategia modernizării* [The Pace and Strategy of Modernisation], Iaşi, 1995.

Ion ILINCIOIU, *Vasile M. Kogălniceanu (1863–1942)*, Anale de Istorie 1967, no. 1, pp. 129–132.

Anastasie IORDACHE, *Instituirea monarhiei constituţionale şi a regimului parlamentar în România 1866–1871* [The Estabilishment of the Consittutional Monarchy and of the Parlamentary Regime in Romania], Bucureşti 1997.

Mircea IOSA, Încercări de modificare a legii electorale în ultimul deceniu al sec. al XIX-lea [Attempts to Change the Electoral Law in the Last Decade of the XIX Century], Revista Istorică vol. 30, 1977, no. 8, pp. 1419–1431.

Mircea IOSA, *Ion I.C. Brătianu şi reformele social-economice liberale (1909–1914)* [Ion I.C. Brătianu and the Liberal Socio-Economic Reforms], Revista de Istorie, serie nouă, vol. 2, 1991, no. 9–10, pp. 541–557.

Nicolae JURCA, *Istoria social-democraţiei din România* [The History of Social-Democracy in Romania], Bucureşti 1994.

Vasile M. KOGĂLNICEANU, *Chestiunea ţărănească* [The Peasant Question], Bucureşti 1906.

Alexandru LAHOVARY, *Discursuri parlamentare (1888–1891)* [Parliamentary Speeches], Bucureşti 1915.

Emil N. LAHOVARY, *Votul universal* [The Universal Vote], Bucureşti 1909.

Georges M. LAHOVARY, *Histoire d'une fiction. Gouvernement des Partis*, Bucarest 1887.

Eugen LOVINESCU, *Istoria civilizaţiei române moderne* [History of Modern Romanian Civilisation], Bucureşti 1997.

Eugen LOVINESCU, *Titu Maiorescu*, Bucureşti 1940.

Titu MAIORESCU, *Discursuri parlamentare* [Parliamentary Speeches], vol. 3, Bucureşti 1899.

Manifestul—program al partidului [The Manifesto—a Party Program], Bucureşti 1911.

George MEITANI, *O pagină din istoria parlamentară a României* [A Page from the Parliamentary History of Romania], Bucureşti 1914.

Ştefania MIHĂILESCU, *Poporanismul şi mişcarea socialistă din România* [Populism and the Socialist Movement from Romania], Bucureşti 1988.

Mişcarea muncitorească din România 1893–1900 [Labour Movement form Romania], Bucureşti 1965.

Florea NEDELCU, *Programele mişcării socialiste din România şi lupta pentru cucerirea votului universal (1880–1914)* [The Programs of the Social Movement in Romania and the Fight for Universal Vote Gain], Revista de Istorie vol. 23, 1970, no. 2, pp. 271–283.

Dimitrie S. NENIŢESCU, *Reprezentarea proporţională a minorităţilor. Studiu asupra sistemelor electorale* [Proportional Representation of the Political Minorities. A Study on Electoral Systems], Bucureşti 1895.

Vasile NETEA, *C. A. Rosetti*, Bucureşti 1970.

George D. NICOLESCU, *Parlamentul român 1866–1901* [Romanian Parliamentary 1866 - 1901], Bucureşti 1903.

Vasile NICULAE, *Liga votului universal* [Universal Vote League], Magazin Istoric vol. 7, 1973, no. 8, pp. 70–73.

Vasile NICULAE, *O istorie a social democraţiei române* [A History of Romanian Social Democracy], Bucureşti 1993.

Vasile NICULAE—Ion ILINCIOIU—Stelian NEAGOE (eds.), *Doctrina ţărănistă în România. Antologie de texte* [Peasant Doctrine in Romania. Text Anthology], Bucureşti, 1994.

Şerban ORĂSCU, *Spiru Haret*, Bucureşti 1976.

Zigu ORNEA, *Viaţa lui C. Stere* [C. Stere Life], vol. 1, Bucureşti 1989.

Alexandru PENCOVICI, *Desbaterile Adunării Constituante din anul 1866 asupra Constituţiunei şi a legei electorale din România* [Debates of the Constituent Assembly and of Romanian Electoral Law], Bucureşti 1883.

Pentru votul universal. Răspunsul d-lui Vasile M. Kogălniceanu [For Universal Vote. The Answer of Mr. Vasile M. Kogălniceanu], Viaţa socială 1, 1910 (August—September), no. 7–8, pp. 17–22

Constantin Titel PETRESCU, *Socialismul în România 1835—6 septembrie 1940* [Socialism in Romania 1835—6 September 1940], Bucureşti 2003.

Cristian PREDA, *Modernitatea politică şi românismul* [Political Modernity and Romanianism], Bucureşti 1998.

Programul Partidei Ţărăneşti din România [Peasant Party Program from Romania], Bucureşti 1895.

Programul Partidului Naţional Liberal din 1892 şi Discursurile Preşedintelui Consiliului de Miniştri D. A. Sturdza [Program of National Liberal Party from 1892 and the Speeches of the President of the Council Of Ministers D. A. Sturdza], Bucureşti 1897.

Programul Partidului social-democrat al muncitorilor din România [Program of Social-Democratic Party of Workers in Romania], Galaţi 1893.

Sorin RADU, *Electoratul din România în anii democraţiei parlamentare (1919–1937)* [Romanian Electorate in the Years of Parliamentary Democracy], Iaşi 2004.

Sorin RADU, *Liberalii şi problema reformei electorale în România (1866–1914)* [Liberals and the Electoral Reform Question in Romania], part 1, Annales Universitatis Apulensis 4–5, 2000–2001, pp. 131–144.

Constantin RĂDULESCU-MOTRU, *Cronica politică. Menirea Partidului Conservator. Educaţiunea opiniunei publice* [Political Chronicle. The Purpose of the Conservative Party. The Education of Public Opinion], Noua Revistă Română pentru Politică, Literatură. Ştiinţă şi Artă 1, 15. 4. 1900, no. 8, pp. 338–340.

Constantin RĂDULESCU-MOTRU, *Cultura română şi politicianismul* [Romanian Culture and the Politicking], Bucureşti 1904.

Vasile RUSSU, *Cauzele luptelor politice dintre grupările liberale şi conservatoare în anii instabilităţii guvernamentale şi parlamentare (1866–1871)* [The Causes of the Political Struggles between Liberal and Conservative Groups in the Years of Governmental and Parliamentary Instability *(1866–1871)*], Cercetări Istorice, vol. 9–10, 1978–1979, pp. 411–437.

Grigore G. PEUCESCU, *Despre partidele politice* [About Political Parties], Iaşi 1878.

Dimitrie ROSETTI-TEŢCANU, *Colegiul unic cu reprezentarea minorităţilor* [Unique College with Political Minority Representation], Bucureşti 1884.

Apostol STAN, *Grupări şi curente politice în România între Unire şi Independenţă* [Political Groups and Currents in Romania in between Union and Independance], Bucureşti 1979.

Apostol STAN, *Ion Mihalache. Destinul unei vieţi* [Ion Mihalache. The Destiny of a Life], Bucureşti 1999.

Apostol STAN, *Putere politică şi democraţie în România 1859–1918* [Political Power and Democracy in Romania 1859–1918], Bucureşti 1995.

Apostol STAN, *Vasile Boerescu (1830–1883)*, Bucureşti 1974.

Apostol STAN—Mircea IOSA, *Liberalismul politic în România. De la origini pînă la 1918* [Political Liberalism in Romania. From Origins to 1918], Bucureşti 1996.

Ioan STANOMIR—Laurenţiu VLAD (eds.), *A fi conservator. Antologie, comentarii şi bibliografie* [To be Conservative. Anthology, Comments and Bibliography], Bucureşti 2002.

Statutele Clubului Conservator şi programul partidului [Statutes of the Conservative Club and the Party Program], Bucureşti 1880.

Constantin STERE, Întregirile necesare reformei electorale [The Necessary Completions for the Electoral Reform], Viaţa Românească 6, 1911, no. 12, , pp. 474–476.

Constantin STERE, *Momentul ("Cronica internă")* [The Moment ("Internal Chronic")], Viaţa Românească 2, 1907, no. 5, pp. 326–328.

Gheorghe TĂTĂRESCU, *Regimul electoral şi parlamentar în România* [Electoral and Parliamentary Regime in Romania], Bucureşti 2004.

Mariu TEODORIAN-CARADA, *Efemeridele. Însemnări şi amintiri* [Ephemeris. Notes and Memories], vol. 1, Bucureşti 1930.

Mariu TEODORIAN-CARADA, *Revizuirea Constituţiei* [Constitution Revision], Bucureşti 1911.

Mariu TEODORIAN-CARADA, *Vasile Lascăr*, Bucureşti 1914.

Alexandru Dimitrie XENOPOL, *Istoria partidelor politice în România. De al origini pînă la 1848* [History of Political Parties in Romania. From Origins to 1848], vol. 1, part 1, Bucureşti 1910.

Alexandru Dimitrie XENOPOL, *Istoria partidelor politice în România. De la origini pînă la 1866*, vol. 1, part 2, Bucureşti 1910.

Alexandru Dimitrie XENOPOL, *Primul proiect de Constituţie a Moldovei din 1822. Originile Partidului Conservator şi ale celui Liberal* [The First Project of the Constitution of Moldavia in 1822. The Origins of the Conservative and Liberal Party], Bucureşti 1898.

List of Contributors

Yuko Kiryu is an Associate Professor of European History at Kobe College, Japan. She is the author of *Kindai Bohemia Nōson to Shiminsyakai* [Czech Nation-Building and the Creation of a Rural Public Sphere in Bohemia] (2012), which examines interrelations between nation-building and the creation of a public sphere in rural Bohemia by analysing the spread of associations and publications among its inhabitants. She is currently working on a project which explores the impact of the First World War and the foundation of Czechoslovakia on the Bohemian lands.

Pavel Kladiwa is a professor at the department of history of the University of Ostrava (Czech Republic). His field of interest is the social history of the Bohemian lands during the "long" 19th century, especially in connection with the formation of civil society, ethnic relations and identity-shaping processes. Recently he worked (with colleagues) on the project "The transformation and social activation of rural areas in Moravia and Austrian Silesia 1861–1914". His current project (together with Andrea Pokludová) is "The Moravian Compromise as a Laboratory for the Nationalization of Politics and Law: The National Partitioning of Moravia's Towns, 1905–1914"

Torsten Lorenz received an M.A. in East European History, Slavic Philology and Political Science from the University of Cologne in 1998 and a PhD in Cultural Studies from the European University Viadrina in Frankfurt/Oder in 2003. Before becoming a DAAD Associate Professor at Charles University in Prague (2011–2016) he worked at the universities in Frankfurt/Oder, Vienna, Dresden, Oldenburg and the Humboldt University in Berlin. He is currently working in Hamburg. He edited the book *Cooperatives in Ethnic Conflicts. Eastern Europe from the late 19th until the mid-20th Century* (2006) and is the co-editor of *Agrarismus und Agrareliten in Ostmitteleuropa* (2013). He is the author of several articles on the cooperative movement in Central and Eastern Europe.

Andrea Pokludová is a historian of social and cultural history of the 19th and 20th centuries with a focus on society in the process of modernization: the formation of social intelligentsia groups, the role and function of associations, the formation of the media landscape and everyday life.

Milan Řepa is head of the Brno branch of the Institute of History of the Czech Academy of Sciences. His research interests include the collective consciousness in the Bohemian lands, the theory and history of historiography, and Moravia in the period 1740–1914. He is the author of *Moravané nebo Češi?* [Moravians or Czechs?] (2001), *Poetika českého dějepisectví* [Poetry of Czech Historiography] (2006), *Moravané—Němci—Rakušané*

[Moravians—Germans—Austrians] (2014), and co-author (with Jiří Malíř) of *Morava na cestě k občanské společnosti* [Moravia towards a Civil Society] (2018).

Sorin Radu is professor habil. at "Lucian Blaga" University of Sibiu (Romania). His fields of research include Romanian history of the 19th and 20th centuries, political culture and modernization in modern and contemporary Romania. He is a convenor for Romania at the International Commission for the History of Representative and Parliamentary Institutions, a member of the European Information and Research Network on Parliamentary History. His latest publications are: *The Countryside and Communism in Eastern Europe: Perceptions, Attitudes, Propaganda* (2016, editor in collaboration with Cosmin Budeancă); *Politics and Peasants in Interwar Romania: Perceptions, Mentalities, Propaganda* (2017, editor in collaboration with Oliver Jens Schmitt).

Kai Struve is a "Privatdozent" of Modern and East European History at the Institute of History at Martin Luther University Halle-Wittenberg. Among his most important publications are *Bauern und Nation in Galizien. Über Zugehörigkeit und soziale Emanzipation im 19. Jahrhundert* (2005) and *Deutsche Herrschaft, ukrainischer Nationalismus, antijüdische Gewalt. Der Sommer 1941 in der Westukraine* (2015). More recently, he co-edited (with Michael G. Müller) *Fragmentierte Republik? Das politische Erbe der Teilungszeit in Polen 1918–1939* (2017).

John C. Swanson is professor of history at the University of Tennessee at Chattanooga. His scholarship focuses on questions of ethnic identity, nationalism and minorities in twentieth-century Central and Eastern Europe. His most recent book, *Tangible Belonging: Negotiating Germanness in Twentieth-Century Hungary*, published by the University of Pittsburgh Press in 2017, won the Barbara Jelavich Book Prize in 2018 and the Hungarian Studies Association Book Prize in 2019. He is also the author of *The Remnants of the Habsburg Monarchy: The Shaping of Modern Austria and Hungary, 1918–1922*. In addition, he is active in documentary film production.